T0093461

Semantic AI in Knowledge Graphs

Recent combinations of semantic technology and artificial intelligence (AI) present new techniques to build intelligent systems that identify more precise results. *Semantic AI in Knowledge Graphs* locates itself at the forefront of this novel development, uncovering the role of machine learning to extend the knowledge graphs by graph mapping or corpus-based ontology learning.

Securing efficient results via the combination of symbolic AI and statistical AI such as entity extraction based on machine learning, text mining methods, semantic knowledge graphs, and related reasoning power, this book is the first of its kind to explore semantic AI and knowledge graphs. A range of topics are covered, from neuro-symbolic AI, explainable AI and deep learning to knowledge discovery and mining, and knowledge representation and reasoning.

A trailblazing exploration of semantic AI in knowledge graphs, this book is a significant contribution to both researchers in the field of AI and data mining as well as beginner academicians.

Semantic AI in Knowledge Graphs

Edited by Sanju Tiwari,
Fernando Ortíz-Rodriguez, Sarra Ben Abbés,
Patience Usoro Usip, and Rim Hantach

CRC Press
Taylor & Francis Group
Boca Raton London New York

CRC Press is an imprint of the
Taylor & Francis Group, an **informa** business

Designed cover image: © Shutterstock

First edition published 2024
by CRC Press
6000 Broken Sound Parkway NW, Suite 300, Boca Raton, FL 33487-2742

and by CRC Press
4 Park Square, Milton Park, Abingdon, Oxon, OX14 4RN

CRC Press is an imprint of Taylor & Francis Group, LLC

© 2024 selection and editorial matter, Sanju Tiwari, Fernando Ortíz-Rodriguez, Sarra Ben Abbés, Patience Usoro Usip and Rim Hantach; individual chapters, the contributors

Library of Congress Cataloging-in-Publication Data

Names: Tiwari, Sanju, 1979- editor. | Ortíz-Rodriguez, Fernando, 1974- editor. |
Ben Abbès, Sarra, 1985- editor. | Usip, Patience Usoro, editor. |
Hantach, Rim, editor. | KGSWC (Conference) (2021 : Online)
Title: Semantic AI in knowledge graphs / edited by Sanju Tiwari, Fernando
Ortíz-Rodriguez, Sarra Ben Abbés, Patience Usoro Usip and Rim Hantach.
Description: Boca Raton : CRC Press, 2023. | "The book...comprises
of extended papers from workshops collocated during the KGSWC 2021" --Preface. |
Includes bibliographical references and index. | Identifiers: LCCN 2023002144 (print) |
LCCN 2023002145 (ebook) | ISBN 9781032321851 (hardback) |
ISBN 9781032321868 (paperback) | ISBN 9781003313267 (ebook)
Subjects: LCSH: Information visualization--Congresses. | Semantic
computing--Congresses. | Artificial intelligence--Congresses.
Classification: LCC QA76.9.I52 S46 2023 (print) | LCC QA76.9.I52 (ebook) |
DDC 001.4/226--dc23/eng/20230607
LC record available at https://lccn.loc.gov/2023002144
LC ebook record available at https://lccn.loc.gov/2023002145

ISBN: 978-1-032-32185-1 (hbk)
ISBN: 978-1-032-32186-8 (pbk)
ISBN: 978-1-003-31326-7 (ebk)

DOI: 10.1201/9781003313267

Typeset in Palatino
by KnowledgeWorks Global Ltd.

Contents

List of Figures

List of Tables

Preface

This book, *Semantic Artificial Intelligence in Knowledge Graphs*, comprises extended papers from workshops collocated during the Knowledge Graph and Semantic Web Conference (KGSWC) 2021. The workshops included the Third International Workshop on Semantic Web (IWSW 2021), First International Workshop on Multilingual Semantic Web (IWMSW 2021), and First International Workshop on Deep Learning for Question Answering (IWDLQ 2021).

The papers explored major roles artificial intelligence (AI) with semantic technologies to present enhanced semantic AI architecture with knowledge graphs. In this book, the role of machine learning toward extending knowledge graphs by graph mapping or corpus-based ontology learning was discovered. Efficient results were obtained via the combination of symbolic AI and statistical AI such as entity extraction based on machine learning, text mining methods, semantic knowledge graphs, and related reasoning power.

Topics covered in this book include Deep Semantics in Knowledge Graphs, Neuro-Symbolic AI and eXplainable AI, Deep Learning, Knowledge Discovery and Mining, Information Retrieval and Question Answering, Knowledge Representation and Reasoning, Natural Language Processing, Entity Linking, etc. this book is made of eight chapters: *Leveraging Semantic Knowledge Graphs in Educational Recommenders to Address the Cold-Start Problem*; *Modeling Event-Centric Knowledge Graph for Crime Analysis on Online News*; *Semantic Natural Language Processing for Knowledge Graphs Creation*; *MSE**: Multi-modal semantic embeddings for datasets with several positive matchings*; *Text-Based Emergency Alert Framework for Under-Resourced Languages in Southern Nigeria*; *Knowledge Graphs in Healthcare*; *Explainable Machine Learning-Based Knowledge Graph for Modeling Location-Based Recreational Services from Users Profile*; and *Building Knowledge Graph from Relational Database*.

Firstly, our thanks go to all the organizers of the main conference and program committee members for ensuring a rigorous review process that led to the successful events. The efforts of the workshop chairs and co-chairs toward the success of the workshops were highly appreciated. We are also very thankful to the authors for their painstaking efforts to write up for the extension. Finally, we are thankful to the editorial board of Taylor & Francis for providing this book opportunity to publish all extended chapters.

Sanju Tiwari, Fernando Ortíz-Rodriguez, Sarra Ben Abbés,
Patience Usoro Usip, and Rim Hantach

Editors

Dr. Sanju Tiwari (CEO and Founder of ShodhGuru Research Labs, India) is a Senior Researcher at Universidad Autonoma de Tamaulipas. She was DAAD Post-Doc-Net AI Fellow for 2021 and visited different German Universities under the DAAD fellowship. She is a Mentor of Google Summer of Code (GSoC 2022-23) at DBpedia and a member of InfAI, Leipzig University, Germany. She is also working as a curator of ORKG Grant Program, at TIB Hannover, Germany. Her current research interests include Semantic Web, Knowledge Graphs, Linked Data, Artificial Intelligence. She has to-date published >50 research papers and 3 Scopus indexed Books. She is working as a General Chair (KGSWC 2020-23, EGETC2022-23, AMLDA 2022-23, AI4S-2023), and Program Chair, Workshop Chair, Publicity Chair, Steering Committee and PC Member in different renowned International Conferences (The Web Conference 2023, SEMANTiCS 2019-23, ESWC2021-23, CIKM2020-22, AICCSA-2021, JOWO-2021, BiDEDE2022-23@ACM SIGMOD, VLIoT@ VLDB2022, SIMBIG2022, ICSC2023). She is working as a Guest Editor for SCI/ Scopus journals (SWJ IoS Press, TEL Emerald, IJWIS Emerald). She is the speaker of IEEE/IETE N2Women and Women's Empowerment and NiWIIT (Nigerian Women In Information Technology).

Fernando Ortíz-Rodriguez is Full Professor, member of the National Research Council, Level C, and Director of the Research Institute UAT at Tamaulipas Autonomous University, Reynosa, Tamaulipas, Mexico. He is a member of the Information Technology research group and part of the knowledge graph and Semantic Web Community. His research interests include Semantic Web, Information Systems, e-Government and Artificial Intelligence. He has been the main Chair and Organizer of the KGSWC multi-series conference. He is a member of National Systems Researchers (SNI) of the National Council of Science and Technology (CONACYT), Mexico's entity promoting scientific and technological activities and high-quality scientific research. He is also a member of the Association for Computing Machinery (ACM). He holds a PhD degree on computer science and Artificial Intelligence and Information Systems from the Technical University of Madrid, Spain.

Dr. Sarra Ben Abbès, PhD, is an R&D Expert on Artificial Intelligence. She has been working for more than 13 years in different domains of Artificial intelligence. She became an expert in these domains following her thesis project focused on the crossroads of knowledge engineering and the semantic web.

She worked as a senior and lead scientist at Storyzy (2013), where she led several innovative projects combining Semantic Web technologies, NLP techniques, and Machine Learning algorithms for real-time news articles.

Since 2018, she has joined Engie as R&D expert on Artificial Intelligence and she mainly worked to improve the use of semantics by bridging NLP, Deep Learning, and Machine Learning techniques. She is working as lead of work-packages and coordinator of several projects (internal and external) related to the energy sector such as the European H2020 project Platoon and Enershare. Her interests are in project management, artificial intelligence, explainable artificial intelligence, semantic interoperability, knowledge engineering, reasoning and inference, semantic information retrieval, decision-making support (machine learning & deep learning) and probabilistic semantic graphs and multi-Agent systems. She supervised the work of many Master trainees, Ph.D. students and consultants. She is an author of different scientific publications related to the artificial intelligence domain. She is also a workshop organizer in national and international conferences like ESWC, FOIS, KG, EGC, ICMLA, etc.

Patience Usoro Usip is a Senior Lecturer of Computer Science, University of Uyo, Uyo, Nigeria. She holds a PhD and MSc in Computer Science from University of Ibadan, Ibadan, Nigeria and BSc in Computer Science from University of Calabar, Calabar, Nigeria. She is a Post-doc fellow, Massachusetts Institute of Technology (MIT), USA and also an All Africa House Fellow, University of Cape Town, South Africa. Her research interests include knowledge representation and reasoning a sub-sub-field of Artificial Intelligence, Formal Representations, Computer Logic, Ontology Development, Knowledge Graphs, Multilingual Sematic Web, Intelligent Systems in several domains including health, etc. She has published locally and internationally in books, book chapters, journals, and conference proceedings. She has served as reviewer to several journals locally and internationally to include MTAP, ASTEJ, etc. She has served as External Examiner for MSc Dissertation, University of Cape Town, South Africa and for PhD Thesis, India, etc. She has served as Speaker, program committee member, and General Chair in winter schools, workshops, and conferences. She has several awards to her credit and is a member of many professional bodies.

Rim Hantach is an artificial intelligence expert and project manager at ENGIE France. She is working on deep learning, computer vision, natural language processing (NLP), knowledge graph, and machine learning techniques for text and image analysis.

List of Contributors

Sanna Aizad
University of Leicester
Leicester, UK

Bilal Arshad
University of Derby
Derby, UK

Daniel Ekpenyong Asuquo
University of Uyo
Uyo, Nigeria

Kingsley Friday Attai
Ritman University
Nigeria

Adrian Basarab
IRIT, Toulouse University
France

Sahan Bulathwela
University College London
UK

Ilham Chaker
Faculty of Science and Technology
Fez, Morocco

Cameron De Sa
Birmingham City University
UK

Hossein Ghomeshi
Birmingham City University
UK

Jeremie Huteau
IRIT, Toulouse University
France

Funebi F. Ijebu
University of Uyo
Uyo, Nigeria

Bilal Ben Mahria
Faculty of Science and Technology
Fez, Morocco

Ryan McGranaghan
NASA Goddard Space Fight Center
Greenbelt, MD, USA

Ikechukwu K. Ollawa
University of Uyo
Uyo, Nigeria

María Pérez-Ortiz
University College London
UK

Laura Po
University of Modena and Reggio
   Emilia
Italy

Federica Rollo
University of Modena and Reggio
   Emilia
Italy

Florence Dupin de Saint-Cyr
IRIT, Toulouse University
France

John Shawe-Taylor
University College London
UK

Ifiok J. Udo
University of Uyo
Uyo, Nigeria

Patience Usoro Usip
University of Uyo
Uyo, Nigeria

Edlira Vakaj
Birmingham City University
UK

Emine Yilmaz
University College London
UK

Azeddine Zahi
Faculty of Science and Technology
Fez, Morocco

1

Leveraging Semantic Knowledge Graphs in Educational Recommenders to Address the Cold-Start Problem

Sahan Bulathwela, María Pérez-Ortiz, Emine Yilmaz, and John Shawe-Taylor

Centre for Artificial Intelligence, University College London, UK

CONTENTS

DOI: 10.1201/9781003313267-1

1

1.1 Introduction

Developing artificial intelligence systems that, mildly at least, understand the structure of knowledge is foundational to building an effective recommendation system for education (Bauman & Tuzhilin, 2018; Jiang, Pardos, & Wei, 2019), as well as for many other applications (Lewis et al., 2020; Yano & Kang, 2016) related to knowledge management and tracing. Many intelligent educational recommenders at present use knowledge components (KCs)/topics to represent the skills that human learner masters over time. But many of these systems assume that these KCs are unrelated to each other when modeling learner knowledge (Yudelson, Koedinger, & Gordon, 2013). Otherwise, human experts are relied upon to annotate the concept relatedness. We identify knowledge bases as a rich source of information that can be utilized to automate harvesting semantic relatedness (SR) information needed for modeling. Our motivation in this work is to use Wikipedia, an open, multilingual, and dynamic encyclopedia to demonstrate that educational recommendation can be improved by leveraging automatically computed SR information, making the next generation of educational recommenders semantically aware.

Through this work, we verify the utility of semantic knowledge graphs in improving educational recommender systems. Our proposal, *Semantic TrueLearn*, is a family of novel and transparent learner models that incorporate automatic entity linking and Wikipedia (a publicly available, humanly intuitive, domain-agnostic, and ever-evolving) knowledge graph, as a first step toward building an educational recommender that automatically labels materials and embeds the structure of universal knowledge using Wikipedia.

Our proposal, Semantic TrueLearn, is a probabilistic graphical model (PGM) that maintains a symbolic representation of learners' knowledge that allows explanations, rationalizations, and scrutiny. The proposed learner model is the perfect example of how probabilistic graphical modeling can harmonize with semantic knowledge graphs to build the accurate and sub-symbolic learner models that are needed in many applications that require interaction and collaboration with the user.

Toward verifying the utility of knowledge graphs to improve informational recommender systems, we:

i. Identify the ability to exploit the SR between entities in Wikipedia.

ii. Propose a novel sub-symbolic Bayesian learner model.

iii. Identify several research questions relating to validating the utility of the proposed learner model.

iv. Validate the research questions using a large dataset of learners engaging with educational resources.

While our experiments focus on the educational domain, we hypothesize these findings may extend to any other informational recommenders.

In this chapter, Section 1.1 introduces the context and outlines the motivation behind this chapter, while Section 1.2 describes the relevant literature on the topic and how they are related/different to our contribution. Section 1.3 formalizes the problem setting and proposes several approaches to model SR between concepts as a solution. Subsequently, Section 1.4 identifies the research questions relevant to the solutions proposed, while outlining the different experiments that are run in order to answer the defined research questions. The latter part of Section 1.4 presents the results observed from the experiments and goes further to discuss the results. Section 1.5 concludes this chapter.

1.2 Related Work

Knowledge tracing (KT) (Yudelson et al., 2013) is one of the most popular methods for user modeling in intelligent tutoring systems (ITS) and educational recommendation (EdRecSys) (Bulathwela, Pérez-Ortiz, Yilmaz, & Shawe-Taylor, 2020b) contexts. Incorporation of SR in KT systems is gaining more attention recently, where it is being utilized in prerequisite modeling (Carmona, Millán, Pérez-de-la Cruz, Trella, & Conejo, 2005; Chen, Lu, Zheng, & Pian, 2018), exercise similarity (Huang et al., 2019; Nakagawa, Iwasawa, & Matsuo, 2019; Pandey & Srivastava, 2020), and various other tasks (Bauman & Tuzhilin, 2018; Thaker, Zhang, He, & Brusilovsky, 2020). However, KT often relies on expert labeling of the KCs (Selent, Patikorn, & Heffernan, 2016) (sometimes also for knowledge hierarchies; Bauman & Tuzhilin, 2018), which is not scalable to large-scale lifelong learning applications in practice. In the majority of the approaches, the similarity between different items (exercises, educational materials) is modeled by using the overlapping KCs or the users' co-consuming pairs of items. Both of these main approaches require either the experts or the learners to invest a substantial amount of human effort in the system before relatedness can be recovered. Another challenge in the above approaches is that the different proposals use different KC taxonomies making the different work hard to compare and inter-operate. The advancement of deep learning and graph neural networks has led to a new generation of neural models that are attempting to exploit the relatedness structures of educational materials using graph neural networks and attention mechanisms (Nakagawa et al., 2019; Song et al., 2021; Yang et al., 2020). However, these approaches require large quantities of data to train and lack interpretability, making them unsuitable for an educational recommendation system. Recent studies have also started questioning the superiority of these neural models over the classical approaches

(Mandalapu, Gong, & Chen, 2021; Schmucker, Wang, Hu, & Mitchell, 2022). Furthermore, neural models do not focus on formulating humanly intuitive graphical models to model the data generation process positioning them beyond the scope of this work.

Wikification, a form of entity linking (Brank, Leban, & Grobelnik, 2017), has shown substantial progress and great promise in automatically capturing the KCs covered in an educational resource addressing the scalable content annotation problem. Another advantage of using Wikification is that it grounds the KCs to a universal knowledge graph like Wikipedia, that is multi-lingual, cross-domain, and temporally dynamic (i.e., its knowledge evolves with time). Using Wikipedia as an ontology or knowledge graph to understand documents is not a new idea. While Wikipedia itself has been used as an ontology using page links and category links to describe "relates to" and "is a type of" relationships, respectively (Kawakami, Morita, & Yamaguchi, 2017; Syed, Finin, & Joshi, 2008), other works have pushed further and used the wealth of information in Wikipedia to build downstream knowledge bases and ontologies (Auer et al., 2007), as well as ontology-driven information retrieval systems (Grefenstette & Rafes, 2015). From the early days of Wikipedia, exploiting different aspects (such as text, link structure, etc.) to model *SR* that represents "relates to" links have been attempted. These SR metrics have evolved over time into recent proposals that are diverse and sophisticated metrics highly predictive of concept relatedness (Ponza, Ferragina, & Chakrabarti, 2020). However, the utility of these proposals with graphical models is underexplored and is investigated in this chapter.

1.2.1 Wikipedia Concept-Based User Modeling

State-based user modeling is a mature topic in personalization (Bulathwela et al., 2021a). As a reliable content-based feature, keywords/concepts/entities/topics are widely used in user state modeling. These techniques in unison are identified as *concept-based* approaches (Zarrinkalam, Faralli, Piao, & Bagheri, 2020) where Wikipedia-based concept features are shown to be effective. Many concept-based approaches use the frequency of user interactions with the items related to a concept to build a concept profile for the user. Once the user profile is available, the similarity between the profile and the items can be used to rank them (Bulathwela, Pérez-Ortiz, Novak, Yilmaz, & Shawe-Taylor, 2021b; Piao, 2021).

Recent works in educational recommendation have also used concept-based user modeling to recommend Massively Online Open Courses (MOOCs) to learners (Piao & Breslin, 2016). In their approach, they consider the user session to be a document where the topics they visit over time are terms (words) in this document. They compute the Term Frequency (TF) for each user over time to build a user profile. The engagement is predicted by measuring the similarity between the user profile and the content using the cosine similarity. In recent work relating to EdRecSys, TrueLearn (Bulathwela, Pérez-Ortiz, Yilmaz, & Shawe-Taylor, 2020c), using Wikification, has demonstrated state-of-the-art performance in building PGMs on top of automatically extracting topics from a semantic knowledge graph, Wikipedia. In this work, Bulathwela, Pérez-Ortiz, et al. also introduce an online multi-skill KT model inspired by Bishop, Winn, and Diethe (2015),which is another PGM that relies on Wikipedia concepts. We identify these two models to be the most relevant prior work to the proposed Semantic TrueLearn model. TrueLearn Novel, the best performing model in Bulathwela et al. (2020c), builds a learner profile where the skill of each KC (Wikipedia topic) is updated based on the learner engagement with a fragment of an educational video. The model is a Bayesian factor graph that uses message passing to learn the KC parameters. This score can be used to rank the recommendations. While these models utilize a rich knowledge graph like Wikipedia, the exploitation of a rich source of semantic information in these cases can be considered a bare minimum as these methods merely use Wikipedia to automatically annotate and represent the KCs/concepts. All these models consider that Wikipedia concepts are independent and thus unrelated, introducing an obvious weakness to the model assumptions. This work breaks from these incorrect model assumptions to exploit the SR between the topics in Wikipedia, making the utility of Wikipedia in the EdRecSys domain rather as an ontology (that also models *relates to* relationships) than a simple taxonomy. More specifically, the contribution of this work is to improve the performance of the TrueLearn Novel model by incorporating the missing assumption of KC relatedness to address the cold-start problem. Our final experiments also demonstrate and validate if the incorporation of relatedness assumptions can apply to other Wikipedia concept-based models (e.g., Piao & Breslin, 2016).

1.2.2 Representations from Graphs

The core technical contribution of this work is proposing a method to infer the latent value of an unobserved skill parameter using observed ones via information sharing based on an SR graph. This requires developing a mechanism to exploit the connectedness structure of Wikipedia topics. Several works have proposed novel ways to use a relationship graph to recover a latent representation for an unknown node using a set of known nodes. Recently proposed Graph Convolutional Neural Networks (Kipf & Welling, 2017) infer hidden node embeddings ($H^{\ell+1}$) by taking the weighted average of the embeddings of its neighbors. This is done using the adjacency matrix A and diagonal D of the relatedness graph as per $H^{\ell+1} = D^{-\frac{1}{2}} A D^{-\frac{1}{2}} H^{\ell} W^{\ell}$. Another popularizing idea in the representation learning research community is the attention mechanism (Bahdanau, Cho, & Bengio, 2015) that uses the concept of alignment. This mechanism learns to quantify the relatedness of the neighboring embeddings to compute the context embedding at a point in order to make a prediction. The alignment is used to compute a normalized weighted sum of the related embeddings, which becomes the context embedding used as part of the feature set when predicting. This method has revolutionized neural modeling significantly improving the state-of-the-art. Our work described in this chapter also uses these ideas, where we utilized the observed embeddings (KC variables) of the TrueLearn learner model in order to infer the value of unobserved variables. In summary, this work lays the foundations for applying SR in an educational recommender using:

   i. A PGM
   ii. The SR values extracted from Wikipedia

1.3 Methodology

Given that there is a gap in exploiting SR to improve concept-based recommendations, our work focuses on developing a method to do so. Specifically, we focus on the instance of cold-start in concept-based user modeling as a foundational step toward using semantic knowledge graphs. In the case of cold-start, the informational concept is novel, i.e., it has not been encountered by the user before in their interaction history. In the conventional user model outlined in Section 1.2, the system will not have any data to infer the learner's interest/skill for such an unobserved concept. In the case of Bayesian probabilistic models such as TrueLearn Novel, the model will use a non-informative prior. To address this issue, we formalize the problem and propose a solution in this section.

1.3.1 Problem Formulation

Consider the case of a learner ℓ interacting with a set of educational resources $S_\ell \subset \{r_1,...,r_Q\}$ over a period of $T = (1,...,t)$ time steps, Q being the total of resources in the system. Each resource r_i is characterized by the top KCs or topics covered $K_{r_i} \subset \{1,...,N\}$ (N is the total of KCs considered by the system) and the depth of coverage d_{r_i} of those. We represent learner knowledge at time t as a multivariate Gaussian distribution $\theta_\ell^t \sim \mathcal{N}(\mu_\ell^t, \Sigma_\ell^t)$, $\mu_\ell^t \in \mathbb{R}^Q$ being the mean of knowledge and Σ_ℓ^t the covariance matrix. TrueLearn assumed that Σ is a diagonal covariance matrix in all cases and thus knowledge topics are completely independent from each other. The work in this chapter builds toward considering a full covariance matrix, assuming that ρ_{ij} (estimated SR) is a proxy for Σ_{ij} for topics i and j when $i \neq j$.

The key idea behind TrueLearn Novel (Bulathwela et al., 2020c) is to model the probability of engagement $e_{\ell,r_i}^t \in \{1,-1\}$ between learner ℓ and resource r_i

at time t as a function of the learner skills/knowledge θ^t_ℓ and resource representation d_{r_i} for the top KCs covered K_{r_i}. When a new learner joins the recommender system, TrueLearn sets $\mu^0_\ell = 0$, $\Sigma_{ii} = \beta$, where β is a hyperparameter of the system, and $\Sigma_{ij} = 0, i \neq j$. Then, when the learner consumes an educational video fragment, TrueLearn updates the learner model/skills accordingly. Every skill that is not updated is set to the value from the last time step, meaning at time t there might be many unobserved skills, especially given the number of topics considered by the system (equal to the number of Wikipedia pages). Thus, TrueLearn assumes that the skill for topics in K_{r_i} can only be obtained through those topics and not semantically related ones. The same problem setting can be generalized to the other concept-based learner models outlined in prior works (Bulathwela et al., 2021b; Piao & Breslin, 2016). The key difference is that these models do not model uncertainty of the skill variables (assuming $\Sigma_{ii} = \Sigma_{ij} = 0$ as well).

1.3.2 Semantic TrueLearn

Extending the TrueLearn model (Bulathwela et al., 2020c), Semantic TrueLearn, is a learner model that infers the knowledge state of learners in an online fashion. Semantic TrueLearn exploits its current knowledge of observed concepts (through interactions from time steps $0 \ldots t-1$) and their SR to the novel concept encountered at time t to make a better prior skill estimate. This approach is graphically illustrated in Figure 1.1.

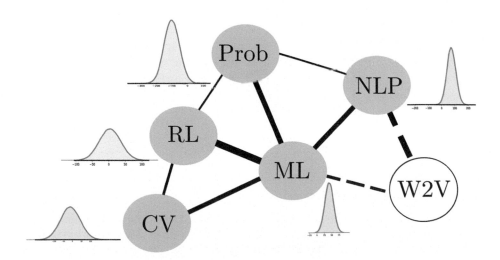

FIGURE 1.1
Inferring the knowledge for the unseen topic (white circle) based on semantically related and seen ones (grey circles) by transferring knowledge (dotted lines). Topics are ML (machine learning), RL (reinforcement learning), Prob (probability), CV (computer vision), NLP (natural language processing), and W2V (Word2Vec).

1.3.2.1 Incorporating Semantic Relatedness between Concepts/KCs

The main assumption when incorporating SR is that knowledge can be shared across semantically related topics. In other words, we assume that the demonstration of having knowledge in certain KCs enables us to reason about their degree of knowledge of related, yet unobserved KCs. By taking inspiration from graph convolution (Kipf & Welling, 2017), we assume the relationship between concepts illustrated in Figure 1.1. The skill of the unobserved KC is calculated as the weighted average of the observed related skills as per Equation 1.1:

$$\theta_{\ell,i}^{t} = \frac{1}{|\Omega_{\ell,i}|} \sum_{j \in \Omega_{\ell,i}} \gamma_{ij} \cdot \theta_{\ell,j}^{t}, \text{where } \theta_{\ell,i}^{t} \sim \mathcal{N}(\mu, \sigma^2) \tag{1.1}$$

where Ω_i represents the set of topics used to infer the representation of topic i (e.g., most semantically related seen topics), where $i \neq j$. The mixing factors γ_{ij} can be set to SR ρ_{ij} or to a factor of the standard error of topic j (meaning most observed topics are used). In the TrueLearn (Bulathwela et al., 2020c) model, which we extend, θ is a Gaussian variable.

Two mathematical formulations are tested to capture the relatedness among the topics, namely the (i) univariate and (ii) multivariate formulations.

1.3.2.2 The Univariate Formulation

This formulation assumes that relatedness exists exclusively between the unobserved topic and the set of observed related topics. The SR between the pairs of observed topics is ignored in this scenario. The motivation behind this is that the relatedness of the observed topics in the user profile doesn't have a significant effect on the final estimation of the unobserved skill parameter. We use Equation 1.2 to calculate the unknown parameter $\theta_{\ell,i}^{t}$ in this formulation:

$$\hat{\theta}_{\ell,i}^{t} \sim \mathcal{N}\left(\sum_{j \in \Omega_i} \frac{1}{|\Omega_i|} \cdot \rho_{ij} \cdot \mu_{\ell,j}^{t}, \sum_{j \in \Omega_i} \left(\frac{1}{|\Omega_i|} \cdot \rho_{ij} \right)^2 \cdot \left(\sigma_{\ell,i}^{t} \right)^2 \right) \tag{1.2}$$

1.3.2.3 The Multivariate Formulation

This formulation, on the contrary to Equation 1.2, assumes that relatedness between all observed KCs also Equation 1.3 presents this formulation where σ in this case represents the covariance matrix:

$$\hat{\theta}_{\ell,i}^{t} \sim \mathcal{N}\left(\sum_{j \in \Omega_i} \frac{1}{|\Omega_i|} \cdot \rho_{ij} \cdot \mu_{\ell,j}^{t}, \sum_{j \in \Omega_i}\sum_{z \in \Omega_i} \left(\frac{1}{|\Omega_i|} \right)^2 \left(\rho_{ij}^2 \sigma_{\ell,j,j}^{t} + \rho_{iz}^2 \sigma_{\ell,z,z}^{t} + 2\rho_{iz}\rho_{ij}\sigma_{\ell,j,z}^{t} \right) \right) \tag{1.3}$$

1.4 Experiments and Results

We ask the following research questions:

- **RQ1**: Which SR Metric is the most suitable (ρ)?
- **RQ2**: How many observed related topics should be used ($|\Omega_i|$)?
- **RQ3**: Can Semantic TrueLearn outperform TrueLearn Novel?
- **RQ4**: Does semantic information contribute to the gains? How?
- **RQ5**: Can this approach generalize to other user models?

1.4.1 Semantic Relatedness Metric (SR Metric)

As mentioned in Section 1.2, different measures of SR for Wikipedia concepts exist (Ponza et al., 2020). We empirically evaluate if the predictive performance of an educational recommender can be improved by incorporating seven different SR Metrics to substitute ρ_{ij} in Equations 1.2 and 1.3. We devise Milne and Witten (M&W), Entity Embeddings (W2V), Point-wise Mutual Information (PMI), Language Model (LM), Jaccard Similarity (Jaccard), Conditional Probability (CP), and Barabasi and Albert (BA) SR Metrics, where SR values are pre-computed and publicly available (Piccinno, 2017).

1.4.2 Models

The core objective of this research tested through RQ 1–4 is to validate if exploiting SR can improve the predictive capability of the TrueLearn Novel model. To test this we integrate the formulations outlined in Section 1.3 by using them whenever the model has not encountered that Wikipedia-based KC in the learner history before. The two models, Semantic TrueLearn Univariate (Semantic TLN Univ.) using Equation 1.2 and Semantic TrueLearn Multivariate (Semantic TLN Mult.) using Equation 1.3, are developed and tested against TrueLearn Novel (Bulathwela et al., 2020c) as the baseline.

To test RQ5, we create the semantic counterparts of a set of relevant baselines that use Wikipedia concepts for user modeling. KT, a different PGM that models learner skills as Bernoulli variables and two user models, the *Cosine* model (Bulathwela et al., 2021b) and *TF(Cosine)* (Piao & Breslin, 2016), that are not PGMs are transformed into semantically aware models by using Equation 1.2. The variance calculation in the equation is omitted as the above models do not explicitly model the variance of the skill variables ($\sigma = 0$). This introduces *Semantic Cosine* and *Semantic TF(Cosine)* for empirically testing RQ5.

1.4.3 Data

As the TrueLearn Novel model deals with video fragment recommendation, we test the new proposals using the same prediction task. We use the PEEK dataset (Bulathwela et al., 2021b), a dataset of more than 20,000 informal learners consuming video lectures in VideoLectures.Net[1] platform. The dataset provides information about how different users consumed fragments of videos over time (Bulathwela, Kreitmayer, & Pérez-Ortiz, 2020a). The majority of videos in this repository are related to computer science. This dataset uses entity linking (Brank et al., 2017) to associate most related Wikipedia concepts to documents. We use the TagMe WAT API (Piccinno & Ferragina, 2014)[2] to source the required SR annotations. As the KCs associated with a video fragment are highly related to each other, we exclusively use the most relevant KC from each video fragment to represent the topic covered by that video fragment ignoring the other KCs associated with that video fragment. Doing this helps us avoid any side effects that can dilute our objective of measuring if exploiting SR improves the predictive abilities of the model. It also exponentially decreases the number of SR annotations we need to run the experiments.

To keep the computational complexity lower, a smaller dataset of the 20 most active users is used when validating RQ 1 and 2. Once the choice of SR metric and the number of related topics have been determined, the full dataset of 20,000 users is used to validate RQ 3–5, which are our primary research questions.

1.4.4 Experimental Design

We used a phased experimental methodology where the results from the early experiments determined the parameters for the subsequent experiments. We empirically evaluated models built with different SR metrics to answer RQ1. The best performant SR metric from the RQ1 experiment was then used to determine how many related topics should be used (RQ2). Then, we used both of these results in RQ3 to test Semantic TLN Univ. and Semantic TLN Mult. against the TrueLearn Novel baseline. Finally, the semantic counterparts of KT, Cosine and TF(Cosine) models were developed as per Equation 1.1 empirically tested for RQ5 with the same SR metric and number of topics that are predetermined in RQ 1 and 2 experiments, respectively. As the latter models used in the RQ5 experiment do not have a variance component, Equations 1.2 and 1.3 reduce to the same formulation as the mean μ is computed similarly.

1.4.4.1 Impact of Semantic Relatedness

We use the topics encountered in user sessions to build a topic-relatedness graph and extract a few attributes linked to graph connectedness for each user. Spearman's Rank Order Correlation Coefficient (SROCC) statistic is then used to evaluate the correlation between the extracted features and the

TABLE 1.1

Predictive Performance of Adding SR to TrueLearn Novel Algorithm. The Different Configurations (SR Metric) of the Semantic TrueLearn Novel Algorithm (Our Proposal) Are Evaluated Using Precision (Prec.), Recall (Rec.), and F1 Score (F1)

Model	SR Metric	Prec.	Rec.	F1
TrueLearn Novel	–	**0.7667**	**0.9476**	**0.8348**
	M&W	0.7701	0.9469	*0.8364*
	W2V	**0.7714**	0.9467	**0.8370**
Semantic	PMI	0.7682	*0.9480*	0.8355
TrueLearn	LM	0.7605	**0.9507**	0.8322
Novel	Jaccard	0.7605	**0.9507**	0.8322
	CP	0.7621	**0.9507**	0.8330
	BA	*0.7704*	0.9469	*0.8364*

Note: The most performant value and the next best value are highlighted in **Bold** and *Italic* faces, respectively. The Semantic TrueLearn algorithms that outperform the baseline model in terms of F1 score are <u>Underlined</u>.

predictive performance. User's *number of events, number of unique topics, topic sparsity rate* (Bulathwela et al., 2020c), *positive label rate, Avg. Connectedness*, i.e., average of the degree distribution of the topics, and *Min. Cut Set Size*, i.e., the minimum number of topics that need to be removed to break the graph into more sub-graphs, are analyzed. The correlation with the recall score is investigated as the improvement in recall attributes to the performance gains of the proposed model (see Table 1.1). To validate if SR is specifically influential in earlier parts of the user session, we plot the mean recall score of all users at event n, for different number of events (n).

1.4.5 Evaluation

In all the empirical evaluations (RQ 1, 2, 3, and 5), a sequential prediction design where engagement at time t is predicted using events 1 to $t-1$ is utilized in this prediction task. A training set of 70% of learners is used for hyperparameter tuning and the remainder is used for testing and reporting. Being a binary classification task, precision, recall, and F1-measure are evaluated whereas F1-measure is used for overall model selection (Bulathwela et al., 2021b). The evaluation metrics are computed for each learner separately and the weighted average of the scores based on the number of learner's events is reported. In cases where the entire dataset is used for evaluation (RQ3 experiment onward), we use a learner-wise one-tailed paired t-test to verify the statistical significance of the improvement.

When measuring the correlation between different learner session-related attributes and the recall score in order to validate RQ4, we use SROCC to assess the degree of correlation between pairs of variables.

TABLE 1.2

The Performance of Semantic TrueLearn Model with W2V SR Metric Is Reported in Terms of Precision (Prec.), Recall (Rec.), and F1 Score (F1)

Number of Topics ($\Omega_{\ell,i}$)	Prec.	Rec.	F1
Most related topic	**0.7717**	0.9431	*0.8359*
Three most related Topics	0.7622	*0.9486*	0.8325
Five most related Topics	0.7659	**0.9490**	0.8345
Ten most related topics	0.7654	**0.9490**	0.8342
All related topics	*0.7714*	0.9467	**0.8370**

Note: The performance of the model is reported when different $\Omega_{\ell,i}$ top semantically related topics are utilized in Equation 1.1. The most performant value and the next best value are highlighted in **Bold** and *Italic* faces, respectively.

1.4.6 Results

We run experiments to answer the research questions outlined above. To identify the most suitable SR metric (RQ1), we evaluate the Semantic TrueLearn model using seven SR Metrics proposed in Section 1.3.2. The results are outlined in Table 1.1. To understand the effect of Ω_i, the Number of Semantically Related Topics (RQ2), we use the identified SR Metric to experiment with different numbers of semantically related topics. The results of this experiment are reported in Table 1.2. Finally, we use the full PEEK dataset to validate if the use of SR data improves the baseline TrueLearn model (RQ3). The results obtained in this experiment are presented in Table 1.3. Figure 1.2 presents the results obtained in investigating the impact of SR (RQ4) where (left) the correlation investigation between topic connectivity of users and recall score and (right) the performance of the model based on a different number of events is reported. The predictive performance of the different user models (left) and their semantic counterparts (right) on the PEEK dataset are outlined in Table 1.4 (RQ5). To ensure fairness of comparisons, Cosine, TF(Cosine), and KT models are trained using the highest ranking topic for

TABLE 1.3

Predictive Performance of Semantic TrueLearn Model (Our Proposal) Using Precision (Prec.), Recall (Rec.), and F1 Score (F1)

	Model	Prec.	Rec.	F1
Baseline	**TrueLearn Novel**	0.5829	0.7924	0.6471
Semantic TLN	Univariate (Univ.)	0.5711	**0.8563**[*]	**0.6512**[*]
	Multivariate (Mult.)	*0.5759*	*0.8251*[*]	*0.6480*[*]

Note: The most performant value is highlighted in **Bold** face. The Semantic TrueLearn model that outperforms the baseline model ($p < 0.01$ in a one-tailed paired t-test) is marked with·[*].

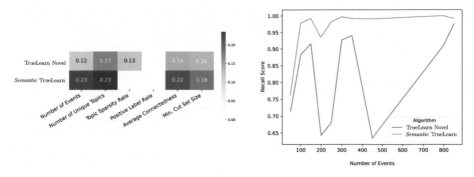

FIGURE 1.2

(Left) Relationship between different behavioral characteristics of user-profiles and model recall performance presented using SROCC. The numbers and the intensity of each cell correspond to the Spearman r coefficient where a significant correlation is present ($p < 0.01$). Empty cells represent the lack of significant correlation. (Right) The average recall performance of the two models for the learner population at a different number of events.

each video fragment in the learner sessions. However, prior work shows that the cosine and the TF(Cosine) models perform best when using the five highest ranked topics. Therefore, we also report the performance of the model trained on five topics in Table 1.4 for a more informative comparison.

1.4.7 Discussion

It is evident from Table 1.1 that incorporating SR leads to improvements in overall F1 score in most of the SR metrics that beat the baseline TrueLearn algorithm. Four Semantic TrueLearn models (ones that use M&W, W2V, PMI, and BA) tend to outperform the baseline TrueLearn Novel model in terms of precision and F1. The remainder demonstrates superiority in the recall. When we consider the F1 score for model comparison, the model that uses

TABLE 1.4

Predictive Performance of Semantic Models (Our Proposals) Using Precision (Prec.), Recall (Rec.), and F1 Score (F1)

Model	Prior Work				Semantic		
	Prec.	Rec.	F1		Prec.	Rec.	F1
Knowledge tracing	0.5325	0.2856	0.3451		**0.5737**[(*)]	0.5613[(*)]	0.5344[(*)]
Cosine	0.4792	0.1599	0.2112		*0.5652*[(*)]	**0.7377**[(*)]	**0.5978**[(*)]
• Five topics	0.5786	0.5845	0.5406		•	•	•
TF(Cosine)	0.5231	0.3355	0.3670		0.5651[(*)]	*0.6805*[(*)]	*0.5728*[(*)]
• Five topics	0.5675	0.6595	0.5711		•	•	•

Note: The most performant value and the next best value are highlighted in **Bold** and *Italic* faces, respectively. The semantic models that outperform the baseline model ($p < 0.01$ in a one-tailed paired t-test) are marked with·[(*)].

the entity embedding-based SR metric (W2V) indicates the best performance among the different semantic models. This is expected, as neural-based SR measures often outperform their graph-based counterparts (Ponza et al., 2020). Therefore, we can observe that the most suitable SR metric for this task (RQ1) is the entity embedding-based metric. Our empirical results in experiments relating to RQ2, outlined in Table 1.2, show that using *all* semantically related topics to infer the skill of the unobserved KC gives the best prediction results in contrast to restricting the number of related topics used. The results in Table 1.3, which attempts to validate if the proposed semantic formulations can help TrueLearn Novel address the cold-start problem (RQ3), show the superiority of Semantic TrueLearn models in comparison to the baseline that does not exploit SR information from Wikipedia. This is a clear indication that a knowledge base such as Wikipedia can be critical to improving the assumptions used for a learner, modeled using a PGM in the education context. Both the Univ. and Mult. Semantic TrueLearn models outperform the baseline to a statistically significant degree in recall and F1. It is observed in Table 1.3 that this improvement of F1 score is attained by significantly increasing the recall of the model by sacrificing a smaller amount of precision. While this is a compromise of this model, the overall performance of the model is improved. It is also interesting to see that modeling the relatedness between the observed topics (Mult. formulation) leads to better precision than not doing it. This indicates that accounting for many different dynamics in the data generation process and capturing them leads to a more precise prediction. However, this precision doesn't translate to overall model superiority in terms of the F1 score in comparison to the Univ. counterpart. It is also noteworthy that the computational complexity of the Mult. version is significantly higher as there is exponentially more SR connections that need to be used in the variance calculation. In an online, lifelong learning platform that needs to scale seamlessly, this can be a disadvantage. The results give promise that the information encoded in a knowledge base such as Wikipedia can be used in ways beyond representing contents in a universal taxonomy. Certain relationships in Wikipedia can be further utilized to improve the model assumptions. In this scenario, SR has shown truly valuable in the early stages of the user session when the interaction data about the user is limited, thus addressing the cold-start problem.

The evaluation of correlations presented in Figure 1.2 (left) investigates the reasons behind the superior performance of the semantic models (RQ4). This sub-figure shows the lack of correlation between Positive Label Rate and recall score across both TrueLearn models. Although it has been demonstrated by the original authors that the TrueLearn algorithm capitalizes on recall, there is no information in the work regarding the positive label rate in the datasets. This observation confirms that the TrueLearn family of algorithms find true patterns in learner data rather than merely capitalizing on the positive labels to boost performance.

Multiple observations in Figure 1.2 (left) give evidence of the superiority of Semantic TrueLearn exploiting the SR between topics to boost recall. The main two observations are the new model's stronger Spearman's rank correlation with learner *Avg. Connectedness* and *Min. Cut Set Size*. This is a strong indication that the Semantic TruLearn model is exploiting the topic correlations. The correlation between the number of events, number of unique topics, and topic connectedness causes the higher correlation between these features and the Semantic TrueLearn model. Figure 1.2 (right) clearly shows how the recall score of predictions is much larger in the Semantic TrueLearn algorithm regardless of the early or later stage of the learner session. Linking this to results in Table 1.1 shows that this impressive gain of recall score is achieved with a much smaller sacrifice of the precision score. Figure 1.2 (right) also shows the nature of this cold-start problem which can occur at any time during the learner's session. Usually, the cold-start problem is associated with the early stages of a learner session, mainly because the scarcity of data is prominent in early stages of a user session in a recommender. However, in educational recommenders and other informational recommenders (e.g., news, podcasts, etc.) where the concept space can be very vast and the learner can journey in the entire knowledge space, the cold-start problem can occur at any given stage of the learner session. The analysis shows that the approach proposed helps combat this phenomenon successfully.

The final question we want to answer is if exploiting SR goes beyond the TrueLearn Novel model (RQ5). The results in Table 1.4 provide solid evidence that this is the case. The table shows that adding the semantic extension proposed in this work to a variety of recently proposed Wikipedia concept-based user models leads to statistically significant improvements across precision, recall, and F1 score. When comparing with the five topic versions of the Cosine and TF(Cosine) models, the table gives evidence that the one topic version of semantic models still outperforms the five topic non-semantic versions by a significant margin in recall and F1 score, the overall evaluation metric. This is further evidence that the utilization of SR coming from Wikipedia can have a strong positive impact on user modeling.

1.4.8 Human-Intuitive Representations

The Semantic TrueLearn model in unison with all the other models used in this work uses Wikipedia-based concepts to build the user representation. This makes the user models humanly intuitive and capable of diagnosis, interpretation, and scrutiny. As the concepts/KCs in the model are symbols familiar to human perception, user-friendly explanations and rationalizations can be produced using the model representation. Specifically, in the context of exploiting SR, the models proposed in this work use the mechanism presented in Figure 1.1. This is already a simple, user-friendly visualization of how the learner model is reasoning. Therefore, approaches such as this that rely on knowledge bases such as Wikipedia have the ability to connect the AI systems to the human users with richer explanations allowing the users to provide a higher degree of engagement and feedback, leading the systems to improve rapidly over time.

1.4.9 Limitations

Amid the significant gains, we observe that most KCs encountered by the model in a session are highly correlated to each other (as the majority of video lectures on the source website are about computer science). This leads to over-lapping information being propagated repeatedly when using Equation 1.1 which may lead to an overestimation of knowledge of unseen KCs. While restricting to exclusively using the top-ranked KC from each video fragment helps us reduce this effect, it doesn't completely solve the problem. Methods to address this effect should be investigated further. As the proposed method primarily infers *unobserved* skills, its use diminishes over time when the user session matures (as new topics are encountered less often). While there is a chance to encounter new topics at any stage of the learner journey, the changes become slimmer over time and so is this approaches usefulness. Mechanisms to retain the use of semantic awareness to refine representations is a much-needed improvement to the proposed method.

1.5 Conclusions

Leveraging SR between Wikipedia topics has demonstrated promise to improve the predictive performance of informational recommenders such as TrueLearn, which are built on Wikipedia ontology and PGMs. In addition, we identify that restricting the number of related topics leads to degraded per-formance, suggesting the use of all available KCs extracted from Wikification. Our analysis also shows that topic connectedness within learner sessions is positively correlated with the performance gains of Semantic TrueLearn, giv-ing clearer evidence of the positive impact of incorporating this aspect when modeling learners and their journey within an education setting. Further investigations also show that the proposed methods generalize to other learner modeling techniques that go beyond the TrueLearn family of models extending to both PGMs and classical concept-based user models.

1.5.1 Future Work

The proposed model is a stepping stone to accounting for SR. However, it still can do better in terms of capturing the correlation among the observed topics. We propose (i) using algorithms such as PageRank (Brin & Page, 1998) to derive uncorrelated skill parameters and (ii) incorporating richer ontolo-gies (Auer et al., 2007) that contain more fine-grained relationships, entity definitions/categorizations, and constraints in the place of the raw Wikipedia graph to incorporate finer grain semantic awareness to the learner model. Mechanisms to continuously utilize SR information (even in the absence of new topics) should be identified and investigated in future work. Moreover, SR measures are not usually built and validated with educational datasets or topics, which is a limitation of the field. In the future, we should aim to validate the usefulness of proposed SR metrics with educational applications and thrive to improve them to align more with educational and information use cases. Also, more advanced model families (e.g., Bulathwela, Pérez-Ortiz, Yilmaz, & Shawe-Taylor, 2022) can benefit from the proposed techniques leading to a generation of semantically aware, integrative educational recommendation systems. As Semantic TrueLearn builds a sub-symbolic representation that is humanly intuitive, it is possible to create narratives and intelligent user interfaces (e.g., Bulathwela et al., 2020a; Pérez-Ortiz et al., 2021) that can be used to interpret and rationalize (Riedl & Bulitko, 2013) the learnings from the model leading toward more *human-in-the-loop* artificial intelligence. This will increase trust and enable verification and scrutinizing of the models (Balog, Radlinski, & Arakelyan, 2019). Going beyond recommendation, SR can be harnessed to improve information retrieval systems as well Ahmed and Bulathwela (2022).

Acknowledgments

This research is conducted as part of the X5GON project (www.x5gon.org) funded by the EU's Horizon 2020 research and innovation program grant number 761758. We gratefully acknowledge support and funding from the US Army Research Laboratory and the US Army Research Office, and by the UK Ministry of Defence and the U.K. Engineering and Physical Sciences Research Council (EPSRC) under grant number EP/R013616/1. This work is also partially supported by the European Commission funded project "Humane AI: Toward AI Systems That Augment and Empower Humans by Understanding Us, our Society and the World Around Us" (grant 820437), EU Erasmus+ project "European Network for Catalysing Open Resources in Education" (project ref: 621586-EPP-1-2020-1-NO-EPPKA2-KA), and the EPSRC Fellowship titled "Task Based Information Retrieval" (grant EP/P024289/1). The AT2030 program is funded by the UK Aid from the UK government and led by the Global Disability Innovation Hub.

Notes

1 www.videolectures.net
2 https://sobigdata.d4science.org/web/tagme/wat-api

References

Ahmed, T., & Bulathwela, S. (2022). Towards proactive information retrieval in noisy text with Wikipedia concepts. In *Proc. of the first workshop on proactive and agent-supported information retrieval at conference of information and knowledge management*.

Auer, S., Bizer, C., Kobilarov, G., Lehmann, J., Cyganiak, R., & Ives, Z. (2007). DBpedia: A nucleus for a web of open data. In *The Semantic Web: 6th International Semantic Web Conference, 2nd Asian Semantic Web Conference, ISWC 2007+ ASWC 2007, Busan, Korea, November 11–15, 2007. Proceedings* (pp. 722–735). Berlin, Heidelberg: Springer.

Bahdanau, D., Cho, K., & Bengio, Y. (2015). Neural machine translation by jointly learning to align and translate. In Y. Bengio & Y. LeCun (Eds.), *Third international conference on learning representations, ICLR 2015, San Diego, CA, USA, May 7–9, 2015, conference track proceedings*.

Balog, K., Radlinski, F., & Arakelyan, S. (2019). Transparent, scrutable and explainable user models for personalized recommendation. In *Proc. of the 42nd international ACM SIGIR conference on research and development in information retrieval (SIGIR '19)*.

Bauman, K., & Tuzhilin, A. (2018). Recommending remedial learning materials to students by filling their knowledge gaps. *MIS Quarterly, 42*(1):313–332.

Bishop, C., Winn, J., & Diethe, T. (2015). *Model-based machine learning*. Early access version (http://www.mbmlbook.com/) (accessed 23-05-2019).

Brank, J., Leban, G., & Grobelnik, M. (2017). Annotating documents with relevant wikipedia concepts. In *Proc. of Slovenian KDD conference on data mining and data warehouses (SIKDD)*.

Brin, S., & Page, L. (1998). The anatomy of a large-scale hypertextual web search engine. In *Proc. of international conference. on world wide web*.

Bulathwela, S., Kreitmayer, S., & Pérez-Ortiz, M. (2020a). What's in it for me? augmenting recommended learning resources with navigable annotations. In *Proc. of international conference on intelligent user interfaces companion* (pp. 114–115).

Bulathwela, S., Pérez-Ortiz, M., Mehrotra, R., Orlic, D., de la Higuera, C., Shawe-Taylor, J., & Yilmaz, E. (2021a, February). Report on the WSDM 2020 workshop on state-based user modelling (sum'20). *SIGIR Forum, 54*(1), Article No.: 5: 1–11. Retrieved from https://doi.org/10.1145/3451964.3451969.

Bulathwela, S., Pérez-Ortiz, M., Novak, E., Yilmaz, E., & Shawe-Taylor, J. (2021b). *Peek: A large dataset of learner engagement with educational videos*. Retrieved from https://arxiv.org/abs/2109.03154.

Bulathwela, S., Pérez-Ortiz, M., Yilmaz, E., & Shawe-Taylor, J. (2020b). Towards an integrative educational recommender for lifelong learners. In *AAAI conference on artificial intelligence*. Retrieved from https://doi.org/10.1609/aaai.v34i10.7151.

Bulathwela, S., Pérez-Ortiz, M., Yilmaz, E., & Shawe-Taylor, J. (2020c). Truelearn: A family of Bayesian algorithms to match lifelong learners to open educational resources. In *AAAI conference on artificial intelligence*. Retrieved from https://doi.org/10.1609/aaai.v34i01.5395.

Bulathwela, S., Pérez-Ortiz, M., Yilmaz, E., & Shawe-Taylor, J. (2022). Power to the learner: Towards human-intuitive and integrative recommendations with open educational resources. *Sustainability, 14*(18). Retrieved from https://www.mdpi.com/2071-1050/14/18/11682.

Carmona, C., Millán, E., Pérez-de-la Cruz, J. L., Trella, M., & Conejo, R. (2005). Introducing prerequisite relations in a multi-layered Bayesian student model. In *Proc. of the international conference on user modeling* (pp. 347–356).

Chen, P., Lu, Y., Zheng, V. W., & Pian, Y. (2018). Prerequisite-driven deep knowledge tracing. In *2018 IEEE international conference on data mining (ICDM)* (pp. 39–48).

Grefenstette, G., & Rafes, K. (2015). Transforming Wikipedia into an ontology-based information retrieval search engine for local experts using a third-party taxonomy. *arXiv preprint arXiv:1511.01259*. Retrieved from https://arxiv.org/abs/1511.01259.

Huang, Z., Yin, Y., Chen, E., Xiong, H., Su, Y., Hu, G., et al. (2019). EKT: Exercise-aware knowledge tracing for student performance prediction. *IEEE Transactions on Knowledge and Data Engineering, 13*(1): 100–115.

Jiang, W., Pardos, Z. A., & Wei, Q. (2019). Goal-based course recommendation. In *Proceedings of international conference on learning analytics & knowledge*.

Kawakami, T., Morita, T., & Yamaguchi, T. (2017). Building Wikipedia ontology with more semi-structured information resources. In *Semantic technology – 7th joint international conference, JIST 2017, proceedings*. Springer.

Kipf, T. N., & Welling, M. (2017). Semi-supervised classification with graph convolutional networks. In *International conference on learning representations (ICLR)*.

Lewis, P., Perez, E., Piktus, A., Petroni, F., Karpukhin, V., Goyal, N., … (2020). Retrieval-augmented generation for knowledge-intensive NLP tasks. *arXiv preprint arXiv:2005.11401*. Retrieved from https://arxiv.org/abs/2005.11401.

Mandalapu, V., Gong, J., & Chen, L. (2021). Do we need to go deep? knowledge tracing with big data. *arXiv preprint arXiv:2101.08349*. Retrieved from https://arxiv.org/abs/2101.08349.

Nakagawa, H., Iwasawa, Y., & Matsuo, Y. (2019). Graph-based knowledge tracing: modeling student proficiency using graph neural network. In *2019 IEEE/WIC/ACM international conference on web intelligence (WI)* (pp. 156–163).

Pandey, S., & Srivastava, J. (2020). RKT: Relation-aware self-attention for knowledge tracing. *arXiv preprint arXiv:2008.12736*. Retrieved from https://arxiv.org/abs/2008.12736.

Pérez-Ortiz, M., Dormann, C., Rogers, Y., Bulathwela, S., Kreitmayer, S., Yilmaz, E., … Shawe-Taylor, J. (2021). X5learn: A personalised learning companion at the intersection of AI and HCI. In *26th international conference on intelligent user interfaces* (pp. 70–74).

Piao, G. (2021). Recommending knowledge concepts on mooc platforms with meta-path-based representation learning. In *Proc. of international conference on educational data mining*.

Piao, G., & Breslin, J. G. (2016). Analyzing MOOC entries of professionals on linkedin for user modeling and personalized MOOC recommendations. In *Proceedings of the 2016 conference on user modeling adaptation and personalization*.

Piccinno, F. (2017). *Algorithms and data structures for big labeled graphs* (Unpublished doctoral dissertation). Universitade Pisa.

Piccinno, F., & Ferragina, P. (2014). From TagMe to wat: A new entity annotator. In *Proc. of the first international workshop on entity recognition & disambiguation (ERD'14)*. Retrieved from https://doi.org/10.1145/2633211.2634350.

Ponza, M., Ferragina, P., & Chakrabarti, S. (2020). On computing entity relatedness in wikipedia, with applications. *Knowledge-Based Systems, 188*.

Riedl, M. O., & Bulitko, V. (2013). Interactive narrative: An intelligent systems approach. *Ai Magazine, 34*(1):67–67.

Schmucker, R., Wang, J., Hu, S., & Mitchell, T. (2022, June). Assessing the performance of online students - new data, new approaches, improved accuracy. *Journal of Educational Data Mining*, 14(1):1–45. Retrieved from https://jedm.educational datamining.org/index.php/JEDM/article/view/541.

Selent, D., Patikorn, T., & Heffernan, N. (2016). ASSISTments dataset from multiple randomized controlled experiments. In *Proc. of the conference on learning @ scale (L@S '16)*. Retrieved from https://doi.org/10.1145/2876034.2893409.

Song, X., Li, J., Tang, Y., Zhao, T., Chen, Y., & Guan, Z. (2021). JKT: A joint graph convolutional network based deep knowledge tracing. *Information Sciences*, 580:510–523.

Syed, Z., Finin, T., & Joshi, A. (2008, March). Wikipedia as an ontology for describing documents. In *Proc. of international conference on weblogs and social media*. AAAI Press.

Thaker, K., Zhang, L., He, D., & Brusilovsky, P. (2020). Recommending remedial readings using student knowledge state. In *Proc. of international conference on EDM*.

Yano, T., & Kang, M. (2016). *Taking advantage of Wikipedia in natural language processing* (Tech. Rep.). Carnegie Mellon University Language Technologies Institute.

Yang, Y., Shen, J., Qu, Y., Liu, Y., Wang, K., Zhu, Y., Yu, Y.... (2020). GIKT: a graph-based interaction model for knowledge tracing. In *Joint European conference on machine learning and knowledge discovery in databases* (pp. 299–315).

Yudelson, M. V., Koedinger, K. R., & Gordon, G. J. (2013). Individualized Bayesian knowledge tracing models. In H. C. Lane, K. Yacef, J. Mostow, & P. Pavlik (Eds.), *Proc. of artificial intelligence in education*.

Zarrinkalam, F., Faralli, S., Piao, G., & Bagheri, E. (2020). Extracting, mining and predicting users' interests from social media. *Foundations and Trends® in Information*, 14(5): 445–617. Boston, MA: Now publishers. Retrieved from http://dx.doi.org/10.1561/1500000078.

2

Modeling Event-Centric Knowledge Graph for Crime Analysis on Online News

Federica Rollo and Laura Po

Department of Engineering, University of Modena and Reggio Emilia, Modena, Italy

CONTENTS

2.1 Introduction

Crime analysis is the set of quantitative and qualitative techniques to analyze crime data, including not only the analysis of actual crimes, criminals, and victims but also the understanding of problems related to the quality of life in a community, the socio-demographic aspects and other factors that can influence the frequency of crime in that community. Also, crime analysis aims at identifying crime patterns and trend correlations that can help law enforcement agencies (LEAs) in crime reduction, prevention, and evaluation. Police reports can be helpful for these scopes since they provide a complete description of crimes; however, these documents are usually private and authorization is required for access.

In this context, newspapers are valuable sources of information. The extraction of structured information on events from online sources for the purpose of crime intelligence gathering has been acknowledged to be of paramount importance by various organizations worldwide. Newspapers provide reliable, localized, and timely data (the time delay between the occurrence of the event and the publication of the related news article does not exceed 24/48 hours). The main drawback is that newspapers do not collect and publish all the facts related to crimes, but only the ones that arouse the readers' interest. Therefore, a percentage of police reports will not be turned into news articles and is lost. Natural language processing (NLP) techniques can be exploited for understanding the content of the news articles and extracting semantically enriched data. Moreover, information about an event is usually spread across multiple news articles. Over time, more details are provided about the dynamics of the event. Identifying the news articles related to the same event is of key importance to merge duplicates and make crime analysis more reliable. On the other hand, clustering similar news articles allows to perform statistical analysis on crime events, e.g., finding the number of car thefts occurred in a specific month in a certain neighborhood of the city or the rate of armed robberies w.r.t. the total number of robberies in the city. For this reason, a representation of the events and their relations is needed.

The Event-Centric Knowledge Graphs are specific knowledge graphs in which information is centered on the event instead of the entities, as defined by Rospocher et al. (2016). These knowledge graphs are able to provide an accurate description of the events and allow for the interconnection between them. Each event is represented by a central node that is connected to other nodes which express the characteristics of the event. These nodes can be connected to more central nodes, which means the corresponding events have something in common. Community detection algorithms can be applied to the graph to distinguish groups of similar event nodes.

In this chapter, we propose a methodology to build in Neo4j an Event-Centric Knowledge Graph related to crime events as they are described in news articles. Centrality algorithms are used to find the importance of the central nodes, and community detection allows to find similar events to perform crime analysis. The methodology is applied to the Italian Crime News dataset[1] demonstrating the advantages of using graph-based analysis in crime monitoring.

The remainder of the contribution is organized as follows: Section 2.2 introduces some previous related work, then Section 2.3 explains the workflow to build our Event-Centric Knowledge Graph, while the experiments on an Italian dataset are presented in Section 2.4 as well as some possible analysis on crime events. We conclude with a discussion and future work in Section 2.5.

2.2 Related Work

In recent years, researchers have taken an increasing interest in the automatic construction of knowledge graphs. Indeed, knowledge graphs have been found to be very helpful representations applied in a multiple number of contexts. In particular, they can be employed for representing events and discovering their relations.

In literature, there are few works focusing on the construction of event-based knowledge graphs for the representation of information contained in unstructured data, e.g., freeform text (Guo, Jiang, and Zhang, 2020; Lakshika and Caldera, 2021). A graph analytical approach was proposed by Po, Rollo, and Lado (2016) to identify the main topics published on social media. The graph is based on the co-occurrence of words across the news articles; however, semantic relationships are not included. An extension was provided by Rollo (2017) to consider also entities for the generation of the graph. In our recent work (Rollo and Po, 2022), we described a method to build knowledge graphs from textual data using Entity Linking and Automatic Keyphrase Extraction.

Moreover, a consistent number of previous works refer to methodologies for the extraction and analysis of named events, e.g., historical events of global importance, from existing knowledge graph (Kuculo, 2022). In most cases, knowledge graphs focus on Entity-Centric knowledge; for example, this is the case of large-scale knowledge graphs such as Wikidata (Vrandecic, 2012), DBpedia (Auer et al., 2007), and YAGO (Mahdisoltani, Biega, and Suchanek, 2015). The concept of Event-Centric Knowledge Graph was defined by Rospocher et al. (2016). In the knowledge graph centered on the event all the data are stored w.r.t. the event, this feature allows to capture the dynamic of the event. Several analyses can be performed on the graph to derive new knowledge about the events, make prediction, generate a storyline of the events, understand their causality (Li et al., 2023; Yan and Tang, 2022). Some works focus on expressing the temporal relation between events (Gottschalk and Demidova, 2018; Knez, 2022; Park et al., 2022).

The use of knowledge graph in the context of criminal data allows to develop technique for investigating, fighting, and preventing crime (Abdul Jalil et al., 2017; Jedrzejek and Bak, 2012; Onnoom et al., 2014; Venkata Srimukh and Shridevi, 2020). Robinson and Scogings (2018) proposed the GraphExtract algorithm to build a weighted graph for proactively identifying criminal events and the actors responsible. Elezaj et al. (2019) extended the SMONT ontology developed by Kalemi et al. (2017) and defined a knowledge graph-based framework to identify the murderer by inferring the person who has the motive, opportunity, and method starting from social networks. Peppes et al. (2020) proposed a visualization tool based on the use of an ontology for performing advanced crime analysis. Szekely et al. (2015) suggested a method to crawl sexual ads from the web and provide LEAs a knowledge graph tool to fight human trafficking and support victims. Data from the web are organized in a predefined ontology, then, the authors address the problem of duplicates through text similarity and entity resolution. Table 2.1 summarizes the main aspects of previous works on the use of knowledge graph in the context of crimes.

With respect to the cited related works, in this chapter, we combine techniques based on graph structure with semantic-based extraction and relationship generation for the analysis of crime events. Adding semantics makes the data not only interconnected but also smarter, allowing for inference,

TABLE 2.1

Previous Works on the Use of Knowledge Graph in the Context of Criminal Data

Reference	Goal(G), Use case(U), Limitation(L)
Abdul Jalil et al. (2017)	**G**: development of a model to match similar crimes and help investigation officer in targeting suspects within the shortest time. **U**: motorcycle thefts **L**: thefts are connected each other just considering the exact match of some data (modus operandi, motorcycle type, crime scene, and time), no semantic approach is used to link semantically similar values
Venkata Srimukh and Shridevi (2020)	**G**: description of an ontology to represent crimes reported to LEAs **L**: the model does not allow to express key information of crimes, e.g., what was used to commit the crime, the stolen objects in a theft. Besides, the ontology is not available for integration and reuse
Onnoom et al. (2014)	**G**: ontology development to recommend words to fill in reports of crime scene investigation **U**: real crime cases from the Forensic Science Police Center 4 of Thailand **L**: the proposed ontology is limited to the specific use case, generalization requires training on new documents
Jedrzejek and Bak (2012)	**G**: extension of a model for representing economic crimes committed by employees **L**: the complexity of the ontology assumes a deep preprocessing of the data to represent, this could be a limit for usability
Elezaj et al. (2019)	**G**: definition of a knowledge graph-based framework for crime analysis starting from social networks **L**: the framework is not implemented; therefore, it is not possible to evaluate its efficiency
Szekely et al. (2015)	**G**: development of an ontology-based knowledge graph from online sexual ads **U**: fighting human trafficking and supporting victims **L**: the text similarity used to find duplicates does not consider synonyms and/or semantic relationships, e.g., connecting the entities to a known vocabulary

analytics, and learning. Moreover, we propose a novel representation of the events that is specific of events as they are described in the news articles. To the best of our knowledge, this is the first work that proposes the construction of such a knowledge graph starting from news articles for crime analysis purposes.

2.3 Event-Centric Knowledge Graph

Our Event-Centric Knwoledge Graph aims at providing a comprehensive representation of the events and highlighting the relationships between different events.

In journalism, the 5W + 1H are the questions the reporter needs to answer in reporting an event:

- What (what is happening?)
- Who (who is involved?)
- Where (where did it happen?)
- When (when did it happen?)
- Why (why did it happen?)
- How (how did it happen?)

Each news article is complete if it contains the answers to all the questions, on the other hand, extracting these answers allows at giving a complete description of the event. In some contexts, the answer to some of these questions may not be present, for instance, this is often the case of question Why. In news articles reporting crime events, the people involved (Who) can be detailed based on the role in the event: the author(s) of the crime, the victim(s), and other participants, e.g., the police. Considering this subdivision, the total number of questions is eight. Since in most cases the scope of the news articles is to provide information related to single events, a single-crime-event-per-document assumption is made. Thus, event and news article can be considered as synonyms in this chapter. Figure 2.1 shows an exemplar representation of a crime event through the Event-Centric Knowledge Graph. The central node E representing the event is connected to eight nodes representing the eight questions. The same answer to a certain question can be extracted from different news articles and shared by multiple events.

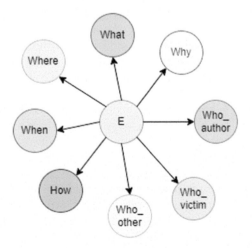

FIGURE 2.1
Crime event representation in the Event-Centric Knowledge Graph.

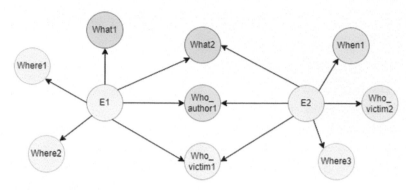

FIGURE 2.2
Interconnection between two crime events.

Representing events in such a way allows to understand the interconnection between the news articles and, consequently, the events. Just as an example, Figure 2.2 illustrates two events (E_1 and E_2) sharing one node What, one Who author, and one Who victim.

Also, the semantically similar answers can be connected each other. Different approaches can be exploited to calculate the semantic similarity of two answers. We propose to use the contextualized word embeddings of BERT (Bidirectional Encoder Representations from Transformers). BERT was introduced in 2019 and is a bidirectional transformer-based language model (Devlin et al., 2019). After training a BERT model on a consistent corpus and extracting the word embeddings, the model can be fine-tuned to perform different tasks. Word embeddings are dense vector representations of words in a lower dimensional space. Despite the static word embeddings of traditional models like Word2Vec, the contextualized word embeddings of BERT are able to capture the meaning of a word based on the context where it is used. In this way, the same word used in two different sentences can have two different vector representations. Similarity links are generated in the graph based on the value of the vectors similarity, i.e., the semantic similarity of the two answers.

The resulting graph appears like the one in Figure 2.3a. Then, the objective is to create connections between the event nodes themselves to express how "connected" two events are. We generated the initial knowledge graph in Neo4j, then several operations are made on the graph using the Cypher query language to create Event-Event connections. As illustrated in Figure 2.3b, two directed connections are generated for each of the 5W + 1H questions if at least one answer is shared. The weight of the relationships is obtained summing the number of shared nodes for that question and the similarity values of the nodes with similarity higher than a certain threshold. The Cypher queries used are reported in Listing 2.1, these queries are executed for each question type.

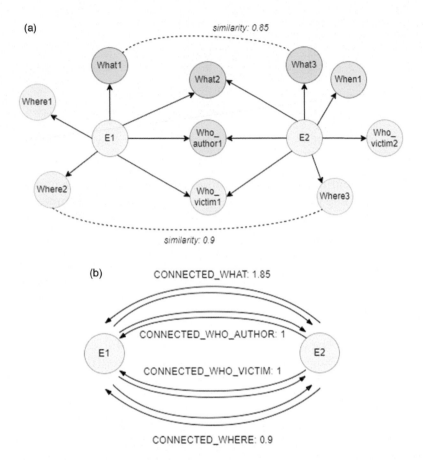

FIGURE 2.3
Representation of two events and their relationships (a) and generation of directed connections between event nodes in the Event-Centric Knowledge Graph (b).

Listing 2.1: Cypher queries to generate relationships between the event nodes based on the shared answers to the 5W + 1H questions.

```
MATCH (c1:CrimeNews)-[w1:WHAT]->(w:What)<-[w2:WHAT]-
(c2:CrimeNews)
WHERE c1.id>c2.id
WITH c1, c2, COUNT(*) AS num_count
CREATE (c1)-[r:CONNECTED_SAME_WHAT]->(c2)
SET r.weight=apoc.convert.toFloat(num_count)
MATCH (c1:CrimeNews)-[r1:WHAT]->(w1:What)-
    [r:SIM_WHAT]-(w2:What)<-[r2:WHAT]-(c2:CrimeNews)
WHERE c1.id>c2.id
WITH c1, c2, r
CREATE (c1)-[r_new:CONNECTED_SIM_WHAT]->(c2)
SET r_new.weight=apoc.convert.toFloat(r.weight)
```

```
MATCH (c1:CrimeNews), (c2:CrimeNews)
OPTIONAL MATCH (c1)-[r1:CONNECTED_SAME_WHAT]-(c2)
OPTIONAL MATCH (c1)-[r2:CONNECTED_SIM_WHAT]-(c2)
WITH c1, c2, sum(r1.weight) AS sumW1, sum(r2.weight) AS sumW2
WHERE c1.id>c2.id
AND apoc.convert.toFloat(sumW1+sumW2) > 0.0
CREATE (c1)-[:CONNECTED_WHAT {weight:apoc.convert.toFloat
(sumW1+sumW2)}]->(c2)
CREATE (c2)-[:CONNECTED_WHAT {weight:apoc.convert.toFloat
(sumW1+sumW2)}]->(c1)
```

Before the identification of communities, the *importance* of the nodes in the obtained weighted graph is calculated by the centrality algorithm.

2.3.1 Node Centrality

In graph theory and network analysis, centrality is a metric of key importance since it helps to better understand the network and navigate through chaos while extracting information from a network. There are a lot of iterative algorithms to calculate the centrality of nodes. Each algorithm has a different perspective and assigns scores based on different factors. If considering a directed graph, each node can have incoming relationships, i.e., links incident on the node, and outgoing relationships, i.e., nodes directed at other nodes.

The *degree centrality* (Freeman, 1978) exploits incoming and/or outgoing relationships to calculate the degree of each node. Given a graph $G := (V, E)$, where V is the set of vertices (i.e., nodes) and E the set of edges (i.e., relationships), the adjacency matrix $A_{v,t}$ is defined. Each element $a_{v,t}$ of that matrix is 1 if vertex v is connected to vertex t, 0 otherwise. The score of vertex v is computed by the formula:

$$x_v = \frac{1}{n-1}\sum_{t=1}^{n}A_{v,t}$$

where n is the number of vertices in the graph. Therefore, in the degree centrality, the importance of a vertex depends only on the number of its neighbors.

The *eigenvector centrality*, as described in Ruhnau (2000), aims at measuring the influence of a node in the graph. It is more suitable for undirected graph. In our graph, eigenvector centrality can measure how much an event influences another event. The algorithm is based on the idea that relationships with high-scoring nodes contribute more to the score of a node w.r.t connections with low-scoring nodes. In other words, a node connected to a few number of nodes with high scores is more important than a node connected to a higher number of low-scoring nodes. The score of node v is given by the formula:

$$x_v = \frac{1}{\lambda}\sum_{t \in M(v)} x_t = \frac{1}{\lambda}\sum_{t \in V}a_{v,t}x_t$$

where $M(v)$ is the set of neighbors of v and λ is a constant. The algorithm can be applied also to weighted graph. In this case, the score of a node sent to its neighbors is multiplied by the normalized weight of the relationship. Therefore, the score depends on the weight of the relationship.

Two extensions of the eigenvector centrality are the page rank and the article rank. The *page rank*, introduced by Brin and Page (1998), assigns a score to the nodes of the graph considering both directed and undirected edges and optional edge weights. Assuming a node v is connected to nodes $\{T_1,\ldots,T_n\}$, its page rank (PR) is calculated as:

$$PR(v) = 1 - d + d \sum_{t=1}^{n} \frac{PR(T_t)}{C(T_t)}$$

where $d \in [0,1)$ is a damping factor and $PR(T_t)$ and $C(T_t)$ are the page rank and the number of outgoing links of the neighbor T_t, respectively. The damping factor controls the convergence speed of page rank algorithm. A low damping factor is used to determine the score of a node based on the score received from external nodes and allows the iterations to quickly converge. In contrast with the eigenvector centrality, the idea beyond page rank is that relationships originating from low-degree nodes have a higher influence than relationships from high-degree nodes.

With respect to page rank, the *article rank* (Li and Willett, 2009) lowers the influence of low-degree nodes. This is a more recent iterative algorithm used to measure the transitive influence of nodes in a graph. The score of node v at iteration i is given by:

$$AR_i(v) = 1 - d + d \sum_{w \in N_{in}(v)} \frac{AR_{i-1}(w)}{|N_{out}(w)| + N_{out}}$$

where $N_{in}(v)$ and $N_{out}(w)$ denote incoming and outgoing neighbors of node v and w, respectively, $d \in [0,1)$ is a damping factor, and N_{out} is the average out-degree.

The implementation of all the described algorithms is available in the Neo4j Graph Data Science library[2] and allows the application to directed and weighted graphs, matching our use case. The algorithms take in input the name of the nodes to consider, the relationships, and their weights. Also, some configuration parameters are allowed. In the degree centrality, it is possible to specify the direction of the relationship to consider for the calculation of the degree. Since in our graph each relationship is generated in both directions, we can consider just one direction in the algorithm. In the eigenvector centrality, the node scores are normalized using the Euclidean norm. The damping factor can be specified in the configuration of the page rank and the article rank algorithms, 0.85 is the default value in Neo4j since it is the one suggested by the authors of the original paper.

2.3.2 Community Detection

Community detection is usually the first step in extracting information from graphs. A community is a dense subgraph within a larger graph that corresponds to a specific function (Aviyente and Karaaslanli, 2022). We are interested in identifying groups of most densely connected nodes, i.e., communities, because if nodes are densely connected each other, the events they represent are similar. Similar events mean that the events have some characteristics in common. Community detection allows identifying these events in short time, then further crime analysis can be performed on the events in the same community. The Neo4j Graph Data Science library mentioned before offers some already implemented community detection algorithms.

The *label propagation* algorithm (Rezaei, Far, and Soleymani, 2015) detects communities exploiting only the graph structure. It assigns to a node the label occurring with the highest frequency among its neighbors. This operation is repeated more times, iteratively. A label can quickly become dominant in a group of closely connected nodes, but will reach with difficulty sparsely connected region. At the end of the iterations, densely connected nodes have the same label that means they are part of the same community.

Louvain is an iterative heuristic algorithm introduced in 2008 by Blondel et al. (2008). It tries to identify communities in a graph by optimizing the modularity score. Modularity is a numerical value between −0.5 (non-modular clustering) and 1 (fully modular clustering) that quantifies the quality of an assignment of nodes to communities and evaluate how densely connected the nodes in the same community are w.r.t. relationships outside communities. The modularity of a community c is given by the formula:

$$Q_c = \frac{\sum_{in}}{2m} - \left(\frac{\sum_{tot}}{2m} \right)^2$$

where m is the sum of all of the relationship weights in the graph, $\sum_{in}$ is the sum of relationship weights between nodes within the community c considering each relationship twice, and $\sum_{tot}$ is the sum of all relationship weights of nodes within the community including relationships which link to nodes of other communities. The iterative procedure of Louvain groups nodes into communities based on how closely connected nodes are and calculates the modularity. The nodes are assigned to a different community if this change leads to increased modularity.

The *weakly connected components* algorithm identifies groups of nodes where each node is connected to all the other nodes (Monge and Elkan, 1997). The result does not depend on the direction of the relationships.

These algorithms have different perspectives; we expect the communities identified by the weakly connected components algorithm to be different from the ones of the previous two algorithms since the scope is slightly different. However, it will be interesting to investigate their results and make some comparisons.

2.4 Application

In this section, we show the application of our methodology to an open-source dataset of Italian news articles reporting crime events occurred in the city of Modena.

2.4.1 Dataset

The dataset contains 10,395 news articles from the Gazzetta di Modena newspaper.[3] The news articles are related to some crime events occurred in the province of Modena from 2011 to 2021 and cover 13 types/categories of crimes (theft, robbery, murder, sexual violence, mistreatment, aggression, illegal sale, drug dealing, scam, fraud, money laundering, evasion, and kidnapping). The dataset has been obtained by the application of web crawler method along with several semantic approaches for information retrieval: crime categorization, named entity extraction, 5W + 1H identification, linked data mapping, geo-localization, time expression normalization, entity linking, and duplicate detection. The framework that allowed to generate the dataset has been described in Rollo and Po (2020) and Rollo, Po, and Bonisoli (2022) while details on the text categorization task developed to understand the type of crime reported in the news articles are provided in Bonisoli, Rollo, and Po (2021) and Rollo, Bonisoli, and Po (2021). The dataset is openly available[1] and is the first one of its kind for the Italian language. The dataset is unbalanced on the crime category: the most news articles are related to thefts (70%), while sexual violence, money laundering, evasion, and fraud are less than 1% of the dataset.

The experiments described in this chapter are related to 285 news articles about thefts occurred in 2020. The answers to the 5W + 1H questions have been manually extracted from the text of the news articles by a group of bachelor students. The annotated dataset is available online in a GitHub repository.[4] The answers to Why and How are rarely reported, so they are excluded from the experiments. The question for What is used to identify the stolen object(s), i.e., bike, jewels, money, car, phone, and other objects. Some answers to When indicate the date of the crime event or the moment of the day, i.e., morning, evening, and so on. The answers to Who author can be generic, such as *il ladro* (the thief), sometimes more specific information are indicated, e.g., the nationality or the age of the thief, or the number of thieves if the responsible for the theft is a gang. The same consideration can be done for Who victim, generic answers are *il titolare del negozio* (the shop owner)

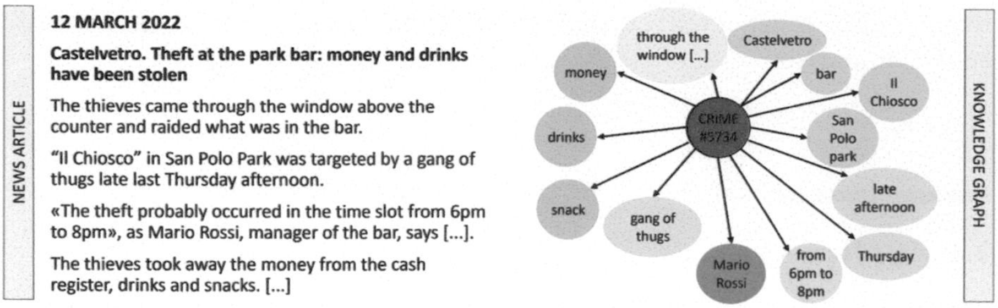

FIGURE 2.4

Exemplar news article related to a theft with the corresponding Event-Centric Knowledge Graph. (News extracted from \url{https://www.gazzettadimodena.it/modena/cronaca/2022/03/12/news/castelvetro-assalto-al-bar-del-parco-spariti-soldi-e-bibite-1.41294303}).

or *il proprietario dell'auto* (the car owner). An example of news article and its knowledge graph is provided in Figure 2.4.

2.4.2 Modena Crime Knowledge Graph

Each news article is represented in the Modena Crime Knowledge Graph as reported in Figure 2.1. Table 2.2 reports the number of nodes and relationships, i.e., the relationships from the crime event node to the answers (incoming relationships) and the ones between the similar answers (similarity relationships). The BERT model used to calculate the similarity is the Italian cased model (Schweter, 2020). Semantic similarity was not calculated for Where nodes since usually the answer to *Dove è avvenuto il crimine?* (Where did the crime event happen?) is the proper name of a place, the name of a city or a specific address. Therefore, semantic similarity in this case is meaningless. In the other cases, the similarity threshold was set to 0.85.

The Cypher queries have been executed to create six types of relationships, named "connected_what," "connected_where," "connected_when," "connected_who_author," "connected_who_victim," and "connected_who_other,"

TABLE 2.2

Number of Nodes and Relationships of the Modena Crime Knowledge Graph

Node	Instances	Incoming rel.	Similarity rel.
CrimeNews	285	–	–
What	318	382	101
Where	270	342	–
When	219	255	320
WhoAuthor	268	398	257
WhoVictim	285	375	75
WhoOther	199	289	437

FIGURE 2.5
Crime news nodes and their relationships.

between the CrimeNews nodes. Thus, we obtain the final weighted directed graph that consists of 285 CrimeNews nodes and 11,047 relationships. Part of the graph is shown in Figure 2.5. As can be noticed in the figure, there are some isolated groups of nodes that do not have external connections with other nodes.

All the centrality algorithms described in Section 2.3.1 have been applied to the graph. The damping factor in the page rank and article rank algorithms was set to 0.5 because in our graph the number of outgoing relationships for each node is equal to the number of its incoming relationships. Analyzing the scores assigned by each algorithm, we notice that the events with the highest scores are approximately the same for all the algorithms. Table 2.3 reports the top five events and the corresponding centrality scores. These nodes are also among the ones with the highest number of relationships with other CrimeNews nodes.

Seven projections of the final graph have been generated in Neo4j: one projection contains all the CrimeNews nodes and the relationships of the final graph, with the relationship weights and the four centrality scores of the nodes, while the other six projections contain only one type of relationship between the CrimeNews nodes, i.e., "connected_what," "connected_where," and so on. The community detection algorithms described in Section 2.3.2 have been applied to all the seven generated graphs. Comparing the communities identified on the same graph by different algorithms, we noticed that

TABLE 2.3

The Five Nodes with the Highest Centrality Scores

	Crime News				
ID	English Title	Degree	Eigenvector	Article Rank	Page Rank
1917556	Hunting the blue car of Modena and Castelnuovo: three thefts in a few hours	140.812	227.173	0.515	2.888
246	Thieves in the apartment "They destroyed everything"	191.455	218.145	0.486	3.640
1773111	Thieves discovered, flight into the night and theft foiled	129.042	217.915	0.479	2.565
1743523	Tevere Street in the crosshairs: robbed and damaged two businesses	131.802	205.752	0.467	2.665
187	New alarms at the deli robbed by a gang	110.226	205.303	0.456	2.204

Note: The English title was derived from the translation of the original Italian title.

there is a very substantial overlap. This means that the result is almost the same regardless the algorithm used.

Table 2.4 shows the number of communities identified by Louvain and the corresponding modularity value based on the centrality score and the type of relationships and nodes (W) included in the graph (in the table, "all"

TABLE 2.4

Results of the Louvain Community Detection Based on the Relationship and Node Type (W) Included and the Centrality Algorithm Used

W	Centrality Algorithm	#Community	Modularity	Centrality Algorithm	#Community	Modularity
What	Degree	156	0.900	Eigenvector	156	0.900
Where		213	0.652		213	0.652
When		142	0.689		142	0.689
Who author		106	0.255		106	0.255
Who victim		169	0.490		169	0.490
Who other		116	0.630		116	0.630
All		10	0.353		15	0.360
What	Page rank	156	0.900	Article rank	156	0.900
Where		213	0.652		213	0.652
When		142	0.689		142	0.689
Who author		106	0.255		106	0.255
Who victim		169	0.490		169	0.490
Who other		116	0.630		116	0.630
All		17	0.360		15	0.350

means that all the relationships – connected_what, connected_where, etc. – are included). The highest value of modularity was reached in the What graph, this is probably due to the fact that in the other graphs the nodes are more densely connected and it is more difficult to identify the communities. Moreover, the centrality score does not seem to affect the results since the same values of modularity is reported regardless the centrality algorithm. Only when all the relationship types are included, the number of identified communities changes based on the centrality algorithm as well as the modularity values. This means that the community detection algorithm exploits the centrality scores associated to the event nodes to generate the communities.

Figure 2.6 shows four graphs, which contain all the relationship types; in each graph a different centrality algorithm was used. The communities identified by Louvain are highlighted with a different color; the size of the nodes depends on the centrality score. In all the graphs, the small groups of nodes connected each other are detected as one single community in most cases. However, sometimes even if the number of nodes connected each other and with no relationship with other nodes is very low, these nodes are

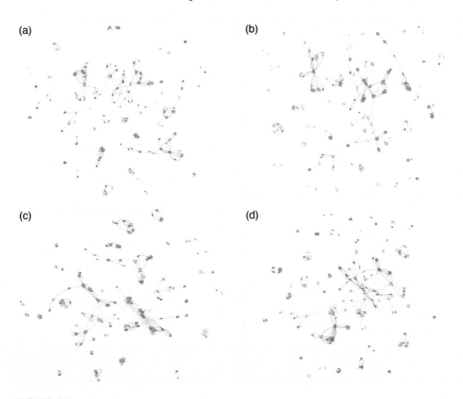

FIGURE 2.6
Louvain Identified communities on the final directed graph with nodes scored by four different centrality algorithms: degree centrality (a), eigenvector centrality (b), page rank (c), and article rank (d).

assigned to different communities while we expect to be part of the same community. The page rank is the algorithm that identifies the highest number of communities (17).

To increase the influence of node centrality, a new weight has been associated to each relationship $r(i, j)$, following the formula:

$$new\_weight_{r(i,j)} = weight_{r(i,j)} + \frac{C_i + C_j}{2}$$

where $weight_{r(i,j)}$ is the weight already associated to the relationship that connects the node i to the node j, and $C(i)$ and $C(j)$ are the centrality scores of the nodes i and j, respectively. Four new weights have been calculated for each relationship, each using a different centrality algorithm. Community detection has been applied to the graph projections including the new weights, one at a time. Using the weakly connected components algorithm or the label propagation, the result is not affected by the centrality score used in the new weight. Probably, this is due to the fact that the scores of the centrality algorithm are very similar each other. Figure 2.7 shows the centrality scores of some nodes in the graph normalized by the min-max scaler. There is a clear overlap of the four lines representing the four algorithms. There are few differences in the obtained communities when Louvain is used. In this case, the highest modularity value was reached when using the weights derived from article rank and considering only the CrimeNews relationships generated by the answers to What. Indeed, as can be seen in Figure 2.8, the communities clearly identify the nodes that are densely connected each other.

2.4.3 Modena Crime Analysis

The data of the Italian Department of Public Security of the Minister of the Interior (published by Sole24Ore[5]) classifies the city of Modena at the 12th position among the other Italian cities based on the number of crimes reported to the police. The total number of police reports in Modena in 2021 was 26,328 (3,722 reports per 100,000 inhabitants). The first city in the national

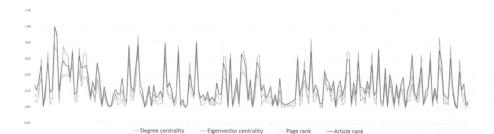

FIGURE 2.7
Normalized scores of CrimeNews nodes according to four different centrality algorithms.

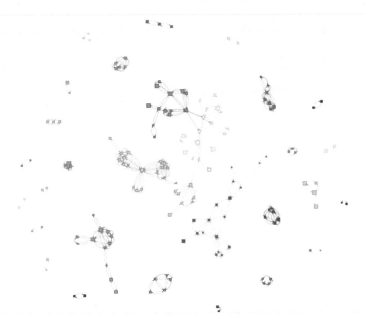

FIGURE 2.8
Communities detected by Louvain in the What graph weighted by the article rank.

ranking is Milan with 159,613 reports (4,866 reports per 100,000 inhabitants). According to the latest report of ISTAT,[6] the most frequent crimes in Modena from 2016 to 2020 are thefts, damages, scams and computer fraud, threats, and willful injury. Figure 2.9 reports the number of the mentioned crimes reported to the authorities. As can be seen, the number of thefts decreases from 2019 to 2020. This is probably due to the lockdown caused by the COVID-19 emergency. In fact, because of the pandemic, the government had imposed severe restrictive measures, allowing only essential displacements. As a result, the population was often at home and worked from home, if allowed. On the other hand, the number of computer fraud increased (from 1,985 in 2019 to 2,773 in 2020).

This kind of reports allows to give an overview of the crime situation of the city, however, there is no detailed information on the victims and the authors, the dynamics, the place where the crime occurred with specification of the address or neighborhood, and so on. Thanks to the extraction of the 5W + 1H answers from the text of the news articles and the use of graph analysis techniques, it is possible to generate these data. Also, it is possible to geolocate the crime events and generate heatmaps as we discussed in a previous work (Po and Rollo, 2018). For example, looking at the graph generated by the 285 news articles related to thefts, it is possible to know which is the most stolen items in Modena. They are the What node with the highest number of incoming relationships. In our graph, these nodes are: handbag, bicycle, safety deposit box, car, phone, wallet, and cash register. The same can

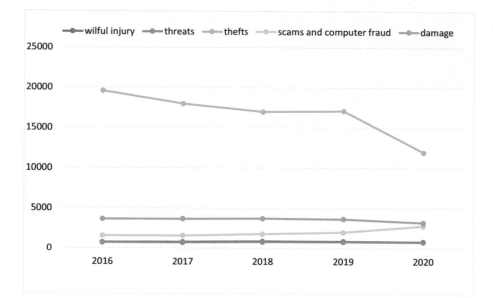

FIGURE 2.9
Crimes reported to the authorities in the province of Modena from 2016 to 2020. (Source: ISTAT, data of the Italian Ministry of the Interior.)

be done to discover the cities and the area of the city where the most crimes occur. These data can be combined with information on the activities/shops located in the same address to understand the cause of the crime events and alerts the police to monitor the situation in that area.

2.5 Conclusion and Future Work

The chapter presented a methodology for the construction of a knowledge graph for the representation of crime events as they are described in news articles. The Event-Centric Knowledge Graph has been generated based on the extraction of the answers to the 5W + 1H journalistic questions from the text of the news. Then, we added direct relationships in the graph among the nodes representing the events to indicate that they share some characteristics. Centrality algorithms were used to determine the importance of the individual nodes, while community detection algorithms allowed to distinguishing groups of similar nodes within the overall graph. The tool used for the creation and the analysis of the knowledge graph is Neo4j. Some experiments have been conducted on a manually annotated Italian dataset containing news articles related to thefts in the province of Modena. We focus on thefts as they are the most frequent crime in Modena. However, the methodology developed depends neither on the language of the news articles nor on the type of event described since all the events can be represented by the answers to the 5W + 1H questions. The results of the experiments are promising and demonstrate how it is possible to develop crime analysis techniques by using knowledge graph.

Since the manual extraction of the 5W + 1H answers is very time consuming, as future work, we will work on automatic approaches through the question answering using BERT. This will allow to increase the amount of annotated news articles and the size of the generated knowledge graph as community detection algorithms work better in large graphs. The increasing dimension of the graph will probably improve also the influence of the centrality scores on the final results. Moreover, further analysis of the graph could be performed to measure the similarity of the text of the news articles in the same community and identify the news articles related to the same event. This analysis should allow to create a storyline of the event. Finally, it could be interesting to explore the possibility of connecting the answers to the 5W + 1H questions to external ontologies, taxonomies, or vocabularies such as WordNet, BabelNet to better understand their similarity. This should allow to increase the number of similarity relationships. Another future work will focus on building a knowledge graph mapping information published in newspapers with respect to the new Crime Event Model, developed by Rollo, Po, and Castellucci (2023).

Disclosure Statement

The authors declare no conflict of interest.

Funding

This work is partially supported by the project "Deep Learning for Urban Event Extraction from News and Social media streams" founded by the Engineering Department "Enzo Ferrari" of the University of Modena and Reggio Emilia.

Notes

1 Italian Crime News dataset: https://paperswithcode.com/dataset/italian-crime-news
2 https://neo4j.com/docs/graph-data-science/

3 https://gazzettadimodena.gelocal.it
4 https://github.com/federicarollo/W-1H-extraction-in-news-articles-for-event-detection
5 https://lab24.ilsole24ore.com/indice-della-criminalita/?Modena
6 http://dati.istat.it/Index.aspx?DataSetCode=dccv_delittips

References

Abdul Jalil, Masita, Chia Pui Ling, Noor Maizura Mohamad Noor, and Fatihah Mohd. 2017. "Knowledge Representation Model for Crime Analysis." *Procedia Computer Science* 116: 484–491. Discovery and innovation of computer science technology in artificial intelligence era: The 2nd International Conference on Computer Science and Computational Intelligence (ICCSCI 2017), https://www.sciencedirect.com/science/article/pii/S1877050917321178

Auer, Sören, Christian Bizer, Georgi Kobilarov, Jens Lehmann, Richard Cyganiak, and Zachary G. Ives. 2007. "DBpedia: A Nucleus for a Web of Open Data." In *The Semantic Web, 6th International Semantic Web Conference, 2nd Asian Semantic Web Conference, ISWC 2007 + ASWC 2007, Busan, Korea, November 11–15, 2007,* edited by Karl Aberer, Key-Sun Choi, Natasha Fridman Noy, Dean Allemang, Kyung-Il Lee, Lyndon J. B. Nixon, Jennifer Golbeck, Peter Mika, Diana Maynard, Riichiro Mizoguchi, Guus Schreiber, and Philippe Cudré-Mauroux, Vol. 4825 of *Lecture Notes in Computer Science,* 722–735. Springer. https://doi.org/10.1007/978-3-540-76298-0_52

Aviyente, Selin, and Abdullah Karaaslanli. 2022. "Explainability in Graph Data Science: Interpretability, Replicability, and Reproducibility of Community Detection." *IEEE Signal Processing Magazine* 39 (4): 25–39. https://doi.org/10.1109/MSP.2022.3149471.

Blondel, Vincent D, Jean-Loup Guillaume, Renaud Lambiotte, and Etienne Lefebvre. 2008. "Fast Unfolding of Communities in Large Networks." *Journal of Statistical Mechanics: Theory and Experiment* 2008 (10): P10008. https://doi.org/10.1088/1742-5468/2008/10/p10008

Bonisoli, Giovanni, Federica Rollo, and Laura Po. 2021. "Using Word Embeddings for Italian Crime News Categorization." In *Proceedings of the 16th Conference on Computer Science and Intelligence Systems, Online, September 2–5, 2021,* edited by Maria Ganzha, Leszek A. Maciaszek, Marcin Paprzycki, and Dominik Slezak, Vol. 25 of *Annals of Computer Science and Information Systems,* 461–470. https://doi.org/10.15439/2021F118

Brin, Sergey, and Lawrence Page. 1998. "The Anatomy of a Large-Scale Hypertextual Web Search Engine." *Computer Networks* 30 (1–7): 107–117. https://doi.org/10.1016/S0169-7552(98)00110-X

Devlin, Jacob, Ming-Wei Chang, Kenton Lee, and Kristina Toutanova. 2019. "BERT: Pre-training of Deep Bidirectional Transformers for Language Understanding." In *Proceedings of the 2019 Conference of the North American Chapter of the Association for Computational Linguistics: Human Language Technologies, NAACL-HLT 2019,*

Minneapolis, MN, USA, June 2-7, 2019, Volume 1 (Long and Short Papers), edited by Jill Burstein, Christy Doran, and Thamar Solorio, 4171–4186. Association for Computational Linguistics. https://doi.org/10.18653/v1/n19-1423

Elezaj, Ogerta, Sule Yildirim Yayilgan, Edlira Kalemi, Linda Wendelberg, Mohamed Abomhara, and Javed Ahmed. 2019. "Towards Designing a Knowledge Graph-Based Framework for Investigating and Preventing Crime on Online Social Networks." In *E-Democracy - Safeguarding Democracy and Human Rights in the Digital Age – 8th International Conference, e-Democracy 2019, Athens, Greece, December 12–13, 2019, Proceedings*, edited by Sokratis K. Katsikas and Vasilios Zorkadis, Vol. 1111 of *Communications in Computer and Information Science*, 181–195. Springer. https://doi.org/10.1007/978-3-030-37545-4_12

Freeman, Linton C. 1978. "Centrality in social networks conceptual clarification." *Social Networks* 1 (3): 215–239. https://www.sciencedirect.com/science/article/pii/0378873378900217

Gottschalk, Simon, and Elena Demidova. 2018. "EventKG: A Multilingual Event-Centric Temporal Knowledge Graph." In *The Semantic Web – 15th International Conference, ESWC 2018, Heraklion, Crete, Greece, June 3–7, 2018, Proceedings*, edited by Aldo Gangemi, Roberto Navigli, Maria-Esther Vidal, Pascal Hitzler, Raphaël Troncy, Laura Hollink, Anna Tordai, and Mehwish Alam, Vol. 10843 of *Lecture Notes in Computer Science*, 272–287. Springer. https://doi.org/10.1007/978-3-319-93417-4_18

Guo, Kaihao, Tianpei Jiang, and Haipeng Zhang. 2020. "Knowledge Graph Enhanced Event Extraction in Financial Documents." In *2020 IEEE International Conference on Big Data (IEEE BigData 2020), Atlanta, GA, USA, December 10–13, 2020*, edited by Xintao Wu, Chris Jermaine, Li Xiong, Xiaohua Hu, Olivera Kotevska, Siyuan Lu, Weija Xu, Srinivas Aluru, Chengxiang Zhai, Eyhab Al-Masri, Zhiyuan Chen, and Jeff Saltz, 1322–1329. IEEE. https://doi.org/10.1109/BigData50022.2020.9378471

Jedrzejek, Czeslaw, and Jaroslaw Bak. 2012. "Application of an Ontology-Based Model to a Wide-Class Fraudulent Disbursement Economic Crimes." In *Multimedia and Internet Systems: Theory and Practice – Proceedings of the 8th International Conference MISSI 2012, Wrocław, Poland, 2012*, edited by Aleksander Zgrzywa, Kazimierz Choros, and Andrzej Sieminski, Vol. 183 of *Advances in Intelligent Systems and Computing*, 109–118. Springer. https://doi.org/10.1007/978-3-642-32335-5_11

Kalemi, Edlira, Sule Yildirim Yayilgan, Elton Domnori, and Ogerta Elezaj. 2017. "SMONT: an ontology for crime solving through social media." *International Journal of Metadata, Semantics and Ontologies* 12 (2/3): 71–81. https://doi.org/10.1504/IJMSO.2017.10011827

Knez, Timotej. 2022. "Multi-task Learning for Automatic Event-Centric Temporal Knowledge Graph Construction." In *Research Challenges in Information Science*, edited by Renata Guizzardi, Jolita Ralyté, and Xavier Franch, 811–818. Springer International Publishing, Berlin/Heidelberg, Germany.

Kuculo, Tin. 2022. "Comprehensive Event Representations Using Event Knowledge Graphs and Natural Language Processing." In *Companion Proceedings of the Web Conference 2022*, WWW '22, New York, NY, USA, 359–363. Association for Computing Machinery. https://doi.org/10.1145/3487553.3524199

Lakshika, M. V. P. T., and H. A. Caldera. 2021. "Knowledge Graphs Representation for Event-Related E-News Articles." *Machine Learning Knowledge Extraction* 3 (4): 802–818. https://doi.org/10.3390/make3040040

Li, Jiang, and Peter Willett. 2009. "ArticleRank: A PageRank-Based Alternative to Numbers of Citations for Analysing Citation Networks." *Aslib Proceedings* 61 (6): 605–618. https://doi.org/10.1108/00012530911005544

Li, Zhipeng, Shanshan Feng, Jun Shi, Yang Zhou, Yong Liao, Yangzhao Yang, Yangyang Li, Nenghai Yu, and Xun Shao. 2023. "Future Event Prediction Based on Temporal Knowledge Graph Embedding." *Computer Systems Science and Engineering* 44 (3): 2411–2423. https://doi.org/10.32604/csse.2023.026823.

Mahdisoltani, Farzaneh, Joanna Biega, and Fabian M. Suchanek. 2015. "YAGO3: A Knowledge Base from Multilingual Wikipedias." In *Seventh Biennial Conference on Innovative Data Systems Research, CIDR 2015, Asilomar, CA, USA, January 4–7, 2015, Online Proceedings*, www.cidrdb.org. http://cidrdb.org/cidr2015/Papers/CIDR15_Paper1.pdf

Monge, Alvaro E., and Charles Elkan. 1997. "An Efficient Domain-Independent Algorithm for Detecting Approximately Duplicate Database Records." In *Workshop on Research Issues on Data Mining and Knowledge Discovery, DMKD 1997 in cooperation with ACM SIGMOD '97, Tucson, AZ, USA, May 11, 1997*.

Onnoom, Boonyarin, Sirapat Chiewchanwattana, Khamron Sunat, and Nutcharee Wichiennit. 2014. "An Ontology Framework for Recommendation about a Crime Scene Investigation." In *2014 14th International Symposium on Communications and Information Technologies (ISCIT)*, 176–180.

Park, N., F. Liu, P. Mehta, D. Cristofor, C. Faloutsos, and Y. Dong. 2022. "EvoKG: Jointly Modeling Event Time and Network Structure for Reasoning over Remporal Knowledge Graphs." In *Proceedings of the Fifteenth ACM International Conference on Web Search and Data Mining (WSDM '22). Association for Computing Machinery*, New York, NY, USA, 794–803. https://doi.org/10.1145/3488560.3498451.

Peppes, N., T. Alexakis, E. Adamopoulou, K. Remoundou, and K. Demestichas. 2020. "A Semantic Engine and an Ontology Visualization Tool for Advanced Crime Analysis." *Procedia Computer Science* 176: 1829–1838. *Knowledge-Based and Intelligent Information & Engineering Systems: Proceedings of the 24th International Conference KES2020*, https://www.sciencedirect.com/science/article/pii/S1877050920321244

Po, Laura, and Federica Rollo. 2018. "Building an Urban Theft Map by Analyzing Newspaper Crime Reports." In *2018 13th International Workshop on Semantic and Social Media Adaptation and Personalization (SMAP)*, Zaragoza, Spain, 2018, pp. 13–18, doi: 10.1109/SMAP.2018.8501866.

Po, Laura, Federica Rollo, and Raquel Trillo Lado. 2016. "Topic Detection in Multichannel Italian Newspapers." In *Semantic Keyword-Based Search on Structured Data Sources - COST Action IC1302 Second International KEYSTONE Conference, IKC 2016, Cluj-Napoca, Romania, September 8–9, 2016*, Revised Selected Papers, edited by Andrea Calì, Dorian Gorgan, and Martín Ugarte, Vol. 10151 of *Lecture Notes in Computer Science*, 62–75. https://doi.org/10.1007/978-3-319-53640-8_6

Rezaei, Aria, Saeed Mahlouji Far, and Mahdieh Soleymani. 2015. "Near Linear-Time Community Detection in Networks with Hardly Detectable Community Structure." In *Proceedings of the 2015 IEEE/ACM International Conference on Advances in Social Networks Analysis and Mining 2015, ASONAM '15*, New York, NY, USA, 65–72. Association for Computing Machinery. https://doi.org/10.1145/2808797.2808903

Robinson, David, and Chris Scogings. 2018. "The Detection of Criminal Groups in Real-world Fused Data: Using the Graph-mining Algorithm "GraphExtract"." *Security Informatics* 7 (1): 2. https://doi.org/10.1186/s13388-018-0031-9

Rollo, Federica. 2017. "A key-entity graph for clustering multichannel news: student research abstract." In *Proceedings of the Symposium on Applied Computing, SAC 2017, Marrakech, Morocco, April 3–7, 2017*, edited by Ahmed Seffah, Birgit Penzenstadler, Carina Alves, and Xin Peng, 699–700. ACM. https://doi.org/10.1145/3019612.3019930

Rollo, Federica, Giovanni Bonisoli, and Laura Po. 2021. "Supervised and Unsupervised Categorization of an Imbalanced Italian Crime News Dataset." In *Information Technology for Management: Business and Social Issues – 16th Conference, ISM 2021, and FedCSIS-AIST 2021 Track, Held as Part of FedCSIS 2021, Virtual Event, September 2–5, 2021, Extended and Revised Selected Papers*, edited by Ewa Ziemba and Witold Chmielarz, Vol. 442 of *Lecture Notes in Business Information Processing*, 117–139. Springer. https://doi.org/10.1007/978-3-030-98997-2_6

Rollo, Federica, and Laura Po. 2020. "Crime Event Localization and Deduplication." In *The Semantic Web – ISWC 2020 – 19th International Semantic Web Conference, Athens, Greece, November 2–6, 2020, Proceedings, Part II*, edited by Jeff Z. Pan, Valentina A. M. Tamma, Claudia d'Amato, Krzysztof Janowicz, Bo Fu, Axel Polleres, Oshani Seneviratne, and Lalana Kagal, Vol. 12507 of *Lecture Notes in Computer Science*, 361–377. Springer.

Rollo, F., Po, L. (2022). Knowledge Graphs for Community Detection in Textual Data. In: Villazón-Terrazas, B., Ortíz-Rodriguez, F., Tiwari, S., Sicilia, MA., Martín-Moncunill, D. (eds) *Knowledge Graphs and Semantic Web. KGSWC 2022. Communications in Computer and Information Science*, vol 1686. Springer, Cham. https://doi.org/10.1007/978-3-031-21422-6_15

Rollo, Federica, Laura Po, and Giovanni Bonisoli. 2022. "Online News Event Extraction for Crime Analysis." In *Proceedings of the 30th Italian Symposium on Advanced Database Systems, SEBD 2022, Tirrenia (PI), Italy, June 19–22, 2022*, edited by Giuseppe Amato, Valentina Bartalesi, Devis Bianchini, Claudio Gennaro, and Riccardo Torlone, Vol. 3194 of *CEUR Workshop Proceedings*, 223–230. CEUR-WS.org. http://ceur-ws.org/Vol-3194/paper28.pdf

Rollo, Federica, Laura Po, and Alessandro Castellucci. 2023. "CEM: An Ontology for Crime Events in Newspaper Articles." In *Proceedings of the 38th ACM/SIGAPP Symposium on Applied Computing, SAC 2023, Tallinn, Estonia, March 27–31, 2023*, ACM. https://doi.org/10.1145/3555776.3577862

Rospocher, Marco, Marieke van Erp, Piek Vossen, Antske Fokkens, Itziar Aldabe, German Rigau, Aitor Soroa, Thomas Ploeger, and Tessel Bogaard. 2016. "Building Event-Centric Knowledge Graphs from News." *Journal of Web Semantics* 37–38: 132–151. https://www.sciencedirect.com/science/article/pii/S1570826815001456

Ruhnau, Britta. 2000. "Eigenvector-Centrality — A Node-centrality?" *Social Networks* 22 (4): 357–365. https://www.sciencedirect.com/science/article/pii/S0378873300000319

Schweter, Stefan. 2020. "Italian BERT and ELECTRA Models." https://doi.org/10.5281/zenodo.4263142

Szekely, Pedro A., Craig A. Knoblock, Jason Slepicka, Andrew Philpot, Amandeep Singh, Chengye Yin, Dipsy Kapoor, et al. 2015. "Building and Using a Knowledge Graph to Combat Human Trafficking." In *The Semantic Web – ISWC 2015 – 14th International Semantic Web Conference, Bethlehem, PA, USA, October 11–15, 2015, Proceedings, Part II*, edited by Marcelo Arenas, Óscar Corcho, Elena Simperl, Markus Strohmaier, Mathieu d'Aquin, Kavitha Srinivas, Paul Groth,

Michel Dumontier, Jeff Heflin, Krishnaprasad Thirunarayan, and Steffen Staab, Vol. 9367 of *Lecture Notes in Computer Science*, 205–221. Springer. https://doi. org/10.1007/978-3-319-25010-6_12

Venkata Srimukh, P., and S. Shridevi. 2020. "Ontology-Based Crime Investigation Process." In *Advances in Smart Grid Technology*, edited by Pierluigi Siano and K. Jamuna, Singapore, 497–509. Springer Singapore.

Vrandecic, Denny. 2012. "Wikidata: A New Platform for Collaborative Data Collection." In *Proceedings of the 21st World Wide Web Conference, WWW 2012, Lyon, France, April 16–20, 2012 (Companion Volume)*, edited by Alain Mille, Fabien Gandon, Jacques Misselis, Michael Rabinovich, and Steffen Staab, 1063–1064. ACM. https://doi.org/10.1145/2187980.2188242.

Yan, Zhihua, and Xijin Tang. 2022. "Hierarchical Storyline Generation Based on Event-centric Temporal Knowledge Graph." In *Knowledge and Systems Sciences*, edited by Jian Chen, Takashi Hashimoto, Xijin Tang, and Jiangning Wu, Singapore, 149–159. Springer Nature Singapore.

3

Semantic Natural Language Processing for Knowledge Graphs Creation

Cameron De Sa[a], Edlira Vakaj[a], Hossein Ghomeshi[a], and Ryan McGranaghan[b,c]

[a]Birmingham City University, Natural Language Processing Lab, UK

[b]Orion Space Solutions. Louisville, CO, USA

[c]NASA Jet Propulsion Laboratory, Greenbelt, MD, USA

CONTENTS

DOI: 10.1201/9781003313267-3

3.1 Introduction

Throughout history, humans have striven to assign categorical mean-ing to concepts in the world around them. However, it was not until 1613 that these practices became a systematic field of study [78], when the term "ontology" (or "ontologia") was separately coined by the philosophers [24] in his Lexicon philosophicum and [45] in his Theatrum philosophi-cum. Ontologics in the philosophical sense refers to a field of study that focuses on the nature of being and the conception of entities and things [40]. However, this is not the only definition. A computational ontology concerns itself with constructing a conceptual model of what it means for a domain to exist, and assign meaning and relationships to the entities in that domain [57]. As a result, a computational ontology provides an effec-tive method for modeling a particular conceptual domain and the entities and relationships therein.

Computational ontologies have wide-ranging applications. Some research domains that have been modeled by ontologies include biomedicine [38, 73], historical research [65], and space data [71, 72, 76]. Although these topics are disparate, they demonstrate that computational ontologies are effective tools for modeling complex, interrelated, heterogeneous data. They can also be used to support a variety of tasks, such as classification, data explora-tion, discovering new topics, and detecting research communities [75]. These factors make ontologies suited for representing information about scientific fields. Overall, being able to capture a domain in an ontology presents par-ticular advantages, such as making complex information accessible, discov-ering new connections, and facilitating the ability to explore data.

However, there are specific challenges related to the development of computational ontologies. The complexity of a domain may mean that scalability is difficult, particularly when manually adding data. Additionally, data properties such as multiple data types, continuous evolution, expansive content, the semantic nature of data, and varying levels of relationships may make information difficult to capture [82]. Tools such as Protégé contain a suite of tools to enable ontology development, including automatic reasoners that create inferences between data [66, 73], although manual intervention is still needed to ensure accuracy. Additionally, evaluating the efficacy and validity of an ontology is an essential step for ensuring its quality. Nevertheless, this aspect of development has been frequently underreported in prior research [42]. Ontology evaluation is also complex, often requiring the manual knowledge of domain experts. Overall, there are many issues related to ontology development, particularly over the matter of how to efficiently capture the complexity of a topic.

Natural language processing (NLP) is a field of Machine Learning (ML) that contains a theoretically motivated range of computational techniques for the analysis and representation of naturally occurring texts at one or more levels of linguistic analysis in order to achieve a human-like level of understanding for a range of tasks and applications [41]. Because NLP techniques can be applied to a text or data corpus, they can be used for automatic or semi-automatic ontology generation. The intersection of NLP ML techniques and ontology creation is known as ontology learning [50]. Many ontologies have utilized NLP techniques, including ones for risk management [51], biomedicine [3, 44], and clinical texts [35]. Owing to the complex nature of many domains, NLP techniques can be helpful for parsing relevant text corpuses, and ontology learning can be used to establish relationships and entities. Then, this may allow for additional resources to be directed toward other aspects of a scientific effort. However, NLP techniques often rely on a rigid corpus of rules in order to create entities and relationships, which tend to be limited to the domain being modeled, and are not easily modified for other domains. In short, NLP techniques have shown promise for the semi-automatic or automatic population of ontologies.

Additional methods have been proposed to address the problem of domain-restricted NLP models. One such technique was utilized by Ayadi et al. [3], who utilized a deep learning-based ontology population system to enhance a biomedical network ontology. An additional technique utilized by Elnagar et al. [15] employed Complex Embeddings (ComplEx) to ensure completeness and reference ontologies to refine the model. However, there is room for additional research into training an NLP model on a text corpus to automatically populate an ontology for a complex scientific domain.

Information extraction (IE) refers to the process of extracting structured information from semi-structured or unstructured text [64]. IE pipelines (IEPs) have been formulated for several IE efforts, ranging from scientific literature [89] to hotel information [82]. Examining these efforts facilitates the creation of an IEP, so that relevant entities and relationships can be generated from a relevant text corpus. This IEP begins with the preprocessing stage, where the text data is cleaned of extraneous information. It then goes through a named entity recognition (NER) stage, where significant entities in the text are extracted based on training information [1]. Finally, a knowledge graph (KG) showing the data nodes and relationships between them can be generated, and analysis can be done on the results of the model. Consequently, the aim of IE is to utilize technology in order to provide meaning to text.

This research utilizes NASA Centre for Helio-Analytics (CfHA) data and NLP techniques to create an ontology learning model centering on the domain of heliophysics. This is done with the goal of examining the techniques used to develop the model in order to determine their efficacy and how they may be applied to future models. As a result, this model provides a case study for examining NLP methods for ontology learning. Furthermore, prior models have been examined in Section 3.2 in order to establish a foundation for this research.

This chapter is organized as follows:

1. Section 3.1 discusses the purpose of the research, the driving questions, and the objectives that organize and guide this effort.

2. Section 3.2 provides a review of existing literature on ontologies and NER models that have been developed for scientific domains.

3. Section 3.3 discusses the journey from text to ontology; from collecting data to developing the NER and ontology learning parts of the model, and evaluating the results.

4. Section 3.4 lays out the results of the model, including a review of the reasoning behind the choices made when developing each part.

5. Section 3.5 provides an exploratory analysis of data generated from each major part of the model.

6. Section 3.6 presents the results along with the research questions, placing the results in context with prior literature. It also brings up the limitations of this project.

7. Section 3.7 summarizes the results of the experiments and provides an overview of areas for further research.

3.1.1 Background

The National Aeronautics and Space Administration (NASA) is an organization that employs individuals who work in a broad range of specializations across space-related disciplines. Consequently, employees collaborate on research projects with diverse aims that reflect their different domains of knowledge. As collaboration facilitates scientific discovery, there is the need to explore methods to enable knowledge-sharing. For example, the NASA Center for Helio-Analytics (CfHA) is a cross-disciplinary community that develops methodologies centered on applications for emerging technologies and techniques to hasten the development of space physics research. McGranaghan et al. [56] developed a KG as a response to the need for facilitating cross-discipline knowledge-sharing. This was proposed to address difficulties faced by members of the CfHA community when attempting to discover information about other members and projects. As a result, this led to the creation of the CfHA ontology, which was manually developed.

By creating a centralized means of accessing community information, gaps in skills and knowledge can be identified, and cross-group collaboration facilitated. In contrast, alternative methods of knowledge representation may face shortcomings when used for these ends. For example, spreadsheets are less structured when compared to many programming languages, which may lead users to cause redundancy, loss of data, and corruption [11]. Furthermore, spreadsheets cannot be searched or queried in the same way as a KG. Meanwhile, databases contain organizational structures that can more accurately model real-world domains, but are often limited by issues of scalability and multi-tenancy when attempting to provide information to many users [32]. Furthermore, querying information from databases frequently necessitates specialist knowledge, unless there is an interface to simplify the process. Therefore, a KG provides a promising avenue for representing a complex domain through its representation of entity nodes and the relationships between them.

Owing to the multidisciplinary emphasis of the CfHA and the projects that its members are involved with, it presents the opportunity for a case study on the benefits and applications of ontology learning in scientific domains. Indeed, there are several potential drawbacks to a purely manual approach that may be addressed by an NLP-based model. For one, although the ontology can be manually updated, it may be difficult to accurately capture current developments in the CfHA in a timely fashion. In addition, introducing automation to ontology population efforts can free up human resources that can go toward other areas of a project. Furthermore, although CfHA data is used to train the ontology learning model, the implications of this research may inform broader approaches to information representation and KG population.

In summary, there is room to study the uses for NLP techniques, and how they can be harnessed to construct a model based on CfHA-related data to automatically populate a CfHA ontology in a way that facilitates knowledge-sharing between the group. In the process, methods for increasing the accuracy and reliability of the model can be analyzed.

3.1.2 Research Questions

In this chapter, the following Research Questions (RQ) around ontology learning and how to utilize state-of-the-art NLP techniques for populating ontologies are addressed.

- **RQ1**: What are the current state-of-the-art approaches to ontology learning?
- **RQ2**: Which NLP techniques for NER are the most relevant to the automatic/semi-automatic population of ontologies?

- **RQ3**: How can an automated approach to ontology population facilitate information sharing between members of the CfHA?
- **RQ4**: How can an automated approach toward ontology population benefit a broader research effort?

3.2 Literature Review

In order to formulate an effective model, research into prior efforts must be undertaken. Critical evaluation of what sources are available is important for understanding both what methodologies have already been formulated, and where there are gaps that can be addressed.

3.2.1 Ontology Learning

The history of ontology learning as a field is inextricable from developments in ML and the Semantic Web. At the beginning of the 21st century, the web was inefficient due to a lack of standardization and quality control measures [2]. As a result, it was difficult to piece together meaningful information. The semantic web was popularized by Berners-Lee et al. [8], who published an article in *Scientific American* that provided an overview of concepts that were vital to the scientific web. Notably, this article detailed the role of ontologies in providing a formally structured method of representing data in a particular domain. Another article on the relevance of ontologies for facilitating cooperative information discovery was published in AI Magazine, where Maedche and Staab [48] used knowledge portals, many of which were domain- or market-specific, as case studies for how ontologies could facilitate better information access.

Ontologies were proposed as a method for organizing the semantic web, but they had use in broader scientific efforts. Maedche and Staab [49] elaborated further on the potential utility of ontologies by proposing the concept of ontology learning. The vision that they put forth built upon structured, semi-structured, or unstructured data to support a semi-automatic, cooperative ontology engineering process. NLP models for ontology learning have been developed since the early 2000s [50, 55]. A two-stage methodology was proposed by Valarakos et al. [85] for automatically populating an allergens ontology. Their model utilized a NER and classification (NERC) model, which was trained by using Hidden Markov Models (HMMs). For the allergens ontology, semi-automation meant that a domain expert would only need to be consulted before the second processing stage, when extraction rules for populating the ontology needed to be created. This methodology was an early adopter of NLP techniques for ontology learning and used Precision and Recall metrics to determine the accuracy of their work.

Nevertheless, the authors were not able to robustly test the entirety of their performance approach and may have benefited from a narrower methodology scope. Overall, the early history of ontology learning was sparser compared to more recent efforts, but the usefulness of NLP techniques in ontology learning was reflected in research at the time.

Ontology learning research efforts became more commonplace in the 2010s. As the field has developed, increasingly sophisticated NLP techniques such as deep learning have been employed. For example, Ayadi et al. [3] utilized a variety of biological documents to populate an already-existing biomolecular network ontology. Their methodology involved using tokenization to preprocess the biological documents, followed by normalization to convert words into a unified format. Word2vec, an algorithm that employs shallow neural networks to learn word embeddings, was employed for the representation of words as vectors. Word2vec was specifically utilized to group semantically close words together, whilst moving unrelated words away from each other. This is useful when attempting to create entities, as entity recognition algorithms may face problems with syntactic disambiguation. When assessing the model, Ayadi et al. [3] used Precision, Recall, and the F-measure to determine the accuracy of their model, whereas in comparison, Valarakos et al. [85] used only Precision and Recall to assess their model. The model developed by Ayadi et al. [3] ultimately performed well in Precision for all measures, whereas Recall fell behind Precision, and the F-measure fell in-between. What this demonstrates is that an approach using shallow neural networks may benefit from additional training in order to ensure that labels are accurately classified. Furthermore, more cutting-edge NLP techniques may not perform better in all measures than traditional NLP approaches.

One additional ontology learning effort was made by Youn et al. [90]. Similarly to [3], they utilized Word2Vec for word embeddings with the aim of populating a food ontology. Unlike [3], they used the GloVe and fastText algorithms to test the efficacy of pre-trained word embeddings. Youn et al. [90] used Precision as the metric for evaluating the algorithms, which demonstrated that those that employed embedding performed better. However, only Precision was used as an evaluation metric. Ayadi et al. [3] used Precision, Recall, and the F-measure to evaluate their algorithm, which demonstrated that a high Precision score may not correlate to a high Recall score, and vice versa. Although the algorithms that Youn et al. [90] tested demonstrated that embedded algorithms scored higher than non-embedded algorithms in Precision, this is not the sole metric that can be used to determine the efficacy of an algorithm. Recall, for instance, would have revealed which proportion of true positives is accurately classified, and the F-score would demonstrate the trade-off between Recall and Precision. Nevertheless, the robustness in comparing different algorithms is important in establishing which models outperform others and analyzing why that may be the case.

An initial analysis of existing research demonstrates that ontology learning efforts have significantly evolved in terms of methodology and NLP

techniques used since they were first introduced. Furthermore, new innovations in NLP have opened up a range of new possibilities for facilitating
the IEP through techniques such as shallow neural networks. Nevertheless,
there is room to explore how the accuracy of ontology learning models can be
improved, particularly when assessing how models extract entities.

3.2.2 Scientific Efforts and Ontologies

The original use for an ontology is rooted in philosophy. Lorhard [45] in
Theatrum philosophicum and Göckel [24] in Lexicon philosophicum both
independently used the term, as "ontologia." The term was used in reference to metaphysics, which is a discipline that studies the philosophical
nature of existence. Subsequent philosophical ontologists sought to provide a definitive and exhaustive classification of all entities in all spheres of
being [79]. The definition of an ontology in computer science is similar, as
ontologies were originally conceived to construct meaning for the semantic web. Ontology-based formalisms were used to add structure where none
had previously existed, and the W3C Web Ontology Language (OWL) was
developed to create a language for constructing ontologies. Similarly, the
Resource Description Framework Schema (RDF/S) was developed as a data
model for storing metadata about an ontology [19]. This transition from philosophy to computer science is united by an aim of representing the nature
of a particular domain.

Although computer science ontologies were initially developed to assign
meaning to the semantic web, they came to be used as a method of modeling data in particular domains. Munir and Sheraz Anjum [61] detail the
use of ontologies as an alternative to databases for managing information.
The authors specify that a major advantage of using a domain ontology is its
ability to define a semantic model of the data combined with the associated
domain knowledge. Zemmouchi-Ghomari et al. [91] detail several primary
differences between ontologies and databases. Where databases are intended
for the closed-world storage of data, ontologies are an open-world representation of a domain. Ontology schemata tend to be more complex than databases,
and ontologies tend to be independent of a specific application or problem.
These features make them appropriate for modeling scientific domains.

Managing space-related data is a particularly pertinent area of application for ontologies. Rovetto [71] mentions that ontologies are useful for the
knowledge management of space-related disciplines due to their knowledge-
rich nature. The author then provides an overview of existing ontologies for
orbital space, the NASA taxonomy, and planetary data. Many of the projects
described are currently ongoing, which demonstrates the open-world, evolving nature of ontologies and provides support for the necessity of efficient
ontology population methods. Describing space systems through ontologies
can help overcome challenges associated with non-ontology methods such
as semantics being ignored for ease of implementation, missing discipline

context information, and there being no existing knowledge capture and mechanism for applying knowledge [28].

A project that has benefitted from the inclusion of an ontology include the Ontology-driven Interactive Search Environment for Earth Sciences (ODISEES). Rutherford et al. [74] describe the purpose of this ontology as aiding researchers aiming to find usable data among a proliferation of closely related data. This effort was aimed at making data easily available to the public, serving both scientists and researchers as well as laymen. An automated approach may be beneficial, considering the scale of the data that the ODISEES handles. Another effort is the Orbital Debris Ontology (ODO), which Rovetto et al. [72] describe as an ontology for monitoring the amount of orbital detritus, particularly the threat it poses to assets in orbit. As a result, timeliness in populating the ontology is vital to ensure that accurate, up-to-date data is reflected. The authors also mention that ontologies are relatively easy to modify, as they do not require code maintenance, and that changing domain knowledge can be reflected in an ontology. Nevertheless, ontologies that reflect domains with time-sensitive information may be hindered if some automation is not employed, especially in larger ontologies. However, the high-risk nature of tracking orbital debris means that some human intervention is still needed.

In conclusion, ontologies present a promising addition to scientific efforts, particularly in domains that are like the CfHA ontology that this chapter uses as a case study. Ontologies also present certain advantages over databases for modeling complex domains. Furthermore, the case studies described by Rutherford et al. [74], Rovetto [71], and Rovetto et al. [72] demonstrate how ontologies are useful for a scientific effort by allowing for large quantities of data to be quickly sorted through and analyzed. These case studies also demonstrate the potential use of automation in ontology population to reduce the need for human intervention.

3.2.3 Named Entity Recognition

One of the most crucial steps of the IEP is the process of extracting meaningful entities from a text corpus. This procedure is known as NER. These NE are nouns – people, places, or things. For example, NER can involve the extraction of Persons, Locations, or Organizations from a selected text [53]. This process is one stage in the information extraction pipeline (IEP), which refers to the whole procedure for taking a text corpus and converting it into data that is meaningful for a particular objective [82]. The Pipeline can be visualized in Figure 3.1. Out of all steps in the IEP, NER is perhaps the most important for ontology creation, as it is this step that deals with identifying and classifying texts into pre-defined ontological classes. Named entities (NEs) often bear important information and must be recognized and translated appropriately, and they are important for the construction of a domain grammar [92]. Consequently, it is worth examining existing research and the efficacy of methodologies for NER.

FIGURE 3.1
Overview of the IEP.

Batbaatar and Ryu [7] present a recurrent neural network approach to ontology-based NER based on Twitter messages. Their work utilized the Pytorch library to implement the BiLSTM-CRF model for NER, which was applied to a corpus of health data extracted from Twitter. The BiLSTM-CRF model has four layers. The embedding layer examines embedding features, character features, and additional word features. The BiLSTM layer learns contextual information. The CRF layer calculates tagging scores for word input. Finally, the Viterbi layer is used to find a tag sequence to maximize the tagging scores. The algorithm evaluation was based on Precision, Recall, and F-score measures alongside a comprehensive comparison against variant models such as LSTM-CRF (word, char, part-of-speech [POS], and combinations) and BiLSTM-CRF (word, char, POS, and combinations). This demonstrated that BiLSTM-CRF scored high on Precision, with a maximum of 94.53% for the Disease or Symptom, 90.83% for Sign or Symptom, and 94.93% for the Pharmacologic Substance predictive performance. Recall scored lower, with a maximum of 73.31% for the word + char + POS metric for Disease or Syndrome, 81.98% for the Sign or Symptom, and 73.47% for the Pharmacologic Substance predictive performance. Overall, the authors presented a thorough approach to model testing for NER.

Another study by Wang et al. [88] explores NERO, a biomedical NER Ontology. This ontology was designed with minimizing arbitrary annotative semantic text labels in mind and aimed to represent textual entities recognized by text mining tools. The Conditional Random Fields (CRF) algorithm was used for the NE recognizer, and the CRF is often used for NER, POS tagging, and gene prediction. The authors measured NER performance using Precision, Recall, and F1-score metrics. The overall performance was measured at 54.9% Precision, 37.3% Recall, and a 43.4% F1-score. This indicates that the CRF algorithm was not as robust as the algorithm presented by Batbaatar and Ryu [7]. The main limitation of the study was that, although the authors aimed for the NERO ontology to cover all entities in the biomedical research literature, not all levels of granularity were covered in classifying entities. Furthermore, many concept types were not well represented due to the heavy-tail distribution in the frequencies of ontology classes. This indicates that ontology learning methods might be ideal for addressing completeness problems in ontologies where there is a lack of sufficient data, especially in complex domains.

A third effort detailed in [31] is the SatelliteNER, a tool for automatically detecting satellite entities from different sources of textual data. This chapter specifically examines NER in the context of a space-related domain, which is relevant to the focus of this research effort. Although the purpose of the SatelliteNER is not ontology population, NER is used specifically for recognizing satellite entities. The spaCy module was selected to build SatelliteNER, and the Pseudo-rehearsal strategy was chosen for the algorithm to run through existing training data and remember assigned weights. However, as there can be common entities, the resultant model is not fast. The authors evaluated several different models to compare them to the SatelliteNER model, including StanfordNer, Stanza, GoogleNER, and MicrosoftNER. The evaluation criteria were based on Precision, Recall, the F1-score, and Processing Time, and the models were tested on three datasets. SatelliteNER had the best Precision, as it was built to only detect models that the authors deemed relevant. SatelliteNER had a high Recall in testing dataset 1, as this was the training dataset, as well as a Recall of over 50% for datasets 2 and 3. The neural network-based models also had higher Recall scores compared to other models. The F1-score of SatelliteNER was also the highest, as the F1-score is the weighted average of Precision and Recall. Finally, SatelliteNER performed the quickest in Processing Time. Ultimately, this demonstrates that custom built NER algorithms for a specific domain tend to outperform generic alternatives and supports the use of a NER model tailored to the CfHA ontology and trained on a quality, relevant data corpus.

In conclusion, several case studies of NER models were examined. Not every case study detailed the use of NER in ontology creation [31, 82], although many did [7, 54, 92]. These studies highlighted the importance of developing an efficient and accurate NER model for extracting labels from a text corpus, as [31] demonstrated by comparing the Precision, Recall, F1-score, and Runtime of a custom-built algorithm that was trained on satellite detection data against other, generic NER algorithms. This demonstrates the benefit of creating an algorithm that is trained on existing CfHA ontology data, because the more accurate the entity extraction is, the more accurate the data for the ontology population will be.

3.2.4 NLP Models for Ontology Learning

Examining existing models that have been developed for the ontology population is important for determining how to represent a particular domain. Because ontology domains are often heterogeneous and feature technical concepts, ontology population models often benefit from an automated or semi-automated mechanism for extracting information and populating ontologies [43]. Some type of ontology-based information extraction (OBIE) is typically used for the population of an ontology. Maynard et al. [55] detail that this involves determining the key terms in a specific text and relating them to existing terms in the ontology. IE usually consists of linguistic preprocessing followed by a NER technique, before an ontology population algorithm is used. However, the authors do not elaborate on specific ontology population methodologies. Thus, examining case studies can provide further insight into existing ontology population algorithms.

di Buono et al. [14] present a case study on applying computational linguistics to the cultural heritage domain. The authors posit that NLP techniques can be used for bridging the information gap and improving access to cultural resources. Lexicon-Grammar (LG) is the NLP theoretical and practical framework used. The authors describe that it is based on the Operator Argument Grammar developed by Harris [27], where human languages are self-organizing systems where word syntactic and semantic properties can be calculated based on their relationships with co-occurring words inside nuclear or simple sentence contexts. Furthermore, electronic dictionaries are used to describe syntax. Finite-State Automata (FSA) variables were used for identifying ontological classes and properties for subjects, objects, and predicates within RDF graphs. The authors developed an FSA with variables that apply to specific POS. Finally, linguistic data was matched to RDF triples and translated into SPARQL and SERQL path expressions. Although the authors describe their methodology for ontology population, they do not provide an evaluation section, so the efficacy of their process is not elaborated on. Nevertheless, it provides insight into how a grammar can be constructed for populating an ontology.

Another case study conducted by Peña et al. [67] focused on Aragon Open Data, a project to open data by the Government of Aragon. Due to the volume of data released, the authors proposed a methodology for allowing unstructured institutional information to become structured data that can be analyzed and browsed. Consequently, an ontology was designed to standardize public administration information. The authors implemented a set of subprocesses through an AI software framework called Moriarty. This is based on two concepts: workitem, a class that implements an atomic function and can be used in multiple contexts, and workflow, which is composed of workitems or other workflows that receive some inputs and perform transformations on them generating and returning outputs. Additionally, a neural network known as the MultiLayer Perceptron (MLP) was used for NER. Extracted knowledge was stored in OpenLink Virtuoso, which uses subprocesses to insert data extracted using the MLP. The algorithm was able to crawl through 667 websites, process 3,963 URLs, and populate the ontology with 95,978 new instances. Although the authors did not provide metrics for specific aspects of their method, the overall results demonstrate how automation can aid in collecting large amounts of information.

One additional study conducted by Makki et al. [51] focuses on automatic ontology population for risk management. It is important to have up-to-date information in order to establish accurate risk assessments. Adopting a fully automated method is dangerous, as risk assessment requires human control and validation, but using NLP techniques can be used to enrich an ontology.

The authors detailed a semi-automated ontology population method on a generic risk management ontology. First, the corpus of risk-related texts was processed using TreeTagger, a POS tagger that annotates texts. Associations between verbs were built through synonyms generated through the lexical resource WordNet, as well as frequent verbs extracted from the annotated corpus and human interference. Finally, triplets were identified and extracted from the list of verbs, which were then validated by a domain expert. The authors formulated a sample experiment to validate their work by using the PRIMA risk management ontology. First, POS tagging was applied to a corpus by the Environmental Protection Agency, and a list of related verbs was built. Then, triplets were extracted and proposed to the syntactic structure recognition procedure, which generated 150 triplets. Eighty-five percent of these were evaluated as acceptable triplets. Although a fully automated method is not ideal for a domain such as risk management, the 85% acceptability rate for triplets indicates that adopting a semi-automated methodology is beneficial. There is still room to test additional parts of the process using evaluation metrics in order to optimize the methodology further.

The reviewed methodologies focused on different domains, ranging from risk management [52] to government data [67] to cultural heritage [14]. There were additional differences in their methodologies. di Buono et al. [14] used LG and FSA variables in order to process relevant keywords, before they were matched to RDF triples. Meanwhile, Peña et al. [67] used OpenLink Virtuoso subprocesses in order to extract data and populate the ontology. Finally, Makki et al. [52] used TreeTagger and WordNet to process and create triplets. Out of these surveys, Makki et al. [51] described an 85% acceptability rate for the ontology triplets. However, the performance of the model was not elaborated on, which indicates that there is room for more detailed survey methods in assessing the acceptability of automatically generated ontology entities.

3.3 From Text to Ontology

This section discusses the steps toward development of the ontology learning model based on the text corpus. It specifies, in detail, the algorithms that have been employed in each stage of the IEP. Although prior research efforts have made use of one or more stages of the IEP employed in this chapter, there are few that contain a model that spans every stage. Nevertheless, examining existing models that correlate to stages in the IEP is useful when developing a methodology. For example, Witte et al. [20] presented a model that utilized NLP for NER, which is the process of assigning meaningful labels to entities extracted from a text corpus. The researchers created a model that went through standard textual preprocessing, including tokenization and POS tagging. NEs were then detected through a two-step process:

1. **Step 1:** An OntoGazetter labeled each word token in the text with all possible ontology classes it could belong to.
2. **Step 2:** Ontology grammar rules written in the JAPE language were used to find NEs.

One additional approach utilized by Jafari et al. [31] used the Spacy library alongside the Pseudo-rehearsal strategy in order to train their model on existing data in order to discover entities. These recognized entities were then added to the training data, to ensure that the model does not forget learned weights. The issue of an NLP model forgetting earlier items after learning a new item is referred to as the "catastrophic forgetting" problem. Therefore, introducing a "pseudorehearsal" strategy is a simple way to solve this problem, in which random inputs are temporarily stored along with their outputs [18]. Jafari et al. [31] also created a from-scratch NER model entitled SatelliteNER, although they did not elaborate on how they developed or trained this model within the paper. Other ontology learning research, including the NERO biomedical ontology [88], also used spaCy for the NER process. Therefore, spaCy has been used for the NER portion of the CfHA model.

The methodology for developing the NLP model built upon the procedures described in this section alongside the literature that has been evaluated in Chapter 3. spaCy has been utilized for IE purposes to label instances with class labels from the CfHA ontology. For the sake of limiting the scope of this project, seven class labels have been chosen: PERSON and ORG, which already exist in the spaCy NER package, and the custom labels ASTROPHYSICS, HELIOPHYSICS, MISSION, PROJECT, and PAPER. All of these labels correspond to class types in the CfHA ontology and have been trained on data pulled from a heliophysics text corpus.

The ontology learning methodology stages are as follows:

- **Step 1:** The text corpus will be tokenized, preprocessed, lemmatized, and stemmed.
- **Step 2:** The spaCy NER library is imported.
- **Step 3:** The dependency tree for each sentence is parsed according to a rule intended to extract subjects, objects, modifiers, and compound words.
- **Step 4:** Relations are extracted as well by using dependency parsing based on the root or verb of the sentence. This process is broken down by step in Figure 3.2.
- **Step 5:** The entities and relationships are converted into RDF triples, and a KG is generated. These triples are then placed into a Protégé ontology.

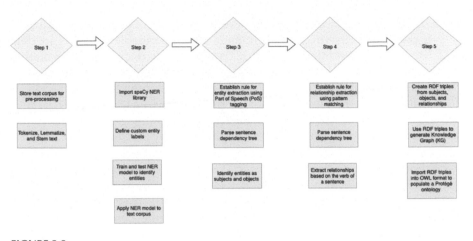

FIGURE 3.2
Overview of ontology learning model methodology.

3.3.1 NLP in Ontology Learning

To construct a foundation for the ontology learning model, the concepts underpinning NLP must be explored. NLP is a field that sits at the intersection between Artificial Intelligence (AI) and linguistics and uses data science techniques to bridge the gap between human forms of communication and machine communication [63]. NLP techniques have been proposed for their use in enhancing ontology development. As an example, Lame [39] implemented an ontology by using Syntex text parsing in order to extract keywords and relationships from legal text corpora and performing statistical analysis in order to assign importance to certain concepts. Statistical approaches are commonly used in NLP, such as dependency analysis, lexico-syntactic analysis, term subsumption, formal concept analysis (FCA), hierarchical clustering, and association rule mining (ARM) [2]. These concepts provide a foundation for the NLP elements utilized in the model.

ML principles underlie NLP. ML can be defined as automated computing procedures that aim to mimic human reasoning and generate classifying expressions that are simple enough to be understood by humans [4]. ML techniques can be divided into supervised learning, where input data and an output target variable are known and a model is trained against this variable, and unsupervised learning, where only input data is available. Supervised learning includes methods such as classification and regression, while unsupervised learning includes methods such as clustering [12]. Hybrid approaches are also possible. These techniques are appropriate for the development of the CfHA ontology learning model, where the aim is to infer classes and relationships similarly to how a human can.

There are additional fields that are relevant to the process of IE. Data mining (DM) involves the extraction of information from structured databases, which is part of the broader field of Knowledge Discovery in Databases

(KDD) [70]. KDD is defined as the non-trivial process of identifying valid, novel, potentially useful, and ultimately understandable patterns in data [84]. Meanwhile, text mining (TM) deals with the extraction of information from unstructured, textual forms. TM holds more relevancy to the aims of this research, as unstructured text is used for developing the model.

TM allows for the systematic extraction of meaningful content from a particular corpus of text, which is relevant to the ontology population from CfHA meeting notes. However, TM applications apply constraints on NLP tools, as they usually rely on large volumes of textual data and do not allow for exponential algorithms to be used. Furthermore, semantic models for a given domain are typically not available, and this limits the sophistication of the semantic and pragmatic levels of a model [70]. This is the reason why models for ontology learning are often rule-based and specific to a particular domain.

The process of creating a KG is divided into two parts. The first half focuses on TM and preprocessing in order to extract information from the text, while the second half focuses on the creation of the ontology from extracted data. TM techniques are used to generate meaning from an unstructured text corpus, based on a trained spaCy model. According to [80], TM is divided into several stages.

1. The first stage involves the collection of unstructured data from different sources that are available in different file formats.
2. The second stage involves preprocessing and cleansing operations, which aim to eliminate abnormalities and capture the essence of the text. Cleansing also aims to remove stop words, as well as stemming and indexing the data.
3. The third stage applies processing and controlling operations in order to audit and clean the data set by automatic processing.
4. The fourth stage involves pattern analysis implemented by the Management Information System (MIS).
5. The fifth stage is to synthesize the information extracted from the text in order to inform decisions and further utilize the processed data.

Extracting meaning from an unstructured text is often done manually. Inniss et al. [30] describe that the typical process for generating a biomedical ontology involves interviewing experts, transcribing the text, and manually mining the text for feature-attribute pairs. Automated TM instead uses speech and language processing concepts in order to construct a structured data object. Where manually parsing a text corpus relies on a human understanding of grammar and disambiguation, NLP for TM must go through several main steps in order to interpret a corpus. These steps include "Lexical Analysis," "Syntactic Analysis," "Semantic Analysis," "Pragmatic Analysis," and "Discourse Analysis," each comprising a different subfield of NLP [62].

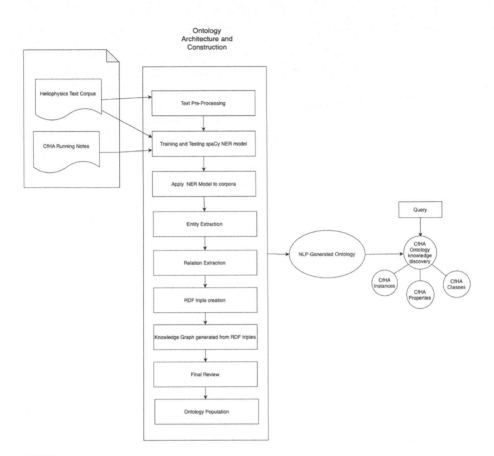

FIGURE 3.3
Architecture of ontology learning model.

For the CfHA ontology learning model, these various sources of information have been synthesized into the theoretical concepts that underlie each step. The overall system architecture is depicted in Figure 3.3.

1. **Step 1:** Here, TM concepts are used to clean and preprocess a text corpus. The corpus is tokenized, stripped of unnecessary symbols and stopwords, and lemmatized.
2. **Step 2:** NER techniques must be employed in order to extract entities from the cleaned text. The model must also be trained to recognize labels that do not already exist in the default model.
3. **Step 3:** Based on the NER labels extracted earlier, concepts and relations must be extracted from the text.
4. **Step 4:** A KG is built from the concepts and relations.
5. **Step 5:** The KG values are processed into RDF triples and inserted into a Protégé ontology.

3.3.2 Prototype Evaluation

To complete the methodology, there needs to be a system for evaluating the efficacy and accuracy of the model. Furthermore, a thorough evaluation of the methodology assesses the quality of the research backing the model. Systematic reviews are preferential, as no type of study should be evaluated in isolation. An assessment should be balanced and draw on a variety of sources [21]. Qualitative data analysis methods provide insight into the suitability of both the text used in TM as well as the ML models themselves. Sonntag [80] defined four categories matching text quality dimensions: contextual, which deals with the amount of data, completeness, relevancy, and timeliness, representational, which deals with consistent, concise representation, ease of understanding, and interpretability, intrinsic, which deals with accuracy, objectivity and reputation, and accessibility. These metrics are listed in Table 3.1.

For the rest of the model, additional metrics suited to assessing NLP models must be used. Siebert et al. [77] provide various metrics for assessing ML models based on quality attributes, such as Accuracy, Precision, Recall, and the F-score, for development and runtime correctness. Additional quality attributes such as robustness can be evaluated using Equalized Loss of Accuracy (ELA), and the level of interpretability can be assessed by using complexity metrics. Gunawardana and Shani [23] survey accuracy evaluation metrics to establish which ones apply to a particular domain. Accuracy metrics that measure truth values such as the Root of the Mean Square Error (RMSE) method, the ROC area curve, and confusion matrices are relevant to classification problems [87].

The performance metrics that are used on the ML model are summarized in Table 3.1.

However, additional focus will be given to Precision, Recall, and the F-Score, as these are commonly employed for NER problems [3, 85, 88]. For these metrics, each object is associated with a binary label L, which corresponds to the correctness of an object. Additionally, there is an assignment A that corresponds to the relevance of an object [22]. This experimental outcome may be summarized in a truth table (Table 3.2).

Here, a true positive would correspond to an entity that was assigned a label, and that the NER model correctly identified as an entity. A false negative would

TABLE 3.1

Performance Measure Metrics for NER Models

Performance Metrics	
Evaluation metric	**Description**
Accuracy	Determines the overall proportion of true results among the total results
Precision	Determines how many predicted positives match up with the true number of positives
Recall	Determines what proportion of true positives is accurately classified
F1-score	Evaluates the accuracy of a test, calculated from the harmonic mean of the precision and recall values

TABLE 3.2

Truth Table for NER Metrics

		Evaluation Metrics	
		Assignment	
		Positive	Negative
Binary label L	Positive	True positive	False negative
	Negative	False positive	True negative

correspond to an entity that was assigned a label and that the NER model did not identify as an entity. A false positive would correspond to a token that was incorrectly identified as an entity by the NER model, and a true negative would mean a token that was correctly identified as not being an entity. From this truth table, the equations for determining Precision and Recall can be calculated. The equation for Precision is displayed in Equation 3.1:

$$precision = (TruePositive)/((TruePositive)+(FalsePositive)) \qquad (3.1)$$

This can be interpreted as the total number of actual entities over the total number of identified entities, whether those be correctly identified or not. The equation for Recall is displayed in Equation 3.2:

$$recall = (TruePositive)/((TruePositive)+(FalseNegative)) \qquad (3.2)$$

This can be interpreted as the total number of actual entities over the total number of actual entities as well as the total number of entities that were not identified.

From here, the F1-score can be calculated. It is the harmonic mean of Precision and Recall. This is displayed in Equation 3.3:

$$F1 = (TruePositive)/(TruePositive+1/2(FalsePositive+FalseNegative)) \qquad (3.3)$$

This can be taken as a measure of the accuracy of a test. As a result, it provides a means of demonstrating an average between Precision and Recall. In cases where Precision or Recall are different values, it can demonstrate the overall efficacy of a model. Consequently, Precision, Recall, and the F1-score are employed to evaluate this model.

3.4 Experimental Study

This section details the development of the NLP model, from selecting the data to the creation of the final ontology. The reasoning behind choices made during development is described in the following sections. The code associated with the development of the model is publicly available online.[2] The developed repository contains an overview of the model prototype, starting from importing text and finishing with the final ontology with all the necessary steps explained in the document.

3.4.1 Overview of the Proposed System

3.4.1.1 Data Sourcing

The data for this research was sourced from both private documents and publicly available research. The CfHA Meeting Notes are running notes that document developments in the CfHA ontology and formed part of the training data for the NER model. Permission was obtained to use these meeting notes for the project. The second portion of the data used for this project came from a JSON file of heliophysics-related paper titles, bibcodes, and abstracts. Permission was also obtained to use this information.

3.4.1.2 Data Preprocessing

Select text snippets were sourced from both the CfHA Meeting Notes and the heliophysics text corpus. These snippets were chosen for the variety in the entities that were contained within them, in order to train the NER model with relevant data. Concepts that were selected for were already reflected in the CfHA ontology. The text was cleaned and preprocessed in order to remove unnecessary information such as stopwords, the process of which is elaborated on in Section 3.4.4. This process was performed on the heliophysics text corpus, which was used for this research due to its robustness and the amount of available data.

3.4.1.3 Model Construction

After preprocessing the text corpus, the NER and KG portions of the model were constructed (see Section 3.4.4.1) in order to identify important entities in the heliophysics text corpus and extract relations between the entities. Additional data analysis was performed on the IEP in order to provide insights into the model (see Section 5.1).

3.4.2 Data Sourcing

3.4.2.1 Heliophysics Text Corpus

Due to the advent of social media and digital information sharing, large swaths of data can be generated and disseminated. Having large amounts of data for a NER model is important to ensure the accuracy of a NER model and should be indicative of the data that the model is used to predict. Consequently, sourcing quality data is an important stage in the model development process. Jafari et al. [31] constructed the SatelliteNER model by using Wikipedia data on governmental and private space agency names, as well as a list of orbital launch systems for each country and for each agency. Wikipedia presents an easily accessible and robust source of information to train a NER model. However, Wikipedia is open-access, and many citations reference news articles, YouTube videos, or other non-peer-reviewed sources [17].

This model focuses on a scientific domain and contains five custom entity labels: Astrophysics, HELIOPHYSICS, PAPER, PROJECT, and MISSION, alongside two default spaCy labels PERSON and ORG. As a result, peer-reviewed research data is particularly valuable for NER training. This is because peer-reviewed research is likely to be written by experts and feature correct usage of entities and relationships in context. As a result, a corpus consisting of heliophysics paper titles, abstracts, and bibliographic codes was sourced to train and test the model.

This heliophysics corpus was provided by Ryan McGranaghan. It consists of a JSON file that contains academic publications, including the title, bibcode, and abstract for all heliophysics-related articles from 2020. All articles in the NASA Astrophysics Data Service were sub-selected using the criteria of only journals that are relevant to the domain of heliophysics.

The data was manually sorted through to identify entities that matched up to instances that were already present in the CfHA ontology. Text snippets containing these entities were selected and used as training and test validation data. The different classes were split up a relatively even amount of instances, and the proportion of classes and instances is visualized in Table 3.3. Subclasses are grouped with superclasses.

TABLE 3.3

Classes and Number of Instances

Word	Number of Occurrences
Action	0
Activity (incl. Affiliate, Match, Meeting, Mission, Project)	8
Event (incl. Presentation, Workshop)	0
Funds	0
Object	0
Organization (incl. Group)	95
Other	0
Output	0
Person	74
Position	0
Program	0
Publication (incl. Data, Paper, Software)	0
Role	0
Skill	0
Team	0
Topic (Astrophysics, Heliophysics, etc.)	159

Table 3.3 demonstrates where there is a need for additional data in the CfHA ontology, with several classes such as Action, Event, and Publication not having any instances. This reveals a gap in the information that is represented in the CfHA ontology. The training and test data has aimed to encompass both instances that are well represented in the ontology and instances that are not. However, the classes without instances cannot be matched to instances in training data. Furthermore, the majority of the entities in the heliophysics text corpus related to heliophysics and astrophysics. Consequently, the data that was extracted from the heliophysics text corpus contained an unbalanced amount of entities. According to [34], training a spaCy model with custom annotations involved around 100 occurrences of each entity. As a result, it is important to ensure that the training data contains a sufficient representative sample for each entity.

3.4.2.2 CfHA Meeting Notes

There was an additional problem to be confronted when it comes to data sources. Because the entities that were manually extracted from the heliophysics text corpus were unbalanced, additional entities representing people and organizations had to be included. Consequently, an appropriate additional data source had to be procured to train the model. The Person entity was the label that primarily lacked sample data, and a text corpus was sought out that contained entities relevant to the CfHA ontology.

While developing the CfHA ontology, a paper that documented the outcomes and important points of each meeting was created. This is referred to as the CfHA Running Notes and contains information about each person involved in the ontology development as well as actions related to the ontology [56]. As a result, it presented a relevant source of training data for the spaCy NER model.

The process of selecting and extracting entities from the CfHA Running Notes was similar to the process outlined in Section 3.4.2.2 for extracting entities from the heliophysics text corpus. Entities were identified through dynamic embedding, which is based on the context of the word as it appears in the sentence [34]. Dynamic embedding is important to the performance of the NER model, as entities may appear in different contexts within a text corpus. For example, NASA may appear as a standalone ORG, or it may appear as part of the title of a PROJECT.

Due to the need for a sufficient amount of examples for each entity, the CfHA Meeting Notes was utilized as an auxiliary text corpus alongside the heliophysics text corpus. It was particularly important to provide data for the custom entities, as those did not have any existing pre-training in the spaCy default English model. However, providing additional data for the PERSON and ORG entity labels is beneficial for further improving the accuracy of the spaCy model.

3.4.2.3 Discussion of Approach

The next stage of the model development is to critically appraise the data collection approach utilized. This includes a discussion of the benefits and limitations. To begin with, choosing an appropriate data source was crucial to facilitate the custom entity label training. Having a robust heliophysics text corpus was vital for this end, especially one that reflected the domain expertise displayed by peer-reviewed research papers. However, the specialized nature of this text corpus caused limitations. There were almost no entities that could be used to train the PERSON class, and less entities for the ORG, PROJECT, and MISSION classes compared to heliophysics and astrophysics-related topics. This meant that the training and test data had plenty of HELIOPHYSICS and ASTROPHYSICS examples, with comparatively less PERSON, ORG, PROJECT, and MISSION instances. As the amount of instances used to train the data was not balanced, this fails to meet the standards outlined by the "Corpus-based" evaluation method for an ontology, as a large amount of the domain cannot be covered [69].

Another problem related to the source of the data was that the language used was at an academic level. Academic descriptions show entities in context, however complex language exacerbates ambiguity problems with disambiguation, or determining the right context that a word appears in. Overcoming this problem is known as Word Sense Disambiguation (WSD), but solutions often necessitate large linguistic databases such as WordNet to have a proper sample size to draw from [25]. This is further exacerbated by the use of custom topics, as the default SpaCy model has no training data to draw from. Heliophysics and astrophysics-related topics have appropriate samples to draw from, but for entities with less examples, this demonstrates the importance of having an appropriately large sample size. If the sample size is small, it may lead to issues with predicting Actual Positive classes and how many of the predicted entities are correctly identified by producing false negatives, or entities that are NEs, but were not labeled as being NEs.

The issues described above presented the opportunity to additionally use the CfHA Running Notes text corpus. As it is a body of work that is relevant to the CfHA Ontology, further examples can be sourced from it. However, there are limitations associated with the CfHA Running Notes text corpus. For example, unstructured phrases in contrast to structured and edited sentences may include abbreviated words, irregular grammar and spelling, and mixed languages which negatively impact entity detection [36]. Furthermore, time restrictions meant that additional data sources could not be utilized to provide more examples for entities.

Nevertheless, there are advantages to this approach. Both bodies of text are relevant to the research and, together, provide sufficient examples for the purposes of this research. The data was provided specifically for this model, so data collection is done with consent and with respect to privacy. The data is at a high academic standard, and there is a wealth of high-quality examples for some labels. Furthermore, the data was easily available and can be further utilized to enhance the model beyond the scope of this research.

3.4.2.4 Ethical Considerations

This research centers on detecting NEs and relationships between NEs relating to the domain of the CfHA and heliophysics research. Informed consent in the use of data is paramount, as the data that the model is trained on involves current research and the work of other individuals. All data was freely provided with the knowledge that it would be used for this research.

Another ethical consideration when it comes to training the model is in being mindful of algorithmic bias. Demographic bias in NER is a recognized phenomenon [13]. For example, the spaCy model surveyed in [59] had the highest accuracy score for recognizing Names that were labeled as White Male. Consequently, this must be accounted for when developing the NER model.

This research was approved by Birmingham City University.

3.4.3 Outline of Model Objectives

3.4.3.1 Objective 1: NER Optimization

In order to guide the performance of the model, suitable objectives must be outlined. The first of these deals with the optimization of the NER portion of the model. There are several factors that may improve the accuracy of a NER model. For one, providing NE information to a dependency parser can improve the accuracy of the parsing [10]. Furthermore, Fernández-Pedauye et al. [16] mention the importance of having a robust training data set with a variety of contexts that entities appear in. It was this factor that contributed the most to the NER optimization. Fernández-Pedauye et al. [16] also detail how selecting appropriate preprocessing techniques can also improve the performance of a NER model. These factors are echoed by Jafari et al. [31].

After evaluating prior methods of optimizing NER models, an important goal of this research is to source an adequate amount of data. As has been discussed in Section 3.4.2, the two text corpora used in this research both provide a large amount of examples for classification. Furthermore, the techniques in textual preprocessing are carefully chosen in order to ensure that the text corpus that goes into the NER model does not face issues with noise or extraneous tokens.

Finally, there are metrics that can be employed to evaluate the performance of a NER model. Siebert et al. [77] suggest various metrics for assessing ML models based on quality attributes, such as Accuracy, Precision, Recall, and the F-score, for development and runtime correctness. Additional quality attributes such as robustness can be evaluated using ELA, and the level of interpretability can be assessed by using complexity metrics. These metrics are further elaborated on in Section 3.2.3.

3.4.3.2 Objective 2: Entity Relationship Modeling Optimization

A suitable objective must also guide the development of the KG portion of the model. Evaluating an ontology can be more difficult than evaluating a NER model, as metrics for evaluation do not rely on numerical values and thus can be subjective. Success metrics include whether the ontology is capable of accomplishing tasks in the target domain, if hierarchical and taxonomical concepts are well represented, and whether the ontology is meeting the technical specifications [29]. A well-functioning ontology that is easy to use is particularly important in a multidisciplinary team such as that of the CfHA.

Ma et al. [46] explore a framework that examines ontology usability based on System Usability Scale (SUS), a ten-item Likert scale. From this, the authors came up with a pool of statements separated into three primary categories: syntax, semantics, and pragmatics. Another survey by Raad and Cruz [69] examines several evaluation methods: gold standard-based, which compares the learned ontology with a previously created "gold standard" reference ontology, Corpus-based, which evaluates how far an ontology covers a given domain, Task-based, which measures how far an ontology goes toward improving the results of a certain task, and Criteria-based, which is divided into Structure-based, which compute various structure properties, and Complex/Expert-based, which involves expert evaluation. Hooi et al. [29] also describe level-based evaluation: Syntax, which assess whether the syntax of the formal language is correct, Structure, which assesses if the concepts and hierarchy are sound, Lexical, which assesses the terms used to represent knowledge, Semantic, which refers to the ontology coping with different terms that relate to the same concept, and Context, which examines how the ontology affects the functionality and usability of ontology-driven applications. Furthermore, Brank et al. [9] add other semantic relations as a level of evaluation. Because different authors use different frameworks for ontology evaluation, it is useful to single out which measures are the most useful for the target domain.

In summary, there are multiple measures that can be used to evaluate an ontology. However, studies focused on evaluating an ontology that has been populated through semi-automated or automated means remain elusive, so selecting measures for evaluation must be carefully done.

3.4.4 Model Implementation

3.4.4.1 Text Corpus Overview

The model utilized the heliophysics text corpus outlined in Section 3.4.2.1 As this corpus was originally in JSON format, it had to be converted into a text file in order to employ preprocessing techniques. The JSON file contained objects with the properties "bibcode," "title," and "abstract." The total size of the file is 13.7 MB, and there are 8990 entries, 1,955,540 words, and it is 13,683,768 characters long. Due to the large size of the file, there were processing problems when attempting to run the model. Running environment and processing restrictions limited the total maximum file size.

Furthermore, using every entry in the document would create a KG that is laden with so much information that it is difficult to read, even when displaying parts of the graph by relationship. Ma et al. [47] found that training a NER model on word embeddings learned from unlabeled data is effective even when data is sparse. Furthermore, Baeza-Yates and Liaghat [5] detail other considerations in regard to the size of a data training corpus, such as training data size, learning time, and quality obtained. They found that, generally, with increased data size came increased quality. However, the performance versus data size curve peaked with a data size of 5 MB.

After considering these restrictions, a sample was procured from the total heliophysics dataset. The size of the file is 354 KB, and there are 249 entries, 50,549 words, and 353,773 characters. This text corpus sample was chosen when considering training data size balanced against the time the model takes to run, as well as the quality of the finished model.

3.4.4.2 Preprocessing for Text Mining (TM)

Employing well-selected textual preprocessing techniques is an important factor in the overall success of a model [16]. Indeed, preprocessing can take up to 80% of the total efforts in knowledge discovery [60]. The primary aims of text preprocessing are to extract key features from a corpus, to improve the relevancy between words and documents, and between words and classes, as well as to convert a text corpus into raw data [33]. Consequently, preprocessing is an important stage to consider.

First, an overview of textual preprocessing methods must be provided. Common techniques for preprocessing a corpus for any TM task include tokenization, which converts raw texts into segmented textual units, stop word removal, which involves the removal of commonly repeated features such as conjunctions and pronouns, and stemming, which involves the removal of affixes (prefixes and suffixes) from a document [33]. More specifically, Asim et al. [2] describe POS tagging, sentence parsing, and lemmatization as the linguistic-based preprocessing techniques that are used in almost every ontology learning methodology. POS tagging involves labeling corpus words with their corresponding POS tags. Parsing is a type of syntactic analysis that discovers the dependencies between words in a sentence and represents them in a parsing tree data structure. Lemmatization is used to bring terms into a normal form by removing word stems. For example, "processing" and "processed" become "process."

This model also utilizes the preprocessing techniques outlined by Asim et al. [2]. First, the heliophysics corpus sample (see Section 3.4.4.1) was saved in a text file and read by the model, before being tokenized using the Natural Language ToolKit (NLTK). Regular expressions used for pattern-matching were employed to remove unnecessary punctuation, whitespace, and characters, before the NLTK toolkit was used to remove stopwords from the text. The cleaned text was then written to a new file for further preprocessing.

After the text went through initial preprocessing, stemming and lemmatization modules from NLTK were imported. This allowed for the text to be converted into a standard format and was done after tokenization and stop word removal so that extraneous characters did not impact the rest of the preprocessing. Vectorization involves the process of converting documents into a numerical vector form, which makes it possible to analyze them and create instances in which the model works [37]. After vectorizing the text, it is stemmed to remove all word stems, and lemmatized to group together different inflections of a word together. This concludes the general preprocessing phase.

3.4.4.3 Named Entity Recognition (NER) Using spaCy

NER is a particularly important step in the IEP for ontology creation, as it involves the identification of entities from texts and categorization of them into predefined ontological classes. NEs are vital for constructing a domain grammar [92]. Therefore, ensuring that the NER portion of the model is accurately constructed is important to ensure that the domain is correctly represented.

The spaCy NER library was used as a basis for developing the NER portion of this model. As spaCy is a common choice for NER in multiple scientific domains [31, 74, 88], it was selected as an appropriate basis for the domain of heliophysics. spaCy NER contains the option for one of several pretrained models to be imported, as well as for creating a model from scratch. The en_core_web_sm pretrained model was selected as a basis for the heliophysics NER model. This decision was made because training a blank NER model would have taken a larger amount of data and resources, and the time scale for this research is limited. Thus, the heliophysics model was already partially trained. This utilizes the principle of transfer learning – where the performance of a target learner on a target domain is improved by transferring the knowledge that is already contained in a different, related source domain [93].

As the NER model must be tailored for the CfHA ontology, the default labels provided by spaCy are insufficient. Thus, additional labels were appended to the heliophysics model. Alongside the default labels PERSON and ORG, which correspond to the Person and Organisation classes, five additional labels were added: ASTROPHYSICS, HELIOPHYSICS, MISSION, PROJECT, and PAPER. Due to time limitations, the seven labels were selected on the basis of representing a cross section of the classes already in the ontology. This was done on the basis of labels representing concepts that are the most important to the ontology, as it is a person-focused ontology that involves research into heliophysics through missions and projects and produces output on this research such as papers.

The next stage of developing the NER model is training it. This step is necessary if there are custom entities, as spaCy relies on in-context examples for entity identification [26]. Jafari et al. [31] detail the process of training the SatelliteNER model to detect custom entities, specifying that a model trained on a particular corpus is suited to detecting entities in a similar corpus. Part of the effort involved updating a pre trained spaCy model, which involved the use of Wikipedia text corpora and an automatic entity tagger to train the model to detect the custom entities orgName, rocketName, and satelliteName – therefore, the trained model was suitable for detecting entities in articles. Similarly, the heliophysics NER model training data was primarily sourced from scientific article abstracts, as the CfHA ontology models scientific data. Therefore, sentences containing instances of the selected entity categories were extracted from the text corpus.

After providing training data, it was appended to the NER model using a "pseudo rehearsal" strategy, in which random inputs are temporarily stored along with their outputs. The NER model also had to be tested for suitability, so an additional corpus of data with labeled entities was utilized to test the NER model. The results are elaborated on in Chapter 6. This testing involved the use of separate data from the training corpus in order to verify the performance of the model.

The next stage involved using the model to extract entities. spaCy contains functionality for visualizing entities, labels, and label descriptions in order to assess the performance of the NER model, so these were utilized in order to assess which entities the model discovered. Further assessment metrics, including TFIDF, word similarity, clustering, and visualization diagrams were applied to the model to determine its quality, which are detailed in Chapter 6.

3.4.4.4 *Entity and Relationship Extraction Using POS Tagging*

The other important stage in the ontology learning pipeline involves the extraction of entities and relationships from a text corpus in order to create a KG Maynard et al. [55] describe that OBIE is usually used for ontology population, which involves determining key terms in a text and relating them to existing terms in the ontology. Therefore, the entity extraction process involves checking for entity categories that relate to already-existing instances in the CfHA ontology.

One additional factor involves determining what constitutes an entity. POS tagging can identify entities that are single words, as they would be nouns and proper nouns – however, the dependency tree of a sentence must be parsed if entities are multiple words long. di Buono et al. [14] describe a system that is based on the Operator-Argument Grammar developed by Harris [27], where FSA variables apply to specific parts of speech, and word syntactic and semantic properties can be calculated based on relationships with co-occurring words inside nuclear or simple sentence contexts. Consequently, dependency tree parsing must be utilized to check the various parts of a sentence and construct entities from there.

Entities are not the only elements that need to be extracted to create a KG. Relations between nodes is the other part, which necessitates discovering the root, or verb of a sentence. Any predicate verb can be taken to indicate a relationship between entities and is taken as the relationship type [58]. This will serve to connect the subject and object entities together.

From here, two distinct algorithms can be developed, one for entity extraction, and one for relationship extraction. The entity extraction algorithm is detailed in Algorithm 1, and the relationship extraction algorithm is detailed in Algorithm 2.

Algorithm 1 is based on a dependency tree parsing approach. Extraneous characters and stopwords are ignored, and tokens are checked for whether they are part of a compound word. The subject and object tokens are checked to ensure that they are NEs that are recognized by the NER portion of the model. Only entities that are identified as NEs are stored as nodes in the KG. After the subject and object are captured, the previous token and dependency tag are updated.

Algorithm 2 utilizes a pattern matching approach. Essentially, a Matcher object can be used to determine relationships within sentences that match a particular pattern. In this case, patterns with the root, or verb of the sentence, are classified as relationships. Once the root is identified, the pattern Matcher checks if it is followed by a preposition. If this is the case, the preposition is appended to the root.

Similarly to the approach elaborated on in [14], POS tagging was employed to match up the roots, or verbs, of a sentence. Furthermore, the subject and object of a sentence were determined to be the entities and checked as to whether they were already recognized as NEs. After cleaning the resulting entity and relation lists to ensure there are no blank nodes, a Pandas graph is employed to visualize the KG. These results are elaborated on further in Section 5 and visualized in Section 5.1.

The final stage of the model involves the importation of the KG into an ontology visualization software. Protégé was chosen for this purpose, as the original CfHA ontology was developed in Protégé. The rdflib library, which represents information as RDF triples, was selected to facilitate the importation. A graph was employed to map the KG triples to, and the nodes were separated out into instances, classes, and object properties based on their status as a source, edge, or target. Classes corresponding to entities were then appended to the graph. Finally, the RDF triples were saved to an already-created tester ontology file to visualize the results. Images of the final Protégé ontology are visualized in Section 5.1.

Algorithm 1 Entity Extraction

```
  function get entities (sentence)
Ensure: contents ← heliophysics ner text
    Initialise Part of Speech variables
    Populate Subject and Object lists
    for token in sentence do
      if token ≠ punctuation then
        if token == compound then
          prefix ← tokentext
          if previous token dependency == compound then
            Add previous token to current token
            if previous token in stopwords then
              prefix ←"
            end if
          end if
        end if
        if token dependency ends with a modifier then
          modifier ← token text
          if previous token dependency == compound then
            Add previous token to current token
            if previous token in stopwords then
              modifier ←"
            end if
          end if
          if token dependency in subjects or token dependency in
objects then
            if token dependency subject exists and token in
contents then
              tokeninfo ← token
              if token dependency subject exists and token in
contents then
                tokeninfo ←"
              end if
              Addmodifier, prefix, and tokeninfo
              Reset prefix, modifier, and previous token
dependency
              if token dependency object exists then
                tokeninfo ← token
                Addmodifier, prefix, and tokeninfo
              end if
            end if
          end if
        Set previous token dependency to current token
dependency
        Set previous token text to token
      end if
    end if
  end for
  return entity 1 and entity 2
end function
```

Algorithm 2 Relationship Extraction

```
function get_relationship (sentence)
Ensure: contents ← heliophysics ner text
  matcher ← Matcher
  Assign dependency patterns to extract sentence roots
  Add patterns to Matcher
  matches ← Apply Matcher to contents
  k ← len (matches) - 1
  span ← the result of pattern matching each sentence in the
text corpus
  return span
end function
```

3.5 Results and Analysis

The results of the model analysis described in Section 3.4 are elaborated on within this section. This covers all major stages of the model, including NER evaluation, word embeddings and clustering, and an analysis of the ontology.

3.5.1 Exploratory Analysis

In order to create a foundation for assessing the model, the performance metrics must be contextualized and examined according to stage. Examining the performance results also provides insight into how the NLP techniques used in the model construction handled the text corpora.

3.5.1.1 NER Performance Metrics

The metrics chosen to evaluate the NER portion of the model were Precision, Recall, and the F1-score. As is described in Table 3.1, precision is a measure of whether a classifier successfully does not label a positive sample as negative. Recall is a measure of whether a classifier successfully finds all positive samples. The F1-score is the harmonic mean of Precision and Recall. It is used to provide an average of the performances of Precision and Recall [77].

It must be noted that the training corpus has been run twice, as spaCy flags an error when NEs span multiple words. Table 3.4 shows the results of running the performance metrics for the en_core_web_sm model that has been trained and tested on heliophysics data. Meanwhile, Table 3.5 shows the same metrics generated from an untrained en_core_web_sm model that has not had the custom labels appended. If the metrics were calculated from an untrained en_core_web_sm model with the custom labels, the scores would be 0, as spaCy would have no frame of reference to extract entities and spaCy

TABLE 3.4

Performance Metrics for Trained
en_core_web_sm Model

Evaluation Metrics	
Precision	100%
Accuracy	100%
Recall	66.6%
F1-score	80%

needs in-context training information [26]. This demonstrates the utility of transfer learning, where less training was necessitated due to the knowledge already contained in spaCy en_core_web_sm.

3.5.1.2 NER Word Embeddings and Clustering

After running performance metrics on the NER model, there are additional metrics that can be applied to the text corpus in order to provide further insight. Term Frequency – Inverse Document Frequency (TF-IDF) is a model that can be used for text to numeric conversion, in order to identify the most important words in a corpus [68]. It assigns higher value to certain words over others, so that even important words that occur infrequently are assigned high weights. A dictionary of words was created from the vectorized heliophysics text corpus and was sorted using TF-IDF in order to produce words with the highest weights and, therefore, importance. Table 3.6 displays the top ten words and their TFIDF scores.

Another tool is word embeddings, which is a language modeling method that is used to map words to vectors that consist of real numbers. Words that occur in similar contexts should hypothetically be closer to each other in vector space. Therefore, related words in the ontology can be extracted by using word embeddings. Word2vec is an algorithm that uses shallow neural networks for word embeddings, and it can be used to represent words as vectors [90]. A Word2Vec model for the heliophysics corpus was constructed and trained. Dimensionality reduction algorithms transform data

TABLE 3.5

Performance Metrics for Untrained
en_core_web_sm Model

Evaluation Metrics	
Precision	0%
Accuracy	100%
Recall	0%
F1-score	0%

TABLE 3.6

Top 12 Words by TFIDF Score

Word	TFIDF Score (Rounded)
Sub	0.29333
Abstract	0.25186
Bibcode	0.25186
Title	0.25186
sup	0.176000
Observations	0.14767
Model	0.14667
Models	0.13655
Climate	0.12846
Data	0.12845
Solar	0.11936
Surface	0.11733

with a high number of dimensions, such as images, into a lower amount of dimensions [86]. This allows for the interpretation of relationships between vectors extracted from the heliophysics text corpus. One such example is determining the top-K most similar words to a particular term and was applied to the word "solar." The results are displayed in text and graph format in Table 3.7.

A final tool that provides insight into the text is clustering. In ML, clustering is an unsupervised technique that groups entities based on similar features. Clustering can be used to discover hitherto unknown patterns in data and can use several different measures for calculating distance [6]. Hierarchical clustering, which divides data into clusters without manually specifying a number of clusters, was initially applied to the TF-IDF features

TABLE 3.7

Top Ten Words Most Similar to "Solar"

Evaluation Metrics	
Word	Similarity Score (Rounded)
The	0.98165
SUB	0.98064
We	0.98041
Global	0.97834
Also	0.97728
Using	0.97676
Abstract	0.97646
Models	0.97641
Data	0.97607

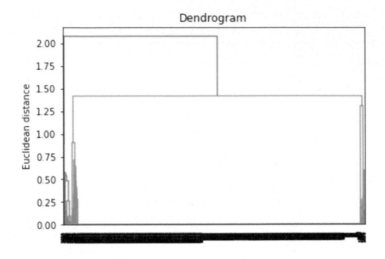

FIGURE 3.4
Dendrogram displaying number of clusters by Euclidean distance.

to determine how the algorithm would divide up the data. The output of the algorithm is displayed in Figure 3.4 and demonstrates that the text corpus can be separated into three clusters.

The hierarchical clustering algorithm demonstrated that the text corpus separates into three clusters. Choosing an appropriate number of clusters is particularly important for K-means clustering. The utility of applying K-means clustering to the data is that it can determine what values are assigned to which clusters. It aims to separate n data values into K clusters, where K = 3 as is established in Figure 3.4. The clusters generated by K-means are visualized in Table 3.8.

TABLE 3.8

Top Ten Terms by Cluster

Cluster 0	Cluster 1	Cluster 2
sub	Title	Magnetic
sup	Bibcode	Measurements
Model	Abstract	Analysis
Models	2020georl	Field
Observations	Mars	Waves
Surface	Climate	Induced
High	2020ssrv	Fields
Data	216	Solar
Results	Global	Pressure
Time	Dust	Signals

3.5.1.3 Ontology Analysis

The final part of the exploratory analysis involves examining the resulting KG and resultant ontology. Assessing an ontology is more challenging than assessing a NER model, as the success of an ontology depends on several measures, many of which are more subjective than NER evaluation metrics such as Precision, Accuracy, and Recall. These measures include whether the ontology is capable of solving tasks in the target domain, whether hierarchical and taxonomic concepts are represented, and ensuring that the ontology meets technical specifications [29].

Additionally, there are systematic frameworks for evaluating ontology performance, some of which were discussed in Section 3.4.3. For the purposes of this research, a level-based evaluation is used. This was chosen for several reasons. The primary aim of this research is populating an already-existing ontology rather than creating one from scratch, so the primary objective that must be assessed is whether the entities and relationships created from the text corpus are similar to entities and relationships in the CfHA Ontology. To this end, the levels that are used to assess the ontology are Syntax, Structure, Lexical, Semantic, and Context, which are based on the metrics described by Hooi et al. [29]. These evaluation metrics and a summary of their performance are summarized in Table 3.9.

TABLE 3.9

Ontology Assessment Metrics

Level	Description	Assessment
Syntax	Assesses whether the syntax of the formal language is correct	Instances are mostly grammatically sound. There are a handful of exceptions with out-of-context numbers or tokens. Entity relationships also make logical grammatical sense
Structure	Assesses if the concepts and hierarchy are sound	Concepts are in-line with those in the CfHA ontology. When examining the assignment of instances to classes, there are some that do not match
Lexical	Assesses the terms used to represent knowledge	Classes and instances reflect terms and concepts used in the CfHA ontology and source heliophysics corpus. Terms reflect many domain concepts
Semantic	Refers to how the ontology copes with different terms that relate to the same concept	Due to text preprocessing, particularly stemming and lemmatization, having multiple similar terms was not a significant issue
Context	Examines how the ontology affects the functionality and usability of ontology-driven applications	The automated results can be integrated with the existing CfHA ontology after some manual annotation, which is the purpose of the tool

3.6 Discussion

This section discusses in detail the model described in Section 3.4 and the results described in Section 3.5, linking back to the literature review done in Section 3.2. It weighs the successes and limitations of the model as well.

3.6.1 Text Mining Implementation

Overall, the TM portion of the model involved the use of well-established TM techniques [2, 33] in order to process the text into a suitable format for constructing the ontology learning model. Removing stop words and special characters was a particularly important step, as many of the tokens in the heliophysics text corpus included special characters. This is particularly important to consider for an ontology creation model, as the process of formatting RDF triples involves the formulation of IRIs, where the inclusion of certain special characters or spaces renders them syntactically invalid.

Stemming and lemmatization were also crucial stages in the model development, which is echoed by Asim et al. [2]. Although these two steps are important when being applied to other text corpora, the heliophysics corpus particularly benefited from this stage. Expert intervention is frequently required for the development of scientific ontologies [30], as scientific domains are particularly open-world and information-rich [91]. Concepts in scientific domains are systematic and frequently interrelated – for example, "sunrise" is related to "presunrise" and "sunset." Therefore, stemming and lemmatization allow for the root concept to be extracted, which results in the most important concepts to be highlighted and terms to be simplified for the NER stage.

3.6.2 Discussion of Spacy NER Model

The NER stage was crucial for determining which entities are relevant to the aims of developing the ontology. Without a robust NER model, constructing an accurate domain grammar would be difficult [92]. Answering RQ1, about already-existing approaches to ontology learning, revealed several existing NER models such as StanfordNER, Stanza, GoogleNER, and MicrosoftNER. However, in the research for this chapter, there were no NER models that covered precisely the same domain as the one detailed in this chapter. This was particularly important when a primary aim of this research is to harness ontology learning to populate an already-existing ontology. Therefore, the NER model had to allow for custom labeling and training.

Training a NER model on custom labels necessitates a large amount of data [34]. However, this research had to be completed in a limited amount of time, and part of compromising for the sake of time involved selecting a pre-trained NER model as a basis and adding additional data for the custom entities. spaCy in particular was chosen after conducting the literature review, as it was frequently used as a NER model for scientific domains [31, 88] and has robust documentation. spaCy did not perform as well as the custom-built SatelliteNER model built by Jafari et al. [31], although the benefits of convenience and the comparatively small difference in performance between a custom-built model and one trained on top of the spaCy en_core_web_sm model justified using a pre-trained spaCy model for this effort. The NER model leveraged transfer learning, where the pre-trained model trained with additional information scored highly on evaluation metrics which worked well within the limited constraints of this effort. A similar methodology was used for time reduction purposes by Kamat Tarcar et al. [34], who harnessed transfer learning by using pre-trained spaCy models on biomedical data.

One additional factor was the performance of the NER model. This research utilized Precision, Recall, and the F1-score for evaluation, which was done to provide a holistic view of how the model performed when identifying entities. Some prior studies only used one or two of these metrics [85, 90]. However, Precision was included to determine whether the NER model was incorrectly classifying non-entities as being entities, whereas Recall was included to determine whether the NER model was overlooking entities. The F1-score was included because it provides a look at the average performance of the model, in order to determine the trade-off between Precision and Recall and whether one needs to be improved at the potential expense of the other.

Comparing the performance of the custom-build spaCy heliophysics model to prior models revealed that it performed similarly and that the patterns resemble those seen in prior research. The custom heliophysics spaCy NER model scored 100% on Precision, 66.6% on Recall, and had an F1-score of 80%. The BiLSTM-CRF model developed by Batbaatar and Ryu (2019) scored higher on Precision (with a maximum of 94.53% for the Disease or Symptom, 90.83% for Sign or Symptom, and 94.93% for the Pharmacologic Substance) and lower on Recall (with a maximum of 73.31% for the word + char + POS metric for Disease or Syndrome, 81.98% for the Sign or Symptom, and 73.47% for the Pharmacologic Substance). This pattern is also demonstrated by the NERO NER model developed by Wang et al. [88], where the overall performance was measured at 54.9% Precision and 37.3% Recall, alongside a 43.4% F1-score.

This demonstrates that the heliophysics NER model performed better, which is attributable to the fact that many concept types were not well represented in the NERO ontology due to the heavy-tail distribution of ontology classes. Additionally, the SatelliteNER model had Precision as the best metric, a high Recall that was still lower than Precision, and an F1-score that sat in-between Precision and Recall. What this reveals is that NER models in general uniformly appear to have significantly lower Recall than Precision, which is attributable to the specialist terms that are used in many scientific domains that a NER model may miss. A comparison of the performance metrics also reveals how vital providing a large enough sample of training data is. While developing the NER model, the Precision, Recall, and F1-score increased as more training data was added, which indicated that the model was able to more easily identify entities in context.

3.6.3 Automated vs. Semi-automated vs. Manual Ontology Creation

The other important facet of the model was the ontology creation mechanism. Two of the driving research questions was how automated approaches to the population of an ontology can facilitate information sharing and how it can benefit a broader research effort. To this end, the literature review revealed that several prior studies had determined the benefits of automation for the ontology population [43, 55, 67]. Therefore, discussing the approach taken can reveal insight into the uses of automation for ontology development.

When the CfHA ontology was first being developed, it required manual effort to analyze texts to extract entities and relationships. Extracting individuals in particular was time consuming, as it required annotating them with classes and relationships. This can be automated through ontology learning, where entities correspond to individuals, edges correspond to properties, and labels correspond to classes. However, the utility of automation depends on the quality of the model – hence, why evaluating the ontology learning pipeline stage-by-stage is necessary.

The KG faced challenges during development. For example, due to the nature of heliophysics as a scientific domain, several entities spanned multiple words – therefore, the entity extraction function had to account for this. Furthermore, the function had to ensure that the identified entities were actually relevant to the CfHA ontology. To address this challenge, the NER stage was crucial in ensuring that extracted terms coincided with identified entities. If this step was not taken, then irrelevant concepts may have been introduced into the ontology, which would require additional time to survey the ontology and remove the relevant items. Therefore, this demonstrates how good design reduces the need for human intervention further down the line.

3.7 Conclusion

Ontologies provide a unique tool for facilitating knowledge-sharing and scientific discovery. Nevertheless, populating an ontology is an involved task. Harnessing ML techniques allows for resources to be freed up to be put toward other areas of scientific efforts. This body of research developed an ML model for ontology learning that contains two components:

a heliophysics NER model and an ontology population tool. The model is able to identify NEs from a text corpus that are relevant to heliophysics, extract relationships, and process this information into RDF triples which are then saved in an ontology. Both components are applications of NER and ontology learning techniques to a novel domain and serve as an extension of the development of the CfHA ontology, which had previously been manually generated and populated. The CfHA ontology and the CfHA community are ever-evolving and necessitate adaptive means of facilitating knowledge-sharing, and the project was limited by time and available data. Consequently, there is room to extend the results of this research further.

One avenue that may potentially be explored further is the development of a from-scratch custom model for the heliophysics domain. This project utilized the spaCy en_core_web_sm model as a basis, although fewer time constraints allow for more focus to be given toward the training component of model development. Jafari et al. (2014) demonstrated the benefits of developing a from-scratch model for SatelliteNER, where it outperformed the default StanfordNer, Stanza, GoogleNER, and MicrosoftNER models. A similar model may be created for the heliophysics domain, which would require additional training data for POS tagging and entity annotating. Alternatively, a transfer learning methodology could be utilized by employing a model that has been trained on a related domain. One particular benefit of the model in this research is that it is adaptable to other domains if applicable data is used to train it. There is also the opportunity to perform a wide-scale test of how other NER models perform compared to spaCy when trained on the heliophysics corpus.

Another opportunity is to involve expert opinion in ontology development. This research effort did not involve a large amount of expert opinion, particularly in the entity recognition stage, due to time constraints. Having input over what would constitute entities in the heliophysics text corpus and how to classify them would improve the quality of the model and ensure that the training data has accurate entity samples. This is a vital step in any future work that extends upon this project, to ensure the accuracy of a model. Training data quality is also vital for the model performance, due to how spaCy learns from entities being displayed in context.

This body of research aimed to build an ML model that automatically detects NEs and entity relationships from a text corpus, create RDF triples from them, and generates a KG from the RDF triples. After fine-tuning the training data corpus, the model showed promising results in-line with the manually constructed CfHA ontology. As scientific communities continue to harness cutting-edge technologies for research efforts, it is of vital importance to develop methodologies that are able to facilitate these efforts and handle research outputs. This research features a case study on how ML methods can be used for rapid ontology population, which in turn presents evidence for how automation can facilitate scientific research.

Notes

1 https://github.com/meganpowers1/SemanticNaturalLanguageProcessingfor KnowledgeGraphsCreation

References

1. K. Adnan and R. Akbar. An analytical study of information extraction from unstructured and multidimensional big data. *Journal of Big Data*, 6:1–38, 2019.
2. M.N. Asim, M. Wasim, M.U.G. Khan, W. Mahmood, and H.M. Abbasi. A survey of ontology learning techniques and applications. *Database*, 2018.
3. A. Ayadi, A. Samet, F.B. de Beuvron, and C. Zanni-Merk. ontology population with deep learning-based NLP: A case study on the biomolecular network ontology. *Procedia Computer Science*, 159:572–581, 2019.
4. T.O. Ayodele. Machine Learning Overview. In Y. Zhang, editor, *New Advances in Machine Learning*, chapter 1, pages 1–10. IntechOpen, London, England, 2010.
5. R. Baeza-Yates and Z. Liaghat. Quality-efficiency trade-offs in machine learning for text processing. In *2017 IEEE international conference on big data (big data)* (pp. 897–904). IEEE, 2017, December.
6. S. Bano and M.N.A. Khan. A survey of data clustering methods. *International Journal of Advanced Science and Technology*, 113(10.14257), 2018.
7. E. Batbaatar and K.H. Ryu. Ontology-based healthcare named entity recognition from Twitter messages using a recurrent neural network approach. *Environmental Research and Public Health*, 16:1–19, 2019.
8. T. Berners-Lee, J. Hendler, and O. Lassila. A new form of Web content that is meaningful to computers will unleash a revolution of new possibilities. *Scientific American*, 1–3, 2001.
9. J. Brank, M. Grobelnik, and D. Mladenić. A survey of ontology evaluation techniques. *Environmental Research and Public Health*, 16:1–19, 2009.
10. N. Colic and F. Rinaldi. Improving spacy dependency annotation and PoS tagging web service using independent NER services. *Genomics & Informatics*, 17:1–6, 2019.
11. J. Cunha, J. Saraiva, and J. Visser. Discovery[CE1] -based edit assistance for spreadsheets. In *IEEE Symposium on Visual Languages and Human-Centric Computing*, pages 233–237, 2009.
12. P. Cunningham. Unsupervised Learning and Clustering. In Cord M. and Cunningham P., editors, *Machine Learning Techniques for Multimedia: Case Studies on Organization and Retrieval*, chapter 1, pages 1–31. Springer, Berlin, Heidelberg, 2009.
13. P. Czarnowska, Y. Vyas, and K. Shah. Quantifying social biases in NLP: A generalization and empirical comparison of extrinsic fairness metrics. *Transactions of the Association for Computational Linguistics*, 9:1249–1267, 2021.
14. M.P. di Buono, M. Monteleone, and A. Elia. How to Populate Ontologies. In *Natural Language Processing and Information Systems*, pages 55–58, Springer International Publishing, Switzerland, 2014.

15. S. Elnagar, V. Yoon, and M.A. Thomas. An automatic ontology generation framework with an organizational perspective. *arXiv preprint*, 2022.
16. J. Fernández-Pedauye, C. Periñán-Pascual, F. Arcas-Túnez, and J.M. Cecilia. Enhancing the spaCy named entity recognizer for crowdsensing. *Intelligent Environments 2020*, 28:361–367, 2020.
17. H. Ford, S. Sen, D.R. Musicant, and N. Miller. Getting to the source: Where does Wikipedia get its information from?. In *Proceedings of the 9th international symposium on open collaboration* (pp. 1–10), 2013, August.
18. M. Frean and A. Robins. Catastrophic forgetting in simple networks: An analysis of the pseudorehearsal solution. *Network Computation in Neural Systems*, 10:227–36, 1999.
19. F. Gandon. A survey of the first 20 years of research on Semantic Web and linked data. *HAL*, 23:11–38, 2018.
20. R. Witte, T. Gitzinger, T. Kappler, and R. Krestel. A semantic wiki approach to cultural heritage data management. In *Proc. Workshop Language Technology for Cultural Heritage Data* (pp. 61–68), 2008.
21. P. Glasziou. Assessing the quality of research. *BMJ*, 328:39–41, 2012.
22. C. Goutte and E. Gaussier. A probabilistic interpretation of precision, recall and F-score, with implication for evaluation. In *Advances in Information Retrieval: 27th European Conference on IR Research, ECIR 2005, Santiago de Compostela, Spain, March 21–23, 2005. Proceedings 27* (pp. 345–359). Springer, Berlin, Heidelberg, 2005.
23. A. Gunawardana and G. Shani. A survey of accuracy evaluation metrics of recommendation tasks. *Journal of Machine Learning Research*, 10:2935–2962, 2009.
24. R. Göckel. *Lexicon philosophicum.* typis viduae Matthiae Beckeri, 1613.
25. S. Hakimov, S.A. Oto, and E. Dogdu. Named entity recognition and disambiguation using linked data and graph-based centrality scoring. In *Proceedings of the 4th international workshop on semantic web information management* (pp. 1–7), 2012, May.
26. C. Hanks, M. Maiden, P. Ranade, and T. Finin. Recognizing and extracting cybersecurity entities from text. In *Conference: Workshop on Machine Learning for Cybersecurity, International Conference on Machine Learning*, pages 1–7, 2022.
27. Z. Harris. *A Grammar of English on Mathematical Principles.* Wiley-Blackwell, New York, 1982.
28. C. Hennig, A. Viehl, B. Kämpgen, and H. Eisenmann. Ontology-Based Design of Space Systems. In *The Semantic Web – ISWC 2016*, pages 308–324. Springer International Publishing, New York, 2016.
29. Y.K. Hooi, M.F. Hassan, and A.M. Shariff. MMI in design process findings and improvement opportunities from a case study. *Procedia Computer Science*, 196:763–771, 2022.
30. T.R. Inniss, J.R. Lee, M. Light, M.A. Grassi, G. Thomas, and A.B. Williams. Towards applying text mining and natural language processing for biomedical ontology acquisition. In *Proceedings of the 1st international workshop on Text mining in bioinformatics* (pp. 7–14), 2006, November.
31. O. Jafari, P. Nagarkar, B. Thatte, and C. Ingram. SatelliteNER: An effective named entity recognition model for the satellite domain. *KMIS*, 3:100–107, 2014.
32. Y. Januzaj, J. Ajdari, and B. Selimi. DBMS as a cloud service: Advantages and disadvantages. *Procedia – Social and Behavioral Sciences*, 195:1851–1859, 2015.
33. A. Kadhim. An evaluation of preprocessing techniques for text classification. *International Journal of Computer Science and Information Security*, 16:22–32, 2018.

34. A. Kamat Tarcar, A. Tiwari, V.N. Dhaimodker, P. Rebelo, R. Desai, and D. Rao. NER Models Using Pre-training and Transfer Learning for Healthcare. In *Proceedings of the 13th international conference on Web Search and Data Mining*, pages 1–6, 2020.

35. M.G. Kersloot, F.J.P. van Putten, A. Abu-Hanna, R. Cornet, and D.L. Arts. Natural language processing algorithms for mapping clinical text fragments onto ontology concepts: A systematic review and recommendations for future studies. *Journal of Biomedical Semantics*, 11:1–21, 2020.

36. M. Khan, S. Khan, and Y. Alharbi. Text mining challenges and applications, a comprehensive review. *International Journal of Computer Network and Information Security*, 20:138–148, 2020.

37. V. Kozhevnikov and E. Pankratova. Research of the text data vectorization and classification algorithms of machine learning. *Theoretical & Applied Science*, 85:574–585, 2020.

38. M. Kulmanov, F.Z. Smaili, X. Gao, and R. Hoehndorf. Machine learning with biomedical ontologies. pages 75–90, 2020.

39. G. Lame. Using NLP techniques to identify legal ontology components: Concepts and relations. *Artificial Intelligence and Law*, 12:379–396, 2006.

40. T. Lawson. A conception of ontology. *Mimeograph, University of Cambridge*, 60, 2004.

41. E.D. Liddy. Natural Language Processing. In A. Kent, editor, *Encyclopedia of Library and Information Science*. Marcel Decker, Inc., New York, 2nd edition, 2009.

42. S.C.J. Lim, Y. Liu, and Y. Chen. Ontology in design engineering: status and challenges. In *International Conference on Engineering Design 2015*, pages 1–10, 2015.

43. R. Lima, B. Espinasse, H. Oliveira, and F. Freitas. Ontology population from the Web: An inductive logic programming-based approach. In *11th International Conference on Information Technology: New Generations*, pages 1–6, 2014.

44. K. Liu, W.R. Hogan, and R.S. Crowley. Natural language processing methods and systems for biomedical ontology learning. *Journal of Biomedical Informatics*, 44:163–179, 2010.

45. J. Lorhard. *Theatrum Philosophicum*. Waldkirch, Switzerland, 1613.

46. X. Ma, L. Fu, P. West, and P. Fox. Ontology population from the web: An inductive logic programming-based approach. *Data Science Journal*, 17:1–11, 2018.

47. Y. Ma, J.-J. Kim, B. Bigot, and M.A. Mateen Khan. Feature-enriched word embeddings for named entity recognition in open-domain conversations. In *ICASSP 2016*, 2016.

48. A. Maedche and S. Staab. Knowledge portals – Ontologies at work. *AI Magazine*, 22:63–75, 2001.

49. A. Maedche and S. Staab. Learning Ontologies for the Semantic Web. In *Semantic Web Workshop 2001*, 2001.

50. A. Maedche and S. Staab. Ontology Learning. In Staab S. and Studer R., editors, *Handbook on Ontologies (International Handbooks on Information Systems)*, pages 193–194. Springer, Berlin, Heidelberg, 2004.

51. J. Makki, A.-M. Alquier, and V. Prince. An NLP-based ontology population for a risk management generic structure. In *Proceedings of the 5th International Conference on Soft Computing as Transdisciplinary Science and Technology*, 2008.

52. J. Makki, A.-M. Alquier, and V. Prince. Ontology population via NLP techniques in risk management. *International Journal of Humanities and Social Sciences*, 3:212–217, 2009.

53. A. Mansouri, L.S. Affendey, and A. Mamat. Named entity recognition approaches. *International Journal of Computer Science and Network Security,* 8:339–344, 2008.
54. D. Maynard, A. Funk, and W. Peters. NLP-based support for ontology lifecycle development. *CEUR Workshop Proceedings,* 514:1–10, 2009.
55. D. Maynard, Y. Li, and W. Peters. NLP Techniques for Term Extraction and Ontology Population. In Buitelaar P. and Cimiano P., editors, *Ontology Learning and Population: Bridging the Gap between Text and Knowledge,* pages 107–127. IOS Press, Amsterdam, 2008.
56. R. McGranaghan, E. Young, M. Powers, S. Yadav, and E. Vakaj. The cultural-social nucleus of an open community: A multi-level community knowledge graph and NASA application. 2022.
57. G.H. Merrill. Ontology, ontologies, and science. *CoRR,* abs/1903.10325, 2019.
58. N. Milosevic and W. Thielemann. Relationship extraction for knowledge graph creation from biomedical literature. *CoRR,* abs/2201.01647, 2022.
59. S. Mishra, S. He, and L. Belli. Assessing demographic bias in named entity recognition. *CoRR,* abs/2008.03415, 2020.
60. K. Morik and M. Scholz. The MiningMart Approach to Knowledge Discovery in Databases. In Kent A., editor, *Intelligent Technologies for Information Analysis,* pages 47–65. Springer, Berlin, Heidelberg, 2004.
61. K. Munir and M. Sheraz Anjum. The use of ontologies for effective knowledge modelling and information retrieval. *Applied Computing and Informatics,* 14(2):116–126, 2018.
62. N. Naderian, M. Shamsfard, and R. Adelkhah. Ontology creation and population for natural language processing domain. *International Journal of Web Research,* 1:56–65, 2018.
63. P.M. Nadkarni, L. Ohno-Machado, and W.W. Chapman. Natural language processing: An introduction. *Journal of the American Medical Informatics Association,* 18:544–551, 2011.
64. B. Oral, E. Emekligil, S. Arslan, and G. Eryiğit. Extracting complex relations from banking documents. In *Proceedings of the Second Workshop on Economics and Natural Language Processing,* pages 1–9, 2019.
65. G. Adorni, M. Maratea, L. Pandolfo, and L. Pulina. An ontology for historical research documents. In *Web Reasoning and Rule Systems: 9th International Conference, RR 2015,* Berlin, Germany, August 4–5, 2015, Proceedings. 9 (pp. 11–18). Springer International Publishing, 2015.
66. J. Park and M. Musen. VM-in-protégé: A study of software reuse. *Studies in Health Technology and Informatics,* 52:644–648, 1998.
67. P. Peña, R. del Hoyo, R. Aznar, and R. Montañés. VM-in-protégé: A study of software reuse. In *XVIII Conferencia de la Asociación Española para la Inteligencia Artificial,* 2018.
68. S. Qaiser and R. Ali. Text mining: Use of TF-IDF to examine the relevance of words to documents. *International Journal of Computer Applications,* 181:25–29, 2018.
69. J. Raad and C. Cruz. A survey on ontology evaluation methods: In *Proceedings of the 7th International Joint Conference on Knowledge Discovery, Knowledge Engineering and Knowledge Management [Internet].* Lisbon, Portugal: SCITEPRESS-Science and and Technology Publications, pages 179–186, 2015.
70. M. Rajman and R. Besançon. Text mining: Natural language techniques and text mining applications. In Spaccapietra S. and Maryanski F., editors, *Data*

Mining and Reverse Engineering. IFIP – The International Federation for Information Processing, pages 50–64. Springer, Boston, MA, 1998.

71. R.J. Rovetto. Ontology-based knowledge management for space data. In *68th International Astronautical Congress (IAC)*, pages 1–13, Adelaide, Australia, 2017.

72. R.J. Rovetto, T.S. Kelso, and D.A. O'Neil. Ontology-based knowledge management for space data. In *First International Orbital Debris Conference*, pages 1–10, 2019.

73. D. Rubin, N. Shah, and N. Noy. Biomedical ontologies: A functional perspective. *Briefings in Bioinformatics*, 9:75–90, 2008.

74. M.T. Rutherford, E.B. Huffer, J.M. Kusterer, and B.M. Quam. Odisees: Ontology-driven interactive search environment for earth sciences. In *World Congress in Computer Science, Computer Engineering, and Applied Computing*, pages 1–5, Las Vegas, Nevada, 2016.

75. A.A. Salatino, T. Thanapalasingam, A. Mannocci, A. Birukou, F. Osborne, and E. Motta. The computer science ontology: A comprehensive automatically-generated taxonomy of research areas. *Data Intelligence*, 2(3):379–416, 2020.

76. C. Shimizu, R. Mcgranaghan, A. Eberhart, and A. Kellerman. Towards a Modular Ontology for Space Weather Research. *arXiv*, 2020.

77. L. Siebert, J. Joeckel and J. Heidrich. Towards Guidelines for Assessing Qualities of Machine Learning Systems. pages 1–12, *ArXiv*. https://doi.org/10.1007/978-3-030-58793-2_2, 2020.

78. B. Smith. *Ontology*, pages 155–166. 01 2003.

79. B. Smith. The Relevance of Philosophical Ontology to Information and Computer Science Download. In Hagengruber R. and Riss U., editors, *Philosophy, Computing and Information Science*, pages 75–83. Pickering & Chatto, London, 2014.

80. D. Sonntag. Assessing the quality of natural language text data. In *Informatik verbindet, Band 1, Beiträge der 34. Jahrestagung der Gesellschaft für Informatik e.V.*, Ulm, Germany, 2004.

81. R. Talib, M. Kashif, S. Ayesha, and F. Fatima. Text mining: Techniques, applications and issues. *International Journal of Advanced Computer Science and Applications*, 7: 11, 2016.

82. A. Teixeira, P. Miguel, M. Rodrigues, J.C. Pereira, and M. Amorim. From Web to Persons – Providing Useful Information on Hotels Combining Information Extraction and Natural Language Generation. In *IberSpeech 2016*, Lisbon, Portugal, 2016.

83. A. Tewari. Medical Ontology: Big Data Big Challenges. 2014.

84. U.M. Fayyad, G. Piatetsky-Shapiro, and P. Smyth From Data Mining to Knowledge Discovery: An Overview. In G. Piatetsky-Shapiro, P. Smyth, R. Uthurusamy, and U.M. Fayyad, editors, *Advances in Knowledge Discovery and Data Mining*. AAAI Press/MIT Press, Palo Alto, 1996.

85. A.G. Valarakos, V. Karkaletsis, D. Alexopoulou, E. Papadimitriou, and C.D. Spyropoulos. From web to persons – providing useful information on hotels combining information extraction and natural language generation. In *Artificial Intelligence in Medicine, 10th Conference on Artificial Intelligence in Medicine*, Aberdeen, UK, 2005.

86. L. van der Maaten, E. Postma, and H. Herik. Dimensionality reduction: A comparative review. *Journal of Machine Learning Research – JMLR*, 10:1–22, 01 2007.

87. Ž. Vujovic. Classification model evaluation metrics. *International Journal of Advanced Computer Science and Applications*, 12:599–606, 2021.

88. K. Wang, R. Stevens, H. Alachram, Y. Li, L. Soldatova, R. King, S. Ananiadou, A.M. Schoene, M. Li, F. Christopoulou, J.L. Ambite, J. Matthew, S. Garg, U. Hermjakob, D. Marcu, E. Sheng, T. Beißbarth, E. Wingender, A. Galstyan, and X. Gao. NERO: A biomedical named-entity (recognition) ontology with A large, annotated corpus reveals meaningful associations through text embedding. *NPJ Systems Biology and Applications*, 7:1–8, 2021.

89. H. Yang, C.A. Aguirre, M.F. De La Torre, D. Christensen, L. Bobadilla, E. Davich, J. Roth, L. Luo, Y. Theis, A. Lam, T.Y.-J. Han, D. Buttler, and W.H. Hsu. Pipelines for procedural information extraction from scientific literature: Towards recipes using machine learning and data science. In *2019 International Conference on Document Analysis and Recognition Workshops (ICDARW)*, volume 2, pages 41–46, Sydney, Australia, 2019.

90. J. Youn, T. Naravane, and I. Tagkopoulos. Using word embeddings to learn a better food ontology. *Frontiers in Artificial Intelligence*, 3, 2020.

91. L. Zemmouchi-Ghomari, A. Djouambi, and C. Chabane. Proposal for a mutual conversion relational database-ontology approach. *International Journal of Modern Education and Computer Science*, 10:13–28, 2018.

92. Z. Zhang and F. Ciravegna. Named entity recognition for ontology population using background knowledge from Wikipedia. *Ontology Learning and Knowledge Discovery Using the Web: Challenges and Recent Advances*: 79–104, 2011.

93. F. Zhuang, Z. Qi, K. Duan, D. Xi, Y. Zhu, H. Zhu, H. Xiong, and Q. He. A comprehensive survey on transfer learning. *CoRR*, abs/1911.02685, 2019.

4

MSE**: Multi-Modal Semantic Embeddings for Datasets with Several Positive Matchings[1]

Jérémie Huteau, Adrian Basarab, and Florence Dupin de Saint-Cyr

IRIT, Toulouse University, France

CONTENTS

4.1 Introduction

Understanding an image or a text, even independently, is an extremely complex task, for which handcrafted methods are both difficult to develop and not very robust. Advances in machine learning have nevertheless made it possible to obtain results about the similarity between two images or between two sentences. These learning methods are part of the deep learning framework: deep convolutional neural networks (CNN, Krizhevsky et al. 2017) for images and deep recurrent neural networks (LSTM-RNN, Hochreiter and Schmidhuber 1997) for texts. To perform a task, a neural network with hidden layers will use these hidden layers to compute a useful representation, which is a latent vector that translates the properties of interest for the task the network was trained on. For example, if one wants to classify images into dogs and cars, a useful representation of the image would be whether or not there are ears, eyes, wheels, or glass panes, from which it is easy to learn which class the image corresponds to. However, the representation that would be learned from such a supervised task would be specialized and might not be useful for other tasks. This is a problem when the task one wants a model for does not have abundant data or when labels are rare and costly: the medical domain is full of such tasks due to data being hard to acquire and labels costly to make.

When the only information is whether two items are related or not (e.g., this image corresponds to this caption, this video sequence follows this sequence), contrastive learning can be used to learn good representations (generic and rich enough to be good starting points) before fine-tuning on a task where labels are sparse/few. In essence, contrastive learning aims to have representations of related elements be close to one another and representations of unrelated elements be far from each other (see Weng 2021) for an introduction to the different methods of contrastive learning). Contrastive learning is particularly useful when dealing with data with several modalities (e.g., an image associated with a caption, a video associated with an audio track, Rohrbach et al. 2013). In this domain, it may be desirable to obtain similar representations for the different modalities of the same object. This common representation can be viewed as a way to capture the meaning of the object represented: this is called semantic embedding. In the case of image and text modalities, the VSE neural architecture (Kiros et al. 2014) uses a CNN and an RNN in parallel in order to obtain a common vector representation for both the image and its associated legend. Once trained on a set of images and legends, the architecture can be used as an encoding-decoding machine in order to produce new legends for unknown images: the legend is generated (decoded) from the vector that encodes the image, or to select images that best suits a new sentence: e.g., select the image from a dataset whose encoding best corresponds to the encoding of the sentence. The idea to use this kind of pipeline comes from the work done in the domain of machine translation (Cho et al. 2014) (with two RNNs), indeed legend generation is a way to translate an image into a description.

Note that obtaining a common representation coming from the two neural networks, i.e., a cross-modality representation, is only possible if the parallels networks are guided with loss functions that aims at making more similar to the data referring to the same object and non-similar to the data referring to a different object. This leads to consider the classical method for contrastive learning which aims at minimizing a triplet loss (Schroff et al. 2015) where triplets are composed of an element which can be considered a query, an element which can be considered a relevant/matching element (w.r.t. the query), and an element which can be considered irrelevant/non-matching. The goal is then to extract a representation from all these elements such that the query and matching elements are more similar to one another than the query and the nonmatching elements are. The representations are extracted with neural networks, whose parameters are learned through the minimization of the triplet loss. The need to define a very accurate loss function was shown by Faghri et al. (2018) where these authors propose a new method VSE++ in which the architecture is the same as the one of VSE (Kiros et al. 2014), but the loss function is more elaborate. Indeed in VSE++, the authors extend VSE with the explicit introduction of hard negatives in the loss for multi-modal embeddings. They show that their proposal improves the results already obtained on the same datasets: experiments were done on Microsoft COCO dataset (Lin et al. 2015) with an out-performance "on the best reported result of almost 9%" (according to the authors).

The two drawbacks of VSE++ are the following: on the one hand, only two modalities are considered namely image and text, while it would be interesting to offer the possibility to express information with other modes like, e.g., text in another language, logical formulas, diagrams, etc. On the second hand, we have encountered datasets where the same image is associated with several texts (in COCO dataset, each image is associated with five legends). Due to the way the loss function is defined, VSE++ is not able to handle such dataset in its integrality. Indeed, let us consider two texts t_1 and t_2 that are both well adapted with an image i. VSE++ can only take into account one of them for being the positive representative of this image, it means that some may be useful and complementary information is lost.

Several approaches have been proposed for improving the learning of joint representations of vision and language. In Li et al. (2019), the authors propose to first transform the images into a more structured representation that relates image regions using Graph Convolutional Networks (Welling and Kipf 2016) to generate features with semantic relationships and then use the triplet ranking loss of *VSE++*. In the same vein, Oscar approach (Li et al. 2020b) performs a pre-training in order to obtain a dataset made of triples (word tokens, object tags, region features) by focusing on some salient elements in the images using Faster R-CNN (Ren et al. 2015). Unicoder-VL (Li et al. 2020a) extends this idea by using three different pre-trainings in order to align the visual and textual modalities: a pre-training using an attention mechanism (Vaswani et al. 2017) is performed in order to learn a "cross-modality contextualized embedding" between regions and word tokens. This pre-training requires first to dispose of the linguistic embeddings (it is done with BERT, Kenton and Toutanova 2019): a pre-trained model for language prediction based on attention mechanism) and image embeddings which are obtained by using Faster R-CNN. In more recent approaches the pre-training is done with self-attention modules that are used for capturing distant dependencies or heterogeneous interactions between regions (Xue et al. 2021), see Dou et al. (2022) for an extensive analysis of the different pre-training models on several image-caption datasets. As we can see all these improvements concern the pre-processing of the dataset in order to focus on salient regions or words and these approach only deal with the two modalities image and text. Note that the object tags used in Oscar approach could be viewed as a third modality, but it is obtained by a pre-processing on the initial dataset, hence obtaining this modality is already a part of the learning process. To sum up, as far as we know there is no approach that proposes both to extend the triple loss notion with multiple positives and to accept multiple modalities in the dataset.

In this chapter, we propose an approach called MSE** which extends VSE++ to many modalities and to the possibility to handle a set of positive items of the same modality for one object. We compare the two methods and show that despite a better expressivity MSE** gives nearly the same results as VSE++ on several datasets. We show that the loss function of *MSE** is more accurate for some hard cases of our dataset.

The rest of this chapter is organized as follows. Section 4.2 presents the new MSE** model, Section 4.3 discusses the particular issues raised in this new framework, Section 4.4 gives the implementation details and analyzes the results obtained on the MS-COCO dataset. The last section summarizes the approach and evokes several perspectives.

4.2 Proposed Model: MSE**

In this section, we describe a new model called MSE** that extends the VSE++ model. The main feature of these two models is the use of triples consisting of an anchor, a positive element, and a negative element and a similarity function between the elements. The goal of the learning process is to learn a representation of each of its elements such that the anchor and the positive element are more similar to each other than the anchor and the negative. We first define the triples and then the loss function used to guide the learning process.

4.2.1 Definitions and Notations

Let us denote by K the number of different modalities contained by a given dataset. For example, for a dataset containing images and text legends, K is equal to 2. We denote by X such a dataset, consisting in I tuples denoted by X_i. Each tuple X_i is formed by K sets denoted by X_i^k, k in $\{1 \dots K\}$, i.e., one set by modality: $X = \{X_i \mid X_i = (X_i^1, \dots, X_i^K), i \in \{1 \dots I\}\}$

Note that within the ith tuple X_i, a set X_i^k contains one or several elements from the modality k, i.e., $X_i^k = \{x_{i,1}^k, \dots x_{i,|X_i^k|}^k\}$, where $|X_i^k|$ stands for the cardinal of X_i^k.

(a)			
	$k=1$	$k=2$	$k=2$
$x_{i,j}^k$	$j=1$	$j=1$	$j=2$
$i=1$		A woman in a red jacket skiing down a slope	A woman posing for the camera standing on skis.
$i=2$		Two giraffes during day in field of grasses.	A couple giraffes staring in the same direction
$i=3$		A close up of a cell phone, scissors and a cup.	A cup of coffee, cell phone and scissor sitting on a desk.

(b)						
Sim	$x_{1,1}^2$	$x_{1,2}^2$	$x_{2,1}^2$	$x_{2,2}^2$	$x_{3,1}^2$	$x_{3,2}^2$
$x_{1,1}^1$						
$x_{2,1}^1$						
$x_{3,1}^1$						

FIGURE 4.1

(a) Toy dataset containing three tuples and two modalities. Each tuple contains one image and two legends. For a given element, index i defines the tuple, k its modality, and j its rank in the modality set. (b) Positive (green) and negative (red) legends for each image of this toy example.

To illustrate these notations, Figure 4.1a shows a small example consisting in three images and six legends. In this example, K is equal to 2 (two modalities). One can observe that this dataset contains three tuples, among which the first consists in a set of images $X_1^1 = \{x_{1,1}^1\}$ (in this example only one image corresponds to one tuple) and a set of two captions $X_1^2 = \{x_{1,1}^2, x_{1,2}^2\}$ (the two legends corresponding to the first image).

In the following, we introduce the notion of triplet, which will be further used to derive the proposed training process.

Definition 2.1 (triplet). A triplet is composed of:

- *an anchor $x^=$: any element from any set of any tuple X_i of dataset X;*
- *a positive x^+: any element extracted from a set belonging to the same tuple X_i as the anchor but from a different modality;*
- *a negative x^-: any element from any set of a different tuple than the anchor, $X_{i'}$ with $i \neq i'$, from a different modality than the anchor.*

Reconsidering the toy example in Figure 4.1a, one valid triplet respecting the definition above is $(x_{1,1}^1, x_{1,1}^2, x_{3,2}^2)$, containing image $x_{1,1}^1$ as anchor, a legend associated with it as positive and a legend associated with another image as negative. Furthermore, Figure 4.1b illustrates how triplets can be formed from this small dataset, by selecting an element of a row as the anchor, an element corresponding to a green cell from the same row as the positive, and an element corresponding to any red cell as the negative. Note that by transposing the matrix, the anchor can correspond to a legend instead of an image.

4.2.2 Loss Function

The triplets defined in the previous section contain two pairs of interest: the anchor and the positive, hereafter referred to as a positive pair, and the anchor and the negative, called negative pair. In general, one can evaluate how close two representations a and b are using a similarity function Sim, which maps the two representations to a scalar $(Sim(a,b) \in \mathbb{R})$, where *a large value corresponds to a high similarity*. One example of such a function is the cosine similarity, which is the dot product of two unit-vectors. It is worth mentioning that one can also use a distance instead of a similarity function, for which the signs and comparison operators are swapped.

Given a triplet, the objective herein is to have a representation of each of its elements such that *the anchor and the positive are more similar to each other than the anchor and the negative*, i.e., $Sim(x^=, x^-) < Sim(x^=, x^+)$. Furthermore, this inequality will be strengthened using a margin parameter α such that $Sim(x^=, x^-) + \alpha < Sim(x^=, x^+)$.

The objective of the learning process is therefore to learn a representation function which leads to the least number of violation of this constraint. Unfortunately, this constraint is not differentiable (because of the comparison operator) and is therefore not suitable for learning a model through gradient descent. In order to facilitate the training of a neural network, one therefore needs to reformulate this inequality into a differentiable loss function as follows:

$$\mathcal{H}(x^=, x^+, x^-) = max(0, Sim(x^=, x^-) + \alpha - Sim(x^=, x^+)) \qquad (4.1)$$

This function, called the triplet $\mathcal{H}$inge loss in the related literature, corresponds to the violation of the constraint on pair similarities. In the case where the positive pair is more similar by a margin of α than the negative pair, the loss is 0. Note that with this loss function the constraint is only imposed to be satisfied, i.e., the degree of constraint satisfaction is not quantified. Otherwise, the loss function becomes strictly positive. Starting from this definition of the loss for a triplet, let us define the loss for a given anchor, from which, as explained previously, one can form several triplets by assigning a positive and a negative.

Definition 2.2

For a given item $x^=$ in a set of modality k, X_i^k, of a tuple X_i, we denote by X^+ the set of its positive elements and by X^- the set of its negative elements (with positive and negative elements defined as in Definition 2.1. With these notations, the loss function for a given anchor, $\mathcal{L}(x^=)$, is given by:

$$\mathcal{L}(x^=) = \mathbb{E}[\mathcal{R}^+_{x^+ \in X^+} \mathcal{R}^-_{x^- \in X^-} \mathcal{H}(x^=, x^+, x^-)], \tag{4.2}$$

where R^+ and R^- are functions mapping a set of elements to one of its subset, called reduction functions and $\mathbb{E}$ is the mathematical expectation.

In our case, these reduction functions select elements based on $Sim(x^=, x)$, their similarity with the anchor. In the case of selecting all elements (no reduction function), this is equivalent to considering the mean of the triplet losses (the traditional triplet loss). In the case of selecting only the hardest positive and negative (respectively the ones with the lowest and highest similarities to the anchor) this is equivalent to taking the hardest triplet as VSE⁺⁺ loss does.

From the definition of the loss for a given anchor, one can define the loss function for a given modality. The loss for the kth modality is defined as the mean of the losses of the elements of this modality, normalized by the margin:

$$\mathcal{L}(X^k) = \frac{1}{\alpha} \mathbb{E}_{x^= \in X^k}[\mathcal{L}(x^=)] \tag{4.3}$$

Note that the interest of the normalization by the margin is to obtain a (soft) loss bounded between 0 and 1. In practice, the worst case is when the representations of all elements collapse to the same vector, leading to a loss of α for all triplets. Finally, the global loss is the mean of the losses of the kth sets for each k:

$$\mathcal{L} = \mathbb{E}_k[\mathcal{L}(X^k)] \tag{4.4}$$

Let us note also that VSE⁺⁺ defines the loss for only one modality and that the global loss is not using the mean of individual losses but rather the sum. The two are equivalent from an optimization point of view, given that the mean is equal to the sum scaled by a constant factor ($\frac{1}{|X^k|}$ for the loss of the kth modality $\mathcal{L}(X^k)$, $\frac{1}{k}$ for the global loss $\mathcal{L}$).

In the general formalism proposed above, we can highlight that VSE⁺⁺ is a particular case where:

- the modality of the anchor and the modality of the positive and negative are different, i.e., cross-modality is imposed;
- there is only one positive by modality, i.e., for each tuple i, for each modality k, $|X_i^k| = 1$;
- the reduction function uses a maximum: it selects the hardest negative taking $\mathcal{R}^-_{x^- \in X^-} = \arg\max_{x^- \in X^-}(Sim(x^=, x^-))$.

The main contribution of VSE^{++} was to compute the loss on the hardest triplet, which in the absence of multiple positives turns to having $\mathcal{R}^- = \arg\max$. The authors of VSE^{++} argued that most negative triplets do not contribute to learning good representations (because they are too easy, i.e., too different from the anchor) while forcing the loss function to local minima in which improving the hard negatives would not help to improve the loss. Therefore, using only the hardest negative example led to better representations.

The main contribution herein is the extension to several positive elements. If the reduction function over positives ($\mathcal{R}^+$) is linear (e.g., a sum), considering multiple positives is equivalent to computing the anchor loss with a different positive each time, i.e., increasing the batch size with same anchor associated with different positive samples. However, similarly to how selecting the hardest negative improves the representations learned by VSE^{++}, we show that selecting the hardest positive has also a positive impact on the representations learned, in particular forcing the representations of the positive to be close to the anchor even in the worst case.

4.3 Particular Issues Raised within MSE** Framework

In this section, we describe how we dealt with two problems raised by the model: the first is due to the fact that we allow an anchor to be associated with a set of negative elements instead of being associated with a single element, the second concerns the constraints induced by the use of different modalities on the data augmentation.

4.3.1 Optimizing the Hardest Negative Selection Process

Although selecting the hardest negative ultimately leads to better learned representations, the optimization process is more difficult when considering all negatives. This is especially the case at the beginning of the training, where the representations are weak and a collapse to the same representation for all elements can occur, which would be a failed training.

The authors of VSE^{++} identified this issue and proposed to train the model by using the mean reduction for a few epochs before switching to the max reduction. It is however not trivial to choose the number of epochs before switching, and as it is a form of pre-training it could lead to worse optima at the end of the training compared to using the max reduction from the beginning.

To meet this challenge, we propose to use the top-f operation as reduction function: it consists in selecting the hardest fraction f of the elements, where "hardest" stands for "most similar to the anchor" for the negatives and "least similar" for the positives. When f equals 1, this function is equivalent to the mean, and when f equals 0 it is equivalent to the max (since we always select at least 1 element). For example, for 100 elements, top-f with $f = 0.3$ will return the 30 elements with the largest values.

By decreasing f from 1 to 0 over the course of the training, one can start the training with a loss easy to optimize and gradually progress to a harder but more productive loss, therefore avoiding a collapse into the same representation for all elements. This method is progressively switching the loss function from mean to max. But sometimes the "pretraining" (with the mean reduction) has a long duration before enabling to switch to the max reduction.

While decreasing f linearly over a small ($\approx 10,000$, out of $\approx 250,000$) number of steps, we noticed that the loss decreased until $f \approx 0.2$, after which it increased to reach 1 when $f = 0$. Therefore, we decided to give priority to a decay rule which spends as few steps as possible in the "easy" regime, in order to do as little "pretraining" as possible. Such a behavior is ensured by the following hyperbola expression scaled between 1 and 0, with the main "inflection point" at $y = 0.2$:

$$\frac{1 - \text{step\_fraction}}{1 + k \times \text{step\_fraction}} \tag{4.5}$$

where step_fraction is the fraction of the decay steps (e.g., 10,000) done at this point and $k = 16$.

Note that this approach can be linked to some forms of curriculum learning. Indeed, curriculum learning is a form of learning in which a model is trained on tasks in a particular order. The tasks can either be the specific examples that the model has to learn: in that case curriculum means to first learn the easy examples then the hard ones or qualitatively different tasks (Pentina et al. 2014): in that case curriculum learning consists in first classifying an object either in animal or machine, then in classifying it either in cat, dog, boat, and plane. In our proposal, we do not alter the order in which the samples are presented to the model, but we start with an "easy" task (the mean reduction) and progressively evolve toward the "hard" task (the max reduction).

The way the transition from easy to hard tasks is done using the top-f reduction can be seen as applying binary weights over the elements and assigning 0 to the weights of the easiest elements as the training goes on. We could instead have used weights between 0 and 1 and have shifted the distribution of these weights toward the hardest elements as the training was going on. This last approach seems more appealing (it avoids to directly take into account the difficulty of the task), but we do not expect it to have much (if any) impact on the accuracy. Therefore, this is left for perspective study.

Even though this careful increase of the difficulty of the task helps with the optimization and makes it possible to train the network, it should be noted that the length of the decay period (how many steps until we reach $f = 0$) is still important: indeed a too short period will still lead to a failed training while a too long one will lead to worse results.

4.3.2 Data Augmentations for Multi-Modal Tuples of Sets

Deep neural networks often suffer from overfitting, and one way to reduce it is to use data augmentation. This consists in applying label conservative transformations to the data, which will artificially increase the amount of data. Training on this augmented data can force the network to encounter some conditions which it would not have met if augmentations had not taken place, this generally helps to learn more robust representations. Examples of such transformations for images are horizontal flip (mirror symmetry), cropping some part of the image, rotations, modifying the color, etc. Concerning texts, one can remove some words or replace them with synonyms.

When working with multi-modal data, some transformations need to be applied to all modalities in order to be label conservative. For example, when applying an horizontal flip to an image, any text describing it must have the words "left" and "right" swapped (Desai and Johnson 2021).

When the multi-modal data is made of sets of elements under the same modality, such a transformation should be applied with the same parameters to all elements of each relevant set. Flipping an image and one of its legend necessarily requires us to flip all the images and legends of the tuple, otherwise we would not preserve left-right positions: a flipped image would not be completely similar to an "unflipped" legend, and trying to match them through the contrastive loss would lead to a network which would be unable to recognize left from right (assuming the flip is done 50% of the time). However, when a transformation is not applied to multiple modalities, it is preferable to apply it with different parameters to the different element of a set. For example, with two images of a tennis ball, modifying the color of the image in the exact same way (say yellow to orange) will result in the tennis ball being the same color in both images. Even though this will still lead to the network having to recognize tennis ball by something else than their color over the course of the training process (and multiple applications of the transformation with different parameters), having the two tennis balls be of different colors will make an update on the parameters which will concern other properties than its specific color. We argue that this is desirable and we implemented it in our experiments. However, we did not run any experiment to confirm it (one would simply need to disable this augmentation parameter difference for the elements of a set) and we think that it will not make any difference on our datasets given the results we obtained.

4.4 Implementation

In order to test our main hypothesis that *using multiple positives in the triplet loss improves the learned representations,* we had to implement the VSE++ model, apply the necessary changes to it, and run the experiment on suitable data.

This implementation is available via the Github repository https://github. com/JeremieHuteau/adria_internship.

4.4.1 Dataset

The triplet loss minimization method can be applied to any dataset if we consider an element as the anchor, an augmentation of this element as the positive and a distinct element as the negative. But as we were originally in the context of cross-modal representations, we stuck with the classic dataset for this task: MS-COCO (Lin et al. 2015). This dataset is suitable for many tasks, but we are mostly interested in the captioning part of the dataset, which contains in its training set about 113,000 images, each described by five different captions generated by humans. The validation/test set contains 5,000 images, again with five captions each. Therefore, only the image modality will have multiple positives.

Due to lack of time to run the experiments, we did not experiment on other datasets. The most suitable one would have been Flicker30K (Young et al. 2014) (similar to MS-COCO but with only 30,000 images). As for the medical domain, a dataset can be built from the PEIR library (Jones et al. 2001), which is way smaller with about 5,000 images but in which the text modality is having multiple positives (a caption can describe a variable number of images). It should be noted that training a complete visual model for medical images with only 5,000 images would not be easy, and using a model trained on natural images as a pre-trained base might not be perfect (see Raghu et al. 2019 for a work on transfer learning for medical imaging).

Let us remark that the MS-COCO dataset is not perfect for our task, as some captions can describe multiple images while only being linked to a single image. For example, a caption stating "A tennis player ready to hit the ball." fits to all images of tennis players in action, but will only be linked to one of them in the dataset. Therefore, many captions which we will consider as negatives are actually false negatives. From a summary exploration of the dataset, we estimate that about 1% of the captions could describe multiple images.

4.4.2 Model

Even if the theoretical model may use more than two modalities and even identical ones, for comparison purposes, we use the same model architecture as the one in VSE++. The model has to be able to process both images and texts.

For the image modality, a CNN is used to extract a representation. The architecture of this CNN is the one of the ResNet family (He et al. 2015). Material constraints did not allow us to use the largest model in the ResNet family (ResNet-152) due to memory requirements, so we ran the biggest network that fits on a single NVidia 1080 Ti GPU: namely, ResNet-34. The model we use is pre-trained on the ImageNet dataset (Russakovsky et al. 2015).

For the text modality, token embeddings of dimensionality 300 are learned for all the words appearing at least four times in the training captions. The captions are then summarized using a Gated Recurrent Unit (GRU) (Cho et al. 2014), which outputs a 1024 dimensional vector. The embedding vectors are initialized from a normal distribution with mean 0 and variance $\frac{1}{300}$. The exact distribution does not seem to matter, but if the initial values are too large (like they are with the default PyTorch embedding initialization, which uses a variance of 1) the results will be hampered. There are some work related with the importance of embedding initialization (Kocmi and Bojar 2017) which further explore and explain this behavior.

When training the model, the image encoding network is frozen (not updated) until some epochs have passed. Therefore, to allow for some flexibility of the image representation, and to help align it with the text representation, and more importantly to make it of the same dimension as the output of the text encoder, a linear projection is appended to the image encoder network. As the text encoder is defined and trained from scratch, it does not need a projection. Before computing the similarities of the representations of images and texts, the vectors are normalized to unit vectors. This, combined with using a dot product as the similarity function, makes it such that the similarity scores are bounded by –1 and 1: the similarity is the cosine similarity. Once the similarity scores are computed, the triplet loss can be computed according to the formulas in Section 4.2.1.

4.4.3 Triplet Loss

Regarding the triplet loss using top-f as the reduction function, naive implementations were responsible for about 50% of the total training time, most likely due to transfers between CPU and GPU as well as being inefficient (not vectorized). Vectorizing this function is not trivial due to anchors having potentially different number of positives (and therefore negatives) in a batch. A user from the PyTorch forums came up with a way to vectorize this function.[2] However, this implementation has a cubic time and space complexity with respect to the number of elements in the batch (the time complexity is acceptable due to running on a GPU, but as we were already memory constrained, this space complexity is not acceptable). We ended up using an implementation which computes the loss on groups of anchors having the same number of positives, which has a quadratic complexity both in time and space, and made the time necessary for the computation of the loss negligible compared to the forward and backward crossing of the network (as it should be). An implementation for the max reduction function was created, using the same techniques as the cubic complexity implementations (masking the irrelevant elements to still allow for vectorization), but it ended up by not being used due to not being always applicable and not providing any run-time benefits (the implementation on groups is already fast enough).

4.4.4 Libraries Used

As with most deep learning projects, Python is the language we use. We chose to use PyTorch (Paszke et al. 2019) as the deep learning framework, combined with PyTorch Lightning (Falcon 2019). PyTorch is responsible of handling the computations, while PyTorch Lightning is there to provide a standardized way to organize the deep learning code (how to define a model, load data, compute metrics, log, etc.). To configure our application, we use Hydra Yadan (2019) which makes modifying the configuration of the application easy due to the way individual configurations (e.g., model architecture, data augmentations) can be composed to form the complete application configuration. Finally, we use GNU Make (Stallman et al. 2004) to link the various scripts (environment configuration generation, data preprocessing, model training).

4.4.5 Model Training

We use the training process from the VSE^{++} paper. As a preprocessing step, all images are resized such that their smallest side has a length of 256 pixels. This is done in order to avoid loading full resolution images (that will not be fed to the network anyway). We also create a dictionary that maps all the words appearing at least four times in the captions to an integer (which is used to index the embedding table).

When loading the data, the following transformations are applied:

- Text is put in lower case.
- Image is cropped at a random position to a size 224×224 pixels.
- Image and text are randomly flipped horizontally (mirror symmetry for image, "left"–"right" swap for text).
- Image is normalized according to ImageNet mean and variance of each channel.
- Text is tokenized (split into individual words) using NLTK's word tokenizer.
- Text is padded with start/end of sentence tokens.
- Text tokens are converted to indices using the dictionary made during preprocessing.

As described in Section 4.3.2, if an image is (not) flipped then all the captions that describe it are also (not) flipped.

We do not apply data augmentations to texts. Simple augmentations which would most likely improve performance exist (Wei and Zou 2019). We could also apply more powerful augmentations to the images, but did not do so to keep our results comparable to the ones from VSE^{++}.

We use a batch size of 128 tuples, which for COCO corresponds to 128 images, and either 128 captions when using one single positive or 640 captions when using all the available positives. We use the Adam Kingma and Ba (2015) optimizer. The learning rate is initialized to $2e^{-4}$ and is set to $2e^{-5}$ after 75 epochs ($\approx 70,000$ steps for COCO) have passed. The image encoder (but not the linear projection following it) is frozen (not updated) until 150 epochs have passed, to avoid to "forget" the pre-trained knowledge while the network still performs poorly on the task.

4.4.6 Results and Analysis

We are interested in two metrics:

- **Retrieval at K:** it is the fraction of the anchors which have one of their positives in their K most similar elements.
- **Mean rank:** it is the average rank of the positives among the elements of the anchors.

We compute the metrics when using images as anchors and texts as anchors and present the values in Table 4.1.

Even though the validation loss is lower using multiple positives, we do not observe improvement on the retrieval metrics. We also computed the mean rank of the positive that is returned last, which is what our method is optimized for, and did not find significant improvements there either (244 vs 247 for VSE^{++} vs MSE**) (Tables 4.2 and 4.3).

We suspect that selecting the hardest positive does not improve the performance due to the low number of positive captions (five on MS-COCO) as well as the simplicity of the captions, which makes it unlikely to find a truly difficult positive (there aren't many ways to describe an image with a short sentence). We expect this method to perform better (relatively to using a single positive/the mean over positives) on datasets containing a lot of variety of positives. One such dataset would be ImageNet, which contains images of concepts in varied scenes, postures, orientations, etc.

TABLE 4.1

Validation Scores of VSE^{++} and Our Method (MSE**) on MS-COCO

		Image to Text			Text to Image		
Model	Method	R@1	R@5	R@10	R@1	R@5	R@10
ResNet-34	VSE^{++}	0.31	0.61	0.74	0.23	0.51	0.65
ResNet-34	MSE**	0.31	0.60	0.72	0.21	0.50	0.63
ResNet-101	VSE^{++}	0.37	0.67	0.80	0.27	0.57	0.70
ResNet-101	MSE**	0.36	0.67	0.79	0.26	0.55	0.68

Note: R@K is the retrieval at K metric: proportion of anchors for which we found positives in the K most similar elements.

TABLE 4.2

Validation Scores of VSE⁺⁺ and Our Method (MSE**) on MS-COCO

			Image to Text		Text to Image
Model	Method	Loss	MeanR	MeanWorstR	MeanR
ResNet-34	VSE⁺⁺	0.98	163	244	35
ResNet-34	MSE**	0.91	177	247	35
ResNet-101	VSE⁺⁺	0.90	134	470	28
ResNet-101	MSE**	0.85	121	393	27

Note: Loss is the triplet loss on the validation set; MeanR, the mean rank of the positives; and MeanWorstR, the mean rank of the hardest positive (only computed for "Image to Text" as captions only have one positive).

Should our method perform better on some other datasets, ablations to identify the important parts would be necessary. The interesting questions to explore would concern the results that we could obtain if we:

- Increase the batch size for the single positive method to match the number of anchors of our method (using a single positive, we have one anchor per tuple, while the multiple positives ends up using every positive as an anchor).
- Use the mean instead of the max for the reduction function over positives (R^+).
- Do not use different data augmentations parameters for all the elements of a set.
- Use augmentations of an anchor as its positives, instead of the native positives (elements in the dataset tuple of this anchor).

Even if our method is only equivalent in results with VSE⁺⁺, it seems to produce a better similarity function, as shown on the example of Figure 4.2.

TABLE 4.3

Similarities between Images a and b with Their Legends

	Image a of Figure 4.2		Image b of Figure 4.2	
Legend	VSE⁺⁺	MSE**	VSE⁺⁺	MSE**
1	0.17	0.57	0.12	0.52
2	0.17	0.53	−0.02	−0.07
3	0.15	0.51	0.10	0.19
4	0.16	0.45	0.13	0.56
5	−0.01	0.15	0.11	0.48
Hardest negative	0.20	0.57	0.17	0.59

Image a	Image b

1. There are two refrigerators in this dirty, rundown kitchen. 2. Two refrigerators standing side by side in a room. 3. An olive green refrigerator next to a white refrigerator in an old kitchen. 4. A small refrigerator in a small kitchen with a window. 5. A kitcken that has two different refrigeratators in it.	1. A herd of elephants standing on top of a field. 2. a number of horses standing near one another 3. Two elephants that are pressing their heads together. 4. A couple of elephants standing in the grass. 5. a couple of elephants out in a large field

FIGURE 4.2

Two images and their five captions from MS-COCO dataset.

We notice that MSE** seems to perform better when one legend has typos (see the fifth legend of Figure 4.2 Image a ["kitcken," "refigeratator"]) and words absent from the vocabulary or is plain wrong (Image b's second legend ["horses"]). There is a difference in the magnitude of similarities between VSE++ and MSE**.

4.5 Conclusion

In this chapter, we have extended the triplet learning method to the case where there are multiple positives associated with an object, this extension does not improve the accuracy of the representations learned w.r.t. the one obtained by the existing method VSE++ in the particular case of the dataset MS-COCO. Nevertheless, the implementation is done to improve the development of this method in future works on different datasets.

This work opens several perspectives: (1) use the triplets method with multiple positives on datasets having many examples of each class; (2) use a VSE model to find new positive pairs and to eliminate false negatives present in some datasets; (3) associate the images not with texts but with logical formulas (in addition to allowing reasoning in post-processing, this would make it possible to introduce degrees of positivity/specificity: if a formula describing an image is more specific than another one, then we will be a priori more intransigent on the respect of the similarity/dissimilarity with this image/another image); generate the most similar captions to the images: is it possible to obtain more exhaustive descriptions of the scenes than those provided by humans?

Notes

1 The experiments presented in this chapter were carried out using the OSIRIM platform (http://osirim.irit.fr/site/en) that is administered by the Institut de Recherche en Informatique de Toulouse (IRIT) and supported by the French National Center for Scientific Research (CNRS), the Occitanie Region, the French Government, and the European Regional Development Fund (ERDF). The work has benefited from a CISA-IRIT funding.
2 https://discuss.pytorch.org/t/how-can-i-vectorize-this-for-loop-loss-function/122407/2

References

Cho, K., van Merrienboer, B., Gulcehre, C., Bahdanau, D., Bougares, F., Schwenk, H., and Bengio, Y. (2014). Learning phrase representations using RNN encoder-decoder for statistical machine translation. In *Proceedings of the 2014 Conference on Empirical Methods in Natural Language Processing (EMNLP)*. October 25–29, 2014, Doha, Qatar, pages 1724–1734.

Desai, K., and Johnson, J. (2021). Virtex: Learning visual representations from textual annotations. In *Proceedings of the IEEE/CVF Conference on Computer Vision and Pattern Recognition* 2021, pages 11162–11173.

Dou, Z.-Y., Xu, Y., Gan, Z., Wang, J., Wang, S., Wang, L., Zhu, C., Zhang, P., Yuan, L., and Peng, N., et al. (2022). An empirical study of training end-to-end vision-and-language transformers. In *Proceedings of the IEEE/CVF Conference on Computer Vision and Pattern Recognition*, pages 18166–18176.

Faghri, F., Fleet, D. J., Kiros, J. R., and Fidler, S. (2018). VSE++: Improving visual-semantic embeddings with hard negatives. In *Proceedings of the British Machine Vision Conference (BMVC), 2018 (BMVC Spotlight)*.

Falcon, W. A. (2019). Pytorch lightning. *GitHub*. https://github.com/PyTorchLightning/pytorch-lightning, 3.

He, K., Zhang, X., Ren, S., and Sun, J. (2015). Deep residual learning for image recognition. In *Proceedings of the IEEE Conference on Computer Vision and Pattern Recognition*, 2016, pages 770–778.

Hochreiter, S., and Schmidhuber, J. (1997). Long short-term memory. *Neural Computation,* 9(8):1735–1780.

Jones, K. N., Woode, D. E., Panizzi, K., and Anderson, P. G. (2001). Peir digital library: Online resources and authoring system. In *Proceedings of the American Medical Informatics Association Symposium* (AMIA 2001), page 1075–1075.

Kenton, J. D. M.-W. C., and Toutanova, L. K. (2019). Bert: Pre-training of deep bidirectional transformers for language understanding. In *Proceedings of the 17th Annual Conference of the North American Chapter of the Association for Computational Linguistics: Human Language Technologies (NAACL-HLT 2019),* pages 4171–4186.

Kingma, D. P., and Ba, J. (2015). Adam: A method for stochastic optimization. In Bengio, Y. and LeCun, Y., editors, *Proceedings of the 3rd International Conference on Learning Representations, ICLR 2015,* San Diego, CA, USA, May 7–9, 2015, Conference Track Proceedings.

Kiros, R., Salakhutdinov, R., and Zemel, R. S. (2014). Unifying visual-semantic embeddings with multimodal neural language models. *arXiv preprint arXiv:1411.2539.* NIPS 2014 deep learning workshop.

Kocmi, T., and Bojar, O. (2017). An exploration of word embedding initialization in deep-learning tasks. In *Proceedings of the 14th International Conference on Natural Language Processing (ICON-2017).* December 2017, Kolkata, India, pages 56–64. NLP Association of India.

Krizhevsky, A., Sutskever, I., Hinton, G. E. (2017). Imagenet classification with deep convolutional neural networks. *Communications of the ACM,* 60(6), 84–90.

Li, K., Zhang, Y., Li, K., Li, Y., and Fu, Y. (2019). Visual semantic reasoning for image-text matching. In *Proceedings of the IEEE/CVF International Conference on Computer Vision,* pages 4654–4662.

Li, G., Duan, N., Fang, Y., Gong, M., and Jiang, D. (2020a). Unicoder-vl: A universal encoder for vision and language by cross-modal pre-training. In *Proceedings of the AAAI Conference on Artificial Intelligence,* volume 34, pages 11336–11344.

Li, X., Yin, X., Li, C., Zhang, P., Hu, X., Zhang, L., Wang, L., Hu, H., Dong, L., Wei, F., et al. (2020b). Oscar: Object-semantics aligned pre-training for vision-language tasks. In *Computer Vision–ECCV 2020: 16th European Conference, Glasgow, UK, August 23–28, 2020, Proceedings, Part XXX 16,* pages 121–137. Springer International Publishing.

Lin, T.-Y., Maire, M., Belongie, S., Bourdev, L., Girshick, R., Hays, J., Perona, P., Ramanan, D., Zitnick, C. L., and Dollár, P. (2015). Microsoft COCO: Common Objects in Context. In Fleet, D., Pajdla, T., Schiele, B., and Tuytelaars, T. (eds), *Computer Vision – ECCV 2014.* Lecture Notes in Computer Science, vol. 8693. Springer, Cham.

Paszke, A., Gross, S., Massa, F., Lerer, A., Bradbury, J., Chanan, G., Killeen, T., Lin, Z., Gimelshein, N., Antiga, L., Desmaison, A., Kopf, A., Yang, E., DeVito, Z., Raison, M., Tejani, A., Chilamkurthy, S., Steiner, B., Fang, L., Bai, J., and Chintala, S. (2019). Pytorch: An imperative style, high-performance deep learning library. In Wallach, H., Larochelle, H., Beygelzimer, A., d' Alché-Buc, F., Fox, E., and Garnett, R., editors, *Advances in Neural Information Processing Systems 32 (NeurIPS 2019),* pages 8024–8035. Curran Associates, Inc. Red Hook, New York, USA.

Pentina, A., Sharmanska, V., and Lampert, C. H. (2014). Curriculum learning of multiple tasks. In *Proceedings of the IEEE Conference on Computer Vision and Pattern Recognition.* 2015. pages 5492–5500.

Raghu, M., Zhang, C., Kleinberg, J., and Bengio, S. (2019). Transfusion: Understanding transfer learning for medical imaging. In *Proceedings of the 32rd International*

Conference on Neural Information Processing Systems (NeurIPS 2019), pages 3347–3357.

Ren, S., He, K., Girshick, R., and Sun, J. (2015). Faster R-CNN: Towards real-time object detection with region proposal networks. In *Proceedings of the 29th Annual Conference on Advances in Neural Information Processing Systems*, 28 (NIPS 2015), pages 91–99.

Rohrbach, M., Qiu, W., Titov, I., Thater, S., Pinkal, M., and Schiele, B. (2013). Translating video content to natural language descriptions. In *Proceedings of the IEEE International Conference on Computer Vision*, pages 433–440.

Russakovsky, O., Deng, J., Su, H., Krause, J., Satheesh, S., Ma, S., Huang, Z., Karpathy, A., Khosla, A., Bernstein, M., Berg, A. C., and Fei-Fei, L. (2015). ImageNet large scale visual recognition challenge. *International Journal of Computer Vision* 115: 211–252.

Schroff, F., Kalenichenko, D., and Philbin, J. (2015). Facenet: A unified embedding for face recognition and clustering. In *Proceedings of the IEEE Conference on Computer Vision and Pattern Recognition (CVPR 2015)*, June 2015, Boston, MA, USA, pages 815–823.

Stallman, R. M., McGrath, R., and Smith, P. D. (2004). *GNU Make: A Program for Directing Recompilation, for Version 3.81*. Free Software Foundation.

Vaswani, A., Shazeer, N., Parmar, N., Uszkoreit, J., Jones, L., Gomez, A. N., Kaiser, Ł., and Polosukhin, I. (2017). Attention is all you need. *Advances in Neural Information Processing Systems*, 30: 5999–6009.

Wei, J., and Zou, K. (2019). EDA: Easy data augmentation techniques for boosting performance on text classification tasks. In *Proceedings of the 2019 Conference on Empirical Methods in Natural Language Processing and the 9th International Joint Conference on Natural Language Processing (EMNLP-IJCNLP)*, Hong Kong, China, pages 6382–6388. Association for Computational Linguistics.

Welling, M., and Kipf, T. N. (2016). Semi-supervised classification with graph convolutional networks. In *5th International Conference on Learning Representations, (ICLR 2017)*, Toulon, France, April 24–26, 2017, Workshop Track Proceedings. OpenReview.net.

Weng, L. (2021). Contrastive representation learning. lilianweng.github.io/lil-log.

Xue, H., Huang, Y., Liu, B., Peng, H., Fu, J., Li, H., and Luo, J. (2021). Probing intermodality: Visual parsing with self-attention for vision-and-language pretraining. *Advances in Neural Information Processing Systems*, 34:4514–4528.

Yadan, O. (2019). *Hydra – a framework for elegantly configuring complex applications*. Github. https://hydra.cc/.

Young, P., Lai, A., Hodosh, M., and Hockenmaier, J. (2014). From image descriptions to visual denotations: New similarity metrics for semantic inference over event descriptions. *Transactions of the Association for Computational Linguistics*, 2:67–78.

5

Text-Based Emergency Alert Framework for Under-Resourced Languages in Southern Nigeria

Patience U. Usip, Funebi F. Ijebu, Ifiok J. Udo, and Ikechukwu K. Ollawa
Department of Computer Science, Faculty of Science, University of Uyo, Uyo, Nigeria

CONTENTS

5.1 Introduction

Language has been the ultimate medium of presenting human experiences from the beginning of time. Without language, humans would be unable to express their feelings, thoughts, emotions, desires, and beliefs. Without language, there could be no society and possibly no religion. Hence, language is what makes us humans. Apart from being a medium of communication, language is also a means of cultural expression and personal identity among people. The power of language in human coexistence cannot be overemphasized as the history and development of speakers are inherent in their language. Although, the world today is described as a global village, this was not the case decades ago. From the inception of civilization, language has been a determinant in people grouping and communal association. This is because the persons with the largest population of unanimous speakers often dominate those with lesser population, otherwise referred to as minorities. But as civilization advances and computers become more powerful, language bridges have continued to emerge, with natural language processing (NLP) and inter-language translations becoming

DOI: 10.1201/9781003313267-5

simpler tasks. Most works that have been undertaken over the years to achieve language translation are done to aid knowledge sharing (Shi et al., 2019).

Knowledge sharing, a major reason for the current rapid growth of technology, would be greatly limited if vital materials and information privy to minority language speakers cannot be accessed and utilized by non-speakers of the minority languages and vice versa. In addition, such knowledge sharing would foster inclusiveness, encourage development, and contribute to making the world further interconnected. Minority languages in this context are well-spoken languages by natives of respective communities but with little or no digital presence in terms of data and information usable for further knowledge generation computationally. Hence, they are referred to low-resourced (Magueresse et al., 2020) or under-resourced (Karim et al., 2020). Whereas languages like English, French, Mandarin, Spanish, Russian, etc., are more easily translated to each other, most native African languages, especially those spoken in southern Nigeria, do not have any structure for computer aided translation (Ezeani et al., 2020). Notwithstanding the fact that the Africa's language diversity is second to none on the planet and Nigeria alone has over 500 under-resourced languages outside the three (Hausa, Igbo, and Yoruba) popular ones.

Prior to modern innovations in natural language translation, an individual would require several weeks, months, or even years to study, understand, and fluently translate words, phrases, and sentences made in their native language to a foreign language. Today, same can be accomplished in seconds following the rapid development of mobile technologies and steady migration of innovations to the web space. One of the most popular and robust digital language translators often patronized for translation tasks is Google Translate. However, as divers and robust as it may be; it fails to capture under-resourced languages like Ibibio, Ijaw, and Itshekiri among others, even though the number of people speaking each of these languages supers the population of some independent countries whose language are supported. With globalization, it is imperative that under-resourced languages growing in popularity be interpretable anywhere in the world using technological devices. To achieve such translations, one can leverage on the several resources finding expression around communities with under-resourced languages. The language-based contents from such communities can form a huge information base that is useful for enhancing intelligence.

It is not strange to find that a sizeable number of natives who are mostly resident in rural areas and uneducated cannot communicate fluently in English, which is the lingua franca in Nigeria. There are vital information and knowledge possessed by such individuals, and English speakers would sometimes possess vital and beneficial information, but because of the language barrier, an exchange cannot happen. In most of these rural areas, custodians of traditional health, cultural, security, and trans-generational information and knowledge live and pass away without documentation or knowledge transfer. Similarly, in the face of current increase in crime and insecurity, people have lost their life because they could not understand the language of personnel giving safety instructions during emergencies. In other cases, making moves contrary to the directives of the attackers due to language barrier has led to the death of persons that may have survived the attack.

Furthermore, there are neighboring communities that speak totally different languages such that if an attack is ongoing in one community and someone safely escapes, communicating the impending danger to residents of the neighboring community for precautionary measures to be taken is very difficult. However, if there are digital alert systems that can notify people of an emergency in their native language, several persons would take well-informed steps to ensure the safety of their life and family. This vacuum in research is identified and noted as one that ought to be filled. Hence, this work presents a framework for a text-based emergency alert system for select under-resourced languages. The proposed system will get text in a sender's preferred language, then translate and transmit same to the target recipient(s) in their native under-sourced language.

The rest of this chapter is structured as follows: Section 5.2 presents related works on machine translation while Section 5.3 highlights methodologies adopted by the proposed framework and the service-oriented architecture (SOA) of the proposed emergency alert system framework with its components. Section 5.4 presents the results of the implementation of the proposed framework while Section 5.5 concludes this chapter with future research directions on possible inclusion of other under-resourced languages in Southern Nigeria.

5.2 Related Works

Machine translation is an applied area of machine learning that involves conversion of words, phrases, or sentences from a source language to a target language or representation (Abiola et al., 2020). Over the years, much of the gains in machine translation have been due to researches into statistical machine translation (SMT) procedures. The efforts have birthed approaches like NLP, example-based translation, and neural machine translation. The direct translation of words, phrases, and sentences is the most primitive or the original approach in machine translation. Here, words in the source language are replaced with words in the target language following the sequence in which the words appear without much linguistic analysis and processing. The major resource used by this approach is a bilingual dictionary, hence it is known as dictionary-driven machine translation. A word-to-word translation of the output text is performed, and the result is obtained in the form of output text. The direct machine translation approach is effective for unidirectional tasks but accesses only one language pair at a time, hence it is not conducive for multilingual machine translation (Abiola et al., 2015; Agbeyangi et al., 2051).

The rule-based approach is another technique adopted in machine translation. It involves the application of morphological, syntactic, and semantic rules in the analysis of the source language file and the synthesis of the target-language text. A database of translation rules is used to translate text from source to target language. This approach deals with the word-order problem and since it uses linguistic knowledge, errors in translation can be traced and resolved more easily by the algorithm. Rule-based machine translation parses the source text and produces an intermediate representation which may be a parse tree or some abstract representation. The target text is then generated from the intermediate representation. Systems implementing this technique rely on the specification of rules for morphology, syntax, lexical selection and transfer, semantic analysis, and generation. It identifies the relationship between source-language words and their structural representations. Although the approach requires a lot of human effort and dedication, it has been effective in early multilingual translation tasks.

The corpus-based technique has also been widely adopted (Ali and Al-Gamal et al., 2021, Tehseen et al., 2018). Corpus-based language translation consists of the SMT and example-based machine translations (EBMT) types. The SMT deals with automatically mapping sentences in one language into another. Using SMT, the translation is modeled either with string-to-string mapping, trees-to-strings, or tree-to-tree models. All these models share the central idea that translation is automatic, with models estimated from parallel corpora and also from monolingual corpora (Post, 2012). In contrast to the rule-based approach, most SMT systems are phrase-based and assemble translations using overlap phrases. In phrase-based translation, the aim is to reduce the restrictions of word-based translation by translating whole sequences of words, where the lengths may differ. The sequences of words are called phrases, but typically are not linguistic phrases, but phrases found using statistical methods from bilingual text corpora. A complexity with this method issue is its need of bilingual content, which can be tricky when it comes to finding content written in under-resourced languages.

Using either the rule-based or corpus-based approaches, a number of works have been undertaken to convert one form of natural language file to another, including text-to-text, speech-to-text, text-to-speech, and speech-to-speech translations (Arikpo and Dickson, 2018). The methods and approaches adapted in each of these efforts continue to achieve varying results from one language to another. A deduction from this is that the semantic and syntactic diversity in languages affects the performance of proposed models. For high-resourced languages, all four forms of machine translation have been greatly investigated; however, the contrary is the case with low-resourced languages. Nevertheless, many machine translation efforts in native African and Nigerian languages have focused more on the area of text-to-text translation, while a few based on speech-to-text.

The submission by Awofolu and Malita (2002) undertook text-based machine translation of English words and sentences to their Yoruba equivalent, using a syntactic and semantic technique. Folajimi and Isaac (2012) also undertook a similar study using statistical approach for bidirectional machine translation between English and Yoruba languages. A bilingual lexicon for building technicians is proposed in Abiola et al. (2020), where the web-based translator uses a direct-based approach for the unidirectional word translation from Yoruba to English. The integrated text-to-speech feature was however for English language which is already a standardized language in terms of text-to-speech machine translation. Many works that have attempted English to Yoruba translation have adopted the rule-based technique for system modeling, except in few, like in Akinwale et al. (2015), where a data-driven approach is adopted. The English to Yoruba translator proposed by Eludiora and Odejobi (2016), however, utilized a combination of NLP tools for the system implementation. Ortíz-Rodriguez et al. (2022) presented MEXIN – a multidialectal ontology supporting NLP approach to improve government electronic communication with the Mexican Ethnic Groups.

In Chinenyeze et al. (2019), English to Igbo language translating system is presented. Although the submission shows evidence of successful translation, the underlying method adopted is not clearly outlined. Furthermore, the number of words and phrases used to train and test the system is not also clearly presented. This is in addition to the absence of system accuracy in terms of its translation of words and phrases from source to target language. Ezeani and collaborators reported an ongoing effort toward creating and making available an Igbo-to-English dataset with over 100,000 sentence pairs and 100,000 monolingual Igbo sentences for machine translation tasks and research (Ezeani et al., 2020). Part of speech (POS) tagging is a prerequisite in most NLP tasks, and the Igbo language also requires this for efficient dataset generation and effective NLP task completion. The work by Onyenwe and colleagues (2019) presented comparative results of six POS tagging techniques and showed the higher accuracy score obtained from their linguistic probabilistic method that took the productive agglutinative morphology of the Igbo language into consideration.

The Ibibio language is the native language of the Ibibio people of Akwa Ibom and Abia States, of Nigeria, belonging to the Ibibio-Efik dialect cluster of the Cross River languages. The name Ibibio is sometimes used for the entire dialect cluster. In precolonial times, it was written with Nsibidi ideograms, similar to Igbo, Efik, Anaang, and Ejagham. Ibibio has also had influences on Afro-American diasporic languages such as African-American Vernacular English words like buckra, and buckaroo, which come from the Ibibio word mbakara, and in the Afro-Cuban tradition of abakua. Ibibio is spoken by 1.5–2 million people in the world and is considered by most to be the fourth most popular language in Nigeria after Hausa, Yoruba, and Igbo. The Ibibio language boasts of a dictionary with English concordance (Urua et al., 2004). Similarly, efforts have been made to translate the Holy Bible into Ibibio language (Okon and Noah, 2004). There are also a number of other informative and educative materials generated in Ibibio and those translated from some other language into Ibibio language. Although these laudable efforts in Ibibio language translation exist with the help of human translators, to the best of our knowledge, there is no automated machine translator. Table 5.1 summarizes the review of the various machine translation approaches.

TABLE 5.1

Tabulated Review Process

Study	Aims	Data	Settings/Method	Key Findings	Critique
Abiola et al. (2015)	Translation of unidirectional tasks	Bilingual dictionary	Direct machine translation approach	Accesses only one language pair at a time	Not conducive for multilingual machine translation
Akinwale et al. (2015)	Involves application of morphological, syntactic, and semantic rules in the analysis	Database of translation rules	Rule-based approach	Produces an intermediate representation, deals with the word-order problem and can easily trace and resolve errors	Requires a lot of human effort and dedication
Ali and Al-Gamal (2021) and Tehseen et al. (2018)	Reduce the restrictions of word-based translation	Models estimated from parallel corpora and also from monolingual corpora	Corpus-based language translation consists of the SMT and EBMT	Translation is modeled either with string-to-string mapping, trees-to-strings, or tree-to-tree models	Complexity due to its need of bilingual content
Awofolu and Malita (2002)	Text-based translation	Bilingual corpora of English/Yoruba words and sentences	Text-based machine translation	Used syntactic and semantic technique	Limited to one language and text-based
Abiola et al. (2020)	Unidirectional word translation from Yoruba to English	Bilingual lexicon	Web-based translator uses a direct-based approach	Integrates text-to-speech feature for English language	Speech not incorporated for Yoruba language

As technology advances, there is need to exploit NLP techniques for automation of Ibibio language. However, the research in this direction is greatly limited, although, great efforts are made in developed countries, where the Multilingual Legacy Emergency Alert System (EAS) and Internet-based EAS (FCC_US, 2022) serve as possible tools for public safety and homeland security. This is the case with the Izon language, which is another under-resourced language spoken by millions of indigenes resident in southern Nigeria. More tasking is the fact that the Izon language, otherwise called Ijaw or Ijo in some quarters, does not yet have a comprehensive human translated dictionary. Efforts toward the Ijaw language demystification are seen in the linguistic identification and classification of Ekiugbo and Ayunku (2018) and Prezi (2014). This submission is therefore designed to cover an available research gap and form a foundation for further knowledge discovery and development of digital content for under-resourced languages of southern Nigeria.

5.3 Methodology

Being that large amount of data is often required for effective model training and efficient language translation systems, natural language understanding by the machine is inevitable. Understanding the patterns in selected under-resourced languages and generating digitally annotated dataset that aids machine training are keys to goal actualization. This section introduces the data source, the hybridized methodology, and the proposed SOA-based emergency alert system framework.

5.3.1 Source – Target Word Concord

Exploiting the strengths of the rule-based and corpus-based language translation approaches, this work presents a hybrid approach that overcomes the weaknesses of the statistical and rule-based translation methodologies. The approach involves rules post-processed by statistics, such that translations are performed using rule-based engine. Statistics are used in an attempt to adjust and correct the output from the rule's engine. Statistical computations are guided by rules that are used to preprocess data for an enhanced statistical engine. Rule-based approach requires declarative component/linguistic knowledge and procedural component. The linguistic knowledge is built from language-specific dictionary of the source under-resourced language. The work by Urua et al. (2004) that produced an Ibibio dictionary serves as a reliable word base. The process of word concordance determination from the bilingual dictionary is depicted in Figure 5.1, where the user's input text is processed and segmented for corresponding words

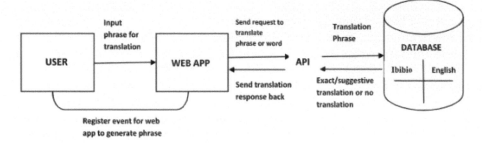

FIGURE 5.1
Description of word concordance determination.

determination in the target language. Output from this stage serves as the input for the SOA-based emergency framework.

5.3.2 Hybridization

In Figure 5.2, the incorporation of rule-based and corpus-based translation approaches into a hybrid technique for efficient language translation is graphically described. From the description, the preprocessing phase incorporates part of speech (POS) tagging, word sense disambiguation, and other standard noise removal activities in NLP. The proposition of a hybrid translation technique is justified by the absence of properly curated corpus in source under-resourced languages, making the corpus-based approach

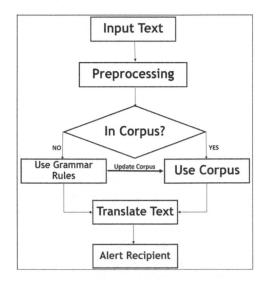

FIGURE 5.2
Flow of the proposed hybridization.

alone inadequate, hence, the inclusion of rule-based approach which allows expert formulation of rules in conformity with syntactic and semantic rules of target language. Another reason for the introduction of the rule-based technique is to handle abbreviated words in text. For instance, words like "Thanks," "because," "before" are often abbreviated or misspelt by writers to "Thks or Tanks," "b/cuz or cus," and "b4 or bfor," respectively. Rules are defined to normalize this kind of word spellings within sentences to achieve proper sentence representation. The need to undertake such word normalization hinges on the fact that being an emergency alert system; users should be given some degree of liberty to use machine interpretable short forms of words for quick communication with intended recipients.

Effective rules generation requires word class identification, taking into consideration that some words in certain languages require certain explanation, unlike others which have direct definitions and meanings. POS tagging is an established means of class identification with successful application in English and well-resourced languages. For the Ibibio English language dictionary being adopted in this study, POS tagging is already done. Our defined rules therefore adapted the POS tags already done for word classification in the input text. This is achieved by putting the sentence into a parse tree and iteratively traversing the tree using a depth-first search algorithm to ensure accurate word sequencing.

Upon sentence sequencing, the corpus is referenced for corresponding sentence in the under-resourced language. When there is none, source words are used to retrieve their corresponding pair in the target language taking into consideration word sense utilization, by getting the words into a parse tree for the under-resourced language. The new translated sentence can now be added to the corpus as an update. Tagged words in both languages are matched to ensure a noun in source language is still a noun in the target language even though their positions in the sentence may differ due to morphological and syntactic characteristics of the target language. This, however, involves morphological and grammar synthesis rules defined for the translator. The rule-based approach in the English-Arabic translation (Shaalan, 2010) and English-Filipino (Tan et al., 2019) is useful for model implementation.

In processing source text for translation using the predefined rules, POS tagging is followed by word sense disambiguation accomplished with supervised machine learning algorithm, Naïve Bayes, described by Equation 5.1.

$$P\left(\frac{C_i}{\nabla V_j}\right) = \frac{P\left(\frac{\nabla V_j}{C_i}\right) \cdot P(C_i)}{P(\nabla V_j)} \qquad (5.1)$$

where $P\left(\frac{\nabla V_j}{C_i}\right)$ is the probability that a test example is of class C_i given values of V. The representation ∇V_j is the conjunction of all feature values in the test example, while $P(\nabla V_j)$ is the probability of ∇V_j. Since the value of $P(\nabla V_j)$ remains constant for all classes of C_i, the equation can be further expressed as in Equation 5.2. During training, naïve Bayes constructs the matrix $P\left(\frac{V_j}{C_i}\right)$, while $P(C_i)$ is estimated from the distribution of training examples among the classes (Ayogu, 2020).

$$P\left(\frac{\nabla V_j}{C_i}\right) = \prod_j P\left(\frac{V_j}{C_j}\right) \tag{5.2}$$

In the process flow description of the hybrid model, the corpus gets updated constantly with new de-noised text not already in the corpus. With this, the system becomes more robust and efficient with continued usage. On the other hand, when an input text corresponds to some predefined translation sequence in the corpus, the grammar rules need not apply for the translation to be completed. As part of the system, the translated text in the under-resourced language is forwarded to the target recipient. For a successful information transmission between users at either end of the system, some type of network must be established. While the network type or design is outside the scope of this work, the sender would require an internet connection to use the system. The emergency alert system is therefore presented using the software as a service principle; hence, implementation is based on SOA.

5.3.3 SOA-Based Framework

As shown in Figure 5.3, the framework is designed based on the SOA. Generally, SOA describes ways to make given software easily reusable through service interfaces that utilize communication protocols like HTTPS for data communication between the tiers. From the architecture, users (both sender and receiver) with the support of application programming interface (API) are connected to services on the infrastructure layer via the platform layer that detects language (in text messages) and translate same to meet the communication needs of the users (i.e., receiver). These layers are distinctive, reliable, and loosely coupled to offer flexibility for distributed language detection and translation in a bilingual (one-to-many) communication scenario with English language as the link language among a community of speakers of any one of the under-resourced languages. It can also lead to an increase in corpus generation and refinement of the under-resourced language at minimal cost due to flexibility offered by the cloud-based services, in terms of billing. Furthermore, to manage message sending from one user (i.e., source) to another user (i.e., receiver), a middleware (i.e., message-processing bus) responsible for point-to-point or publish to subscribe (García-Valls and Basanta-Val, 2017) delivery patterns across networks is proposed for effective message delivery to users.

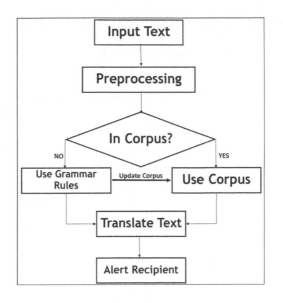

FIGURE 5.3
An SOA-based emergency alert system framework.

Further describing the components of the architecture, the input and expected output from the system are both plain texts. However, the text would be in different languages. The emergency alert system is designed to receive natural language text in a user preferred language at the API layer; this language is automatically detected by the system using the Language Detector module integrated into the message-processing bus of the platform layer. Every language is different from the next in terms of its syntax and morphology (Ekiugbo and Ayunku, 2018), as such the proposed system by Chinenyeze et al. (2019) incorporated a customized keyboard that considered characters in the native Igbo language that are not tenable in the standard QWERTY, DVORAK, or any other everyday computer keyboard. Because languages are different, grammar rules are incorporated within the message-processing bus to hold rules (apart from the generic ones,) that are unique to the source language's definition. These rules cover word sense, usage context, subject-verb agreement, and other linguistic uniqueness associated with the source language.

Based on the detected language, a rule selector selects the predefined associated rules of the source language. This selector concurrently scans the infrastructure layer to identify the appropriate corpus with structured words, phrases, or sentences in the source language. Using the specific bilingual corpus in combination with the grammar rules, the inputted text is passed to the language translator module aided by internet service, where the actual conversion is done automatically. This process which generates the text in the target under-sourced language is followed by an instant transmission of the under-sourced language text to the mobile device(s) of the intended individuals. The action or reaction of the recipients of the message is not considered by this system, except the recipient decides to also respond via the system.

5.4 Result and Discussion

The semantics of Ibibio and a number of other under-resourced languages makes direct machine translation inaccurate sometimes. As such, interviews and interactions with native speakers on syntax and order of words in Ibibio translated sentences provided insight necessary for rules formulation. Contextual word and grammar usage in Ibibio is another insight derived from the data collection process. Although the proposed rules have not been presented in this work, SOA-based translation have been achieved and presented. The implementation that uses two-tier network architecture leverages on the Ibibio dictionary (Urua et al., 2004) identified in this work. For translation of words and phrases, system accomplished tasks in an average time of 0.5 seconds. This is a relatively short time, but being an emergency alert system, further work would be undertaken to reduce the turnaround time.

Although the Ibibio–English dictionary is available, it is not useable in our work in it's as-is form, hence, its conversion into a useable database using the MongoDB technology. MongoDB is a NoSQL database technology that's robust and easily scalable. Over 2000 words were annotated with their corresponding POS tags in the database. Built as a web-based application, the API can be integrated with all common everyday browsers save Internet Explorer. Whereas the emergency notification system is intended to be mobile based, with event describable emogies for quick and easy composition of text and graphics messages, this initial phase has been developed to be highly reusable. Hence, its implementation with Node.js, a JavaScript framework built on C++. Other technologies adopted include Vue.js and TailwindCSS.

The SOA-based emergency alert framework proposes translation of multilingual text messages for the purpose of alerting designated receiver with vital and emergency information. Normally, such messages are short and most times they do not constitute a complete sentence. As such, translations sometimes may not make complete sense in the under-resourced language. However, the Ibibio to English bidirectional translator implemented in this work as a plug-in ensures near exact translations from source to target language. An interface of the plug-in installed on a web browser is shown in Figure 5.4. In Figure 5.5, an example translation from Ibibio to English and vice versa is shown. Based on the proposed framework's design that combines several bilingual corpora into a robust multilingual corpus, other languages can be integrated into the API, while new APIs can also be developed following this hybrid translation approach.

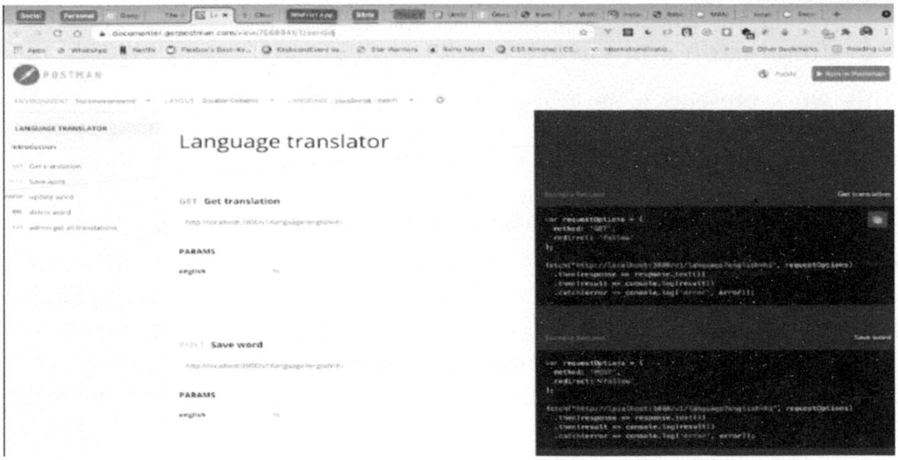

FIGURE 5.4
Ibibio–English Translator interface.

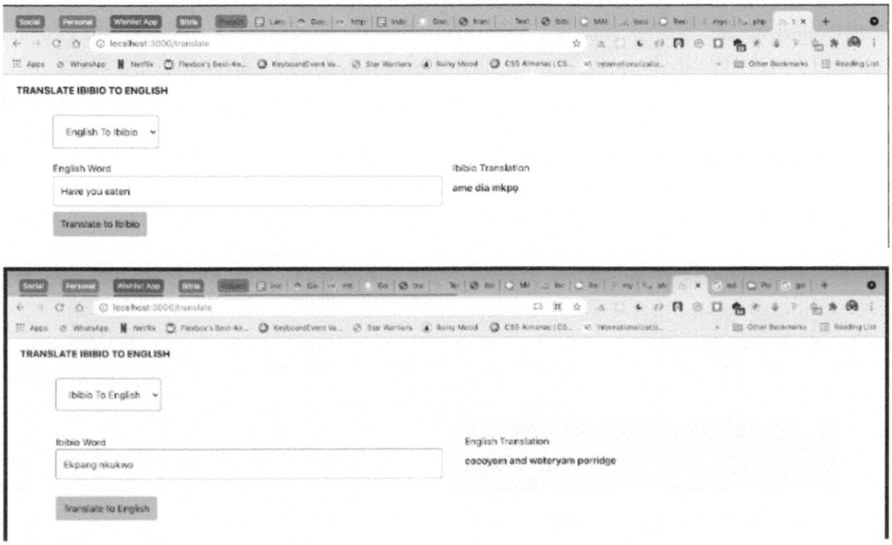

FIGURE 5.5
Bidirectional translation sample.

5.5 Conclusion and Future Work

This work presents a multilingual text translation framework for under-resourced languages of southern Nigeria. Although a usable Ibibio-English bilingual corpus has not been produced as part of this work, the framework is robust and implementable with machine learning techniques based on the SOA. The framework has been designed in such a way that multiple bilingual corpuses following predefined standard configurations can be integrated to form the multilingual translator of under-resourced languages using English as an intermediate language. The dynamics of subject-verb agreements and morphemes in most under-resourced languages makes rule definition in rule-based translation complex. However, the message-processing bus would hold rules that effectively perform the bidirectional translations.

The choice of the SOA architecture in the work is partly due to our desire to implement bilingual APIs that are loosely coupled, so that it can be easily integrated onto different platforms, and for reusability which will aid the extension of the API functionality to support the targeted under-resourced languages, thus making the system fully multilingual. Through the adoption of the SOA, a platform that supports flexibility in language detection and translation to service a community of different language speakers, usage, standardization, and maintenance of corpora of the under-resourced language can be achieved. Bridging the gap of communication between speakers of different languages through NLP techniques can provide reliable corpus for accurate detection and translation of under-resourced languages. As such, the focus in the future would be to implement the framework and include other under-resourced languages widely spoken in southern Nigeria by millions of people. Target languages would include Ijaw, Ibibio, Oro, Itshekiri, and Isoko among others.

References

Abiola O. B., Adetunmbi A.O., and Oguntimilehin A. (2015). Review of the Various Approaches to Text to Text Machine Translations. *International Journal of Computer Applications*, Vol. 120(18). Pp.: 7–12.

Abiola O.B, Adeyemo O.A., Saka-Balogun O.Y., and Okesola F. (2020). A Web-Based Yorùbá to English Bilingual Lexicon for Building Technicians, *International Journal of Advanced Trends in Computer Science and Engineering*, Vol. 9(1). Pp.: 793–800, DOI:10.30534/ijatcse/2020/114912020

Agbeyangi A.O., Eludiora S.I., and Adenekan D.I. (2015). English to Yorùbá Machine Translation System Using Rule-Based Approach. *Journal of Multidisciplinary Engineering, Science and Technology*, Vol. 2(8). Pp.: 2275–2280.

Akinwale O.I., Adetumbi A.O., Obe O.O., and Adesuyi A.T. (2015). Web-Based English to Yoruba Machine Translation. *International Journal of Language and Linguistics*, Vol. 3(3). Pp.: 154–159.

Ali M.A.E., and Al-Gamal M.A.A. (2021). Corpus-Based Machine Translation. *International Journal of Research and Analytical Reviews*, Vol. 8(3). Pp.: 1–4.

Arikpo I., and Dickson I. (2018). Development of an Automated English-to-Local-Language Translator Using Natural Language Processing. *International Journal of Science & Engineering Research*, Vol. 9(7). Pp.: 378–383.

Awofolu O., and Malita M. (2002). The Making of a Yoruba-English Machine Translator. *Journal of Computing Science in Colleges*, Vol. 17(6). Pp.: 236–237.

Ayogu I.I. (2020). Exploring Multinomial Naïve Bayes for Yoruba Text Document Classification. *Nigerian Journal of Technology*, Vol. 39(2). Pp.: 528–535.

Chinenyeze C.E., Bennett O.E., and Taylor E.O. (2019). A Natural Language Processing System for English to Igbo Language Translation in Android. *International Journal of Computer Science and Mathematical Theory*, Vol. 5(1). Pp.: 64–75.

Ekiugbo O.P., and Ayunku V.T. (2018). Affixation Processes in Izon. *International Journal of Linguistics, Literature and Translation (IJLLT)*, Vol. 3(1). Pp.: 1–4.

Eludiora I.S., and Odejobi A.O. (2016). Development of an English to Yoruba Machine Translator. *International Journal of Modern Education and Computer Science*, Vol. 11. Pp.: 8–19.

Ezeani I., Rayson P., Onyenwe I., Uchechukwu C., and Hepple M. (2020). Igbo-English Machine Translation: An Evaluation Benchmark. 8th International Conference on Learning Representations (ICLR2020), Addis Ababa, Ethiopia. April 20–30.

FCC_US (2022). Multilingual Alerting for the Emergency Alert System and Wireless Emergency Alerts Updated by Public Safety and Homeland Security on Wednesday, September 28, 2022. Available on https://www.fcc.gov/MultilingualAlerting_EAS-WEA.

Folajimi Y.O., and Isaac O. (2012). Using Statistical Machine Translation (SMT) as a Language Translation Tool for Understanding Yoruba Language. EiE's 2nd International Conference on Computing, Energy, Networks, Robotics and Telecommunication. Pp.: 86–91.

García-Valls M., and Basanta-Val P. (2017). Analyzing Point-to-Point DDS Communication Over Desktop Virtualization Software. *Computer Standards & Interfaces*, Vol. 49, Pp.:11–21.

Karim M.R., Chakravarthi B.R., Arcan M., McCrae J.P., and Cochez M. (2020). Classification Benchmarks for Under-resourced Bengali Language based on Multichannel Convolutional-LSTM Network. 2020 IEEE 7th International Conference on Data Science and Advanced Analytics (DSAA). Pp.: 390–399.

Magueresse A., Carles V., and Heetderks E. (2020). Low-resource Languages: A Review of Past Work and Future Challenges. ArXiv, abs/2006.07264.

Okon M.M., and Noah N.P. (2004). Translation of the Bible into the Ibibio Language: Experiences of the Translator. *Journal of Linguistics Association of Nigeria*, (8), 2001–2004. Pp.: 92–99.

Onyenwe E.I., Hepple M., Chinedu U., and Ezeani I. (2019). Towards an Effective Igbo Part-of-Speech Tagger. *ACM Transactions on Asian and Low Resourced Languages. Information Processing (TALLIP)*, Vol. 18(4). Pp.: 1–26.

Ortíz-Rodriguez F., Tiwari S., Panchal R., Medina-Quintero J.M., and Barrera R. (2022, June). MEXIN: Multidialectal Ontology Supporting NLP Approach to Improve Government Electronic Communication with the Mexican Ethnic Groups. In DG. O 2022: The 23rd Annual International Conference on Digital Government Research. Pp. 461–463.

Post M., Callison-Burch C., and Osborne M. (2012, June). Constructing Parallel Corpora for Six Indian Languages via Crowdsourcing. In Proceedings of The seventh Workshop on Statistical Machine Translation. Pp. 401–409.

Prezi T.G. (2014). The State of Ịzọn in Bayelsa State Schools. *US-China Foreign Language*, Vol. 12(4). Pp.: 262–275.

Shaalan K. (2010). Rule-Based Approach in Arabic Natural Language Processing. *International Journal on Information and Communication Technologies*, Vol. 3(3). Pp.: 11–19.

Shi X., Huang H., Wang W., Jian P., and Tang Y.-K. (2019). Improving Neural Machine Translation by Achieving Knowledge Transfers with Sentence Alignment Learning. Proceedings of 23rd Conference on Computational Neural Language Learning (CoNLL). Pp: 260–270. https://doi.org/10.18653/v1/k19-1025

Tan M.W., Ang R.I., Bautista N.G., Cai Y.R., and Tamlo B. (2019). Learning Translation Rules from Bilingual English-Filipino Corpus. Proceedings of the 19th Asia-Pacific Conference on Language, Information and Computation. Pp.: 1–10

Tehseen I., Tahir R.G., Shakeel K., and Ali M. (2018). Corpus Based Machine Translation for Scientific Text. In: *Artificial Intelligence Applications and Innovations*. Pp.: 196–206. https://doi.org/10.1007/978-3-319-92007-8_17.

Urua E.-A., Ekpenyong M., and Gibbon D. (2004). Uyo Ibibio Dictionary. ABUILD Language Documentation Curriculum Project. *Preprint Draft*, Vol. 1. Pp.: 1–132.

6

Knowledge Graphs in Healthcare

Sanna Aizad[a] and Dr. Bilal Arshad[b]

[a]*School of Computing and Mathematical Sciences, University of Leicester, Leicester, UK*
[b]*School of Computing and Engineering, University of Derby, Derby, UK*

CONTENTS

6.1 Introduction

Recent times have seen a spike in interest in graphs. They are seen to be employed everywhere from search engines to social media to recommendation systems [1]. The main reason for this is that graphs allow a technical way to integrate data from different sources in a structured manner and enable the capturing of relationships between the different data types. A graph is a data structure that maps entities and their connections. One category of graphs is the knowledge graph which is a system of interconnected data entities, representing real-world objects and their relationships. It provides a way to represent the world as it exists in data.

Knowledge graphs are also viewed as semantic networks or a database of interconnected concepts and their relationships. Knowledge graphs are made up of nodes (representing entities, i.e., things) and edges (representing relationships between things). Nodes can be seen as 'places' or 'locations' in the world, while edges can be seen as 'connections' or 'relationships' between these places. Knowledge graphs are typically created by extracting data from large volumes of unstructured text in the form of natural language and other sources. This process is known as 'knowledge extraction' or 'knowledge harvesting.'

DOI: 10.1201/9781003313267-6

Other definitions suggest that knowledge graphs are ontologies based on taxonomies, i.e., a knowledge base [2]. This is because ontologies formalize the representation of entities in a graph and can contain multiple taxonomies. In other words, knowledge graphs provide a hierarchical classification of the world's knowledge. For example, if you were to search for 'car' in a knowledge graph, you would find out that cars fall under the category of vehicles and then under the category of transportation.

Knowledge graphs can be used for a variety of purposes such as information retrieval, data integration and analysis, personalization for users, and more. Knowledge graphs can help you find answers to questions like 'Where does this term come from?' or 'What is the definition?' Representing the data as graphs has many benefits. It can be used to represent complex information in a way that makes it easier to understand. It can find concealed information between entities by allowing users to query the data and apply graph analytical techniques in addition to generating inferences between previously unknown entities. It allows easy access and interaction with data by multi-hopping relationships between entities. It also allows users to visualize data.

Healthcare has also benefited from the use of knowledge graphs. Since the beginning of time health has been a vital part of our lives. The healthcare industry was established to enable prolonged and good health. It is responsible for giving proper diagnoses and treatments in a timely manner. Furthermore, it is responsible for making future predictions to allow preventive care by making timely changes in lifestyles. A timely diagnosis and treatment are of utmost importance to save lives from progressive diseases such as cancer. Therefore, over the years, many analytical applications with genomics and clinical datasets have been developed [3]. Researchers have identified the need to consolidate genomic and clinical data for better analytics [4]. Knowledge graphs can play an important role in this.

Healthcare data is structured but heterogeneous in nature. To have a broad and clear picture of the data, it is essential to bring all the data together. Health knowledge graphs are an excellent option for this as they enable doctors, service providers, and researchers to easily find information from a wide array of variables and data sources. However, many challenges come with the construction of health knowledge graphs [5]. Some of these are listed below:

- Data is not centralized and so may not always be accessible
- Data is structured and heterogenous making it challenging to map relationships and complex biological concepts
- Data follows various, non-central medical standards
- Data may be of poor quality or not properly captured

There is a wide range of use-cases of health knowledge graphs which address one or more of the challenges. This chapter provides insight into knowledge graphs based on two real-world scenarios. The first use-case illustrates how knowledge graphs can be utilized to organize genomic data for representation and analysis by providing details on how genomic data is mapped onto knowledge graphs. This is followed by a discussion on how to capture and visualize variations within the knowledge graphs as the genome sequence is altered due to diseases over the course of time. It further provides details on how to enrich these knowledge graphs even more by incorporating additional details. The second use-case discusses how knowledge graphs can be utilized to integrate clinical and genomic datasets to provide value in the long-term preservation of data, analytics, and decision-making process. This is followed by details on how to ensure the results are accurate when integrating these heterogeneous sources in silos by using entity relationships to avoid deduplication of records along with consistency mechanisms to preserve the integrity of the results. This chapter concludes with a discussion on results and some future avenues for employing knowledge graphs within the healthcare domain. The following section looks at related work from the literature.

6.2 Related Work

Knowledge graphs are a great way to identify the relationships in healthcare services, which is why they are being used more often. Not only can they map the relationships between different data points, but they can also use machine learning to find connections. Table 6.1 summarizes some uses of knowledge graphs in healthcare.

Electronic health records (EHR) are widely used in healthcare. They are non-centralized and may have missing or poor-quality data. Capturing the data and its nuances from EHR can be very beneficial especially because it is used by a wide variety of personnel such as doctors, clinicians, nurses, and technicians. It is no surprise that knowledge graphs have been used to create

TABLE 6.1

Summary of Use of Knowledge Graphs in Healthcare

Data Type	Information Extracted
Electronic health record	Prediction and validation
	Question-answer framework
Visual genome datasets	Object detection
	Relationship detection
Drug – Target	Drug-target interaction prediction
Repositories	Data centralization

graphs from EHR which relate symptoms to diseases [6]. This overcomes the challenge of mapping relationships and complex biological concepts from structured and heterogeneous data.

A knowledge graph-based question-and-answer framework for EHR has also been developed which is an intelligent EHR agent answering questions from users [7]. This makes the EHR data more centralized. It also helps overcome the use of non-central medical standards by providing a more accessible and unified view. Knowledge graphs have also been used to predict and validate unknown adverse drug reactions from EHR [8]. This is beneficial when trying out new drugs by mapping relationships and complex biological concepts. Knowledge graphs have been applied to other areas of healthcare besides EHR. Object detection and relationship detection in biomedical images is important for diagnosis and treatment. Objects in image detection have used knowledge graphs to infer relationships between semantic objects detected using images (i.e., visual relationship detection) from visual genome datasets [9].

Drugs can have beneficial as well as harmful effects on their targets. It is important to make a prediction of the effect before a drug is given. Also, it is vital to verify the effect on real data. In order to understand the effects of a drug on a target, drug-target interaction predictions have also made use of knowledge graphs to quickly predict and verify the effects of drugs [10].

Rich repositories of information are found scattered across the different fields of biomedicine. Centralizing and extracting meaningful information from these can be very beneficial. Knowledge graphs provide a way of doing this. A knowledge base for biomedical sciences called KnowLife has been developed [11]. It uses distant supervision of pattern-based extractions of data from different sources. It then uses these patterns for automated and scalable knowledge base construction.

The use of knowledge graphs in healthcare is fairly new. The next section looks at two uses-cases that can employ knowledge graphs.

6.3 Proposed Methodology

The relationships between the genomic and clinical datasets can be easily represented as graphs using nodes and edges. Biological concepts such as genes and chromosomes can be organized with relative modesty using taxonomical hierarchies and, in turn, giving us knowledge graphs. This gives immediate benefits in terms of the knowledge which can be extracted from the datasets using graph algorithms and machine learning techniques. Furthermore, exploiting knowledge graphs for decision-making processes based on the provenance of datasets provides a deeper understanding and knowledge of the processes involved and generates trust in the results.

6.3.1 Use-Case 1: Knowledge Graph in Genomics to Organize Genomic Data for Easy Access and Analysis

Knowledge graphs can support analytics in the field of genomics. They can be employed for mapping relationships between heterogeneity and structure of healthcare data. To do this, taxonomies and ontologies are used to organize data as knowledge graphs. Graphs have been known to provide a unified representation of the human genome and its variations [12].

The reference genome comes from the file type FAST-All (commonly known as FASTA), which is an accepted standard in bioinformatics for representing nucleotide or protein sequences. As shown in Figure 6.1, the file contains the sequence of the genome as single-letter codes representing the nucleotides within the genome. These nucleotides appear in the same sequence as they are present in the chemical structure of the genome. The file begins with a '>' sign followed by a short description of the sequence. The rest of the lines under this are the nucleotides represented by the codes 'A,' 'C,' 'G,' and 'T.'

To generate a graph of the reference genome, the information is extracted from the FASTA file as three types of entities, 'reference genome,' 'chromosome,' and 'nucleotide.' These entities are presented as nodes with properties in a graph as shown in the schema in Figure 6.2. There are three types of relationships between these nodes. The relationship between the 'reference genome' node (with property 'Version') and the 'chromosome' node (with property 'Number') is 'HAS.' Similarly, the relationship between the 'chromosome' node and the 'nucleotide' node (with property 'Position') is 'HAS.' The relationship between the 'nucleotide' nodes is 'NEXT' indicating the sequence of appearance within the genome. Intuitively, the graph schema in Figure 6.2 can be read as: 'the Reference Genome' with a version number 'GRChxx' has Chromosome number x which contains the 'nucleotide' at Position x. Furthermore, the nucleotides are arranged in a sequence indicated by the 'NEXT' relationship between the nucleotide nodes.

```
>Hypothetical Sequence
ACGTGCGCGTAGCGGCATGCGAGGCGATGCGAGCTGCGCAGTCGCATACGACGTGCGCGTAGCGGCATGCGA
GGCGATGCGAGCTGCGCAGTCGCATACGACGTGCGCGTAGCGGCATGCGAGGCGATGCGAGCTGCGCAGTCG
CATACGACGTGCGCGTAGCGGCATGCGAGGCGATGCGAGCTGCGCAGTCGCATACGACGTGCGCGTAGCGGC
ATGCGAGGCGATGCGAGCTGCGCAGTCGCATACGACGTGCGCGTAGCGGCATGCGAGGCGATGCGAGCTGCG
CAGTCGCATACGACGTGCGCGTAGCGGCATGCGAGGCGATGCGAGCTGCGCAGTCGCATACGACGTGCGCGT
AGCGGCATGCGAGGCGATGCGAGCTGCGCAGTCGCATACGACGTGCGCGTAGCGGCATGCGAGGCGATGCGA
GCTGCGCAGTCGCATACGACGTGCGCGTAGCGGCATGCGAGGCGATGCGAGCTGCGCAGTCGCATACGACGT
GCGCGTAGCGGCATGCGAGGCGATGCGAGCTGCGCAGTCGCATACGACGTGCGCGTAGCGGCATGCGAGGCG
ATGCGAGCTGCGCAGTCGCATACGACGTGCGCGTAGCGGCATGCGAGGCGATGCGAGCTGCGCAGTCGCATA
CGACGTGCGCGTAGCGGCATGCGAGGCGATGCGAGCTGCGCAGTCGCATACG
```

FIGURE 6.1
Example of FASTA file.

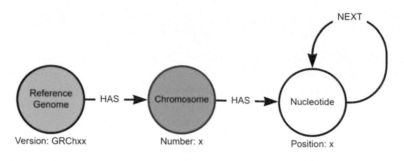

FIGURE 6.2
Graph schema of the reference genome.

With this graph model as a base, further information from other data sources can now be mapped onto this graph. One such data source is the VCF (Variant Call Format) file. The VCF file contains variations discovered from the variant call process which aligns the sample genome to a reference genome, identifies the differences, and writes these as variations to the VCF file. The VCF file is a standardized file and has two parts – a header section and a data section. The header section contains the meta-information about the data in the data section. The data section is tab delimited and is divided into eight mandatory columns as can be seen in Figure 6.3.

Each row represents one variant with the corresponding information about it arranged into columns. Each variation (or row) in the VCF file can be mapped to the graph model of a reference genome modeled above by using the chromosome (CHROM), Position (POS), Reference (REF), and Alternate

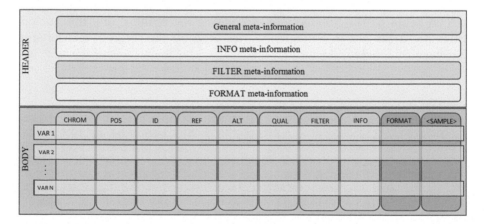

FIGURE 6.3
Structure of the VCF file. (Reproduced from Aizad, S., & Anjum, A. (2019, August). Graph Data Modelling for Genomic Variants. In 2019 IEEE SmartWorld, Ubiquitous Intelligence & Computing, Advanced & Trusted Computing, Scalable Computing & Communications, Cloud & Big Data Computing, Internet of People and Smart City Innovation (SmartWorld/ SCALCOM/UIC/ATC/CBDCom/IOP/SCI) (pp. 1577–1584). IEEE. [12].)

(ALT) columns. The reference genome version number is extracted from the header section of the VCF file.

Within the data section of the VCF, the first column reads the chromosome number on which the variation lies. The second column reads the position of the variation on this chromosome. The fourth column indicates the nucleotide(s) expected at this position on the reference genome. The fifth column reads the alternate nucleotide(s) found at the position instead of the expected nucleotide(s). The rest of the columns contain various information about the variant found. The variant can be a Single Nucleotide Polymorph (SNP) or a Structural Variant. An SNP can be a mutation of the kind of substitution, deletion, or insertion. The VCF file also allows multiple alleles at a given position. This means that there can be more than one variant present at a given position.

The SNP mutations were mapped onto the reference genome by [12]. Additional nodes were added to the graph of the reference genome (explained above) by finding the position on the chromosome and creating relations between them. Figure 6.4 shows a snapshot of a VCF file. The lines starting with ## belong to the header section. The data section begins with the line starting with #. This line contains the labels of the columns. The rest of the file contains the variations as rows.

The first variation row in Figure 6.4 shows a substitution, the second row shows an insertion, and the third row shows a deletion. These are mapped onto the reference genome graph at the corresponding positions.

Figure 6.5 shows the substitution row in Figure 6.4 mapped to the reference genome graph. A single nucleotide in the reference genome is replaced by another single nucleotide. This is shown as a new variant node being created at the position this change has occurred. The relationships between the variant nodes at the reference node show the alternate path that can be traversed to reach this variation from the reference genome graph.

Figure 6.6 models the insertion row in Figure 6.4 mapped to the reference genome graph where more than one nucleotide is added to the reference genome at the indicated position. Several new variant nodes are added

```
##fileformat=VCFv4.1
##FILTER=<ID=PASS,Description="All filters passed">
##fileDate=20150218
##reference=ftp://ftp.1000genomes.ebi.ac.uk//vol1/ftp/technical/reference/
phase2_reference_assembly_sequence/hs37d5.fa.gz
##source=1000GenomesPhase3Pipeline
##contig=<ID=1,assembly=b37,length=249250621>
#CHROM POS ID REF ALT QUAL FILTER INFO
1    15274    rs62636497  A    G    100 PASS
AC=1739,3210;AF=0.347244,0.640974;AN=5008;NS=2504;DP=23255;EAS_AF=0.4812,0.5188;AMR_AF=0.2752
1    15274    rs62636497  C    CGG 100 PASS
AC=1739,3210;AF=0.347244,0.640974;AN=5008;NS=2504;DP=23255;EAS_AF=0.4812,0.5188;AMR_AF=0.2752
1    104118   rs566244561 CAC  C    100 PASS
AC=1;AF=0.000199681;AN=5008;NS=2504;DP=26384;EAS_AF=0;AMR_AF=0;AFR_AF=0.0008;EUR_AF=0;SAS_AF=
X    195405   .    C    CAA,CAAA,CAAAA 100 PASS
AC=30,27,47;AF=0.00599042,0.00539137,0.00938498;AN=5008;NS=2504;DP=16961;AMR_AF=0.0072,0.0058
```

FIGURE 6.4
VCF records from VCF file.

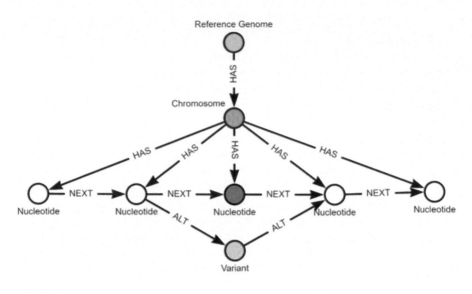

FIGURE 6.5
Substitution mutations mapped to the reference genome.

to the reference genome graph at the given position. The relationships between the variant nodes and the reference nodes show the alternate path created to reach this variation from the genome graph. The relationships between the variant nodes show the order in which they are connected to each other.

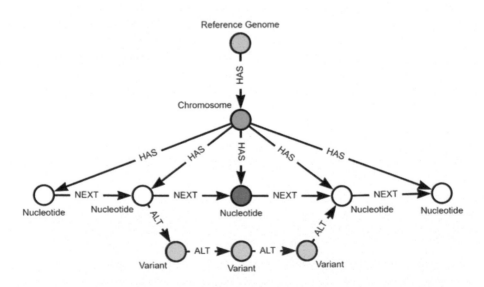

FIGURE 6.6
Insertion mutations mapped to the reference genome.

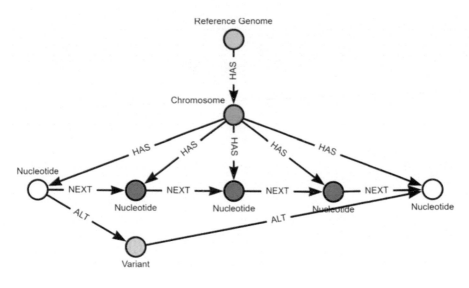

FIGURE 6.7
Deletion mutations mapped to the reference genome.

Figure 6.7 depicts the deletion row in Figure 6.4 mapped to the reference genome graph. One or more of the reference nucleotides are missing. A single variant node is added to represent the deletion. It is connected to the reference genome nodes by a relationship which connects to a position after the missing nucleotides.

As can be seen from the examples above, it becomes relatively easy to organize genome data. Chromosomes, nucleotides, and variants are taxonomies within this knowledge graph as they are using basic constructs of categories and hierarchical relationships. Ontologies can be used to further represent collections of data. For example, genes can be added to the knowledge graph. To show how this can be done, let's look at Chromosome 21, which is the smallest human autosome chromosome. It is made up of a sequence of 48 million nucleotides. There are 234 protein-coding genes associated with Chromosome 21 as estimated by the Ensembl genome database [13]. The gene called APP (Amyloid-beta precursor protein) is found on Chromosome 21 from nucleotide position 25,880,550 to nucleotide position 26,171,128. This can be mapped to the graph by creating a gene node with two relationships indicating the start and end of the gene as shown in Figure 6.8.

As can be seen, with a relatively modest organization of data using taxonomical hierarchies, we get immediate benefits in terms of the knowledge that can be extracted. Multiple hierarchies can be dynamically layered on top of data. For example, the gene APP on Chromosome 21 is attributed to Alzheimer's disease. There are other genes associated with this disease, but they are found on different chromosomes. These can be linked together by

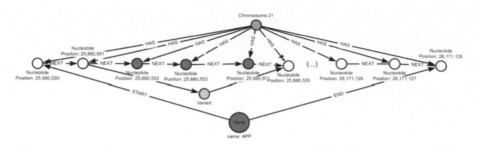

FIGURE 6.8
Gene ontology on the knowledge graph.

adding a disease hierarchy by creating a disease node and linking it to the genes associated with this disease. This is shown in Figure 6.9.

In the knowledge graph described above, genes and diseases can be described as ontologies or classification schemes which describe the categories of data and the relationships between them. However, these are biological concepts and cannot be restricted to just being hierarchical structures looking at broader to narrower views. These ontologies allow us to define the complex relationships between the different categories such as 'gene is part of a chromosome,' 'disease has genes associated with it,' etc. If need be, they also allow us to define the hierarchy of relationships for further classification (e.g., symmetrical relationships).

The benefit of using knowledge graphs for these biological concepts is that ontologies are built on top of already present data, so they are modular in nature. This makes them composable allowing each layer to be queried independently. They also allow for looking at data across categories and hierarchies giving us the ability to carry out studies across domains. Furthermore,

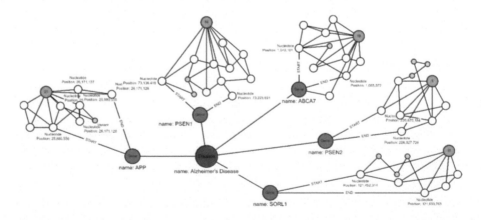

FIGURE 6.9
Disease mapped to the knowledge graph.

clinical data and treatments can also be added to this knowledge graph, making it richer.

6.3.2 Use-Case 2: Distributed Knowledge Graphs for Scalable Integration, Analytics, and Decision-Making Process

Another avenue for knowledge graphs is the integration of clinical and genomic data sources in silos to unearth relationships and biomarkers for diseases such as colorectal cancers [14]. These diseases are becoming increasingly common among populations across Europe. The challenge with such diseases is the fact that even in this age and time they are unrecoverable. Admittedly, the diagnosis of such diseases is particularly complicated. In general terms, due to the volume and velocity of data involved to detect and analyze the conditions, it frequently involves large-scale computing infrastructures. As the challenge of volume and velocity of change increases so does the challenge of inconsistencies in integrating these data sources [15].

A prime example in a healthcare use-case to integrate various data sources to determine additional information for patients and clinicians is IBM Watson [16]. It aims to combine data from a variety of sources including but not limited to genes, chemical compounds, patents, drugs, and published studies. Inconsistencies can arise promptly as sources evolve, addition/deletion of a column, change in the column name, or merging of columns for instance [17] [20]. The consequence of inconsistencies is startling for data integration, particularly in the context of linking inaccurate records or faulty associations between data entities. This deluge of actions leads to false reports and analyses. Coupled with the volume and velocity of changes, the repercussions of inconsistencies can be very detrimental to the overall distributed system.

The fundamental guideline is to guarantee that the elements from these heterogeneous datasets address similar elements inside a knowledge base or across different knowledge bases. This can be achieved by linking and grouping. For instance, in data integration, one would like to find different records (with possible contradictions) in one or multiple databases that refer to the same object in the real world. Also, there could be multiple ways of referring to the same person or an object in text, different drug details for medicines, etc. One more illustration of it very well may be when combining two databases or cleaning a database, the user might want to decide when two records are alluding to a similar real-world entity (deduplication or potentially record linkage). In data integration, determining approximate join is significant for merging data from various sources; most frequently there won't be a one-of-a-kind key that can be utilized to join tables in dispersed databases, and the user should deduce if two records are from various databases, perhaps with various data structures, both referring to a similar entity.

In order to resolve the above-mentioned issue, entity resolution is employed within knowledge graphs to provide a true representation of integrated sets of data. Most of the prior entity resolution approaches were designed to find matches in a single source or between two sources only. In the case of a single source, the matching entities are generally put together in a disjoint cluster with the determination that any of the two entities in a cluster should not be able to match the other. Also, none of the entities in the cluster should be able to match with the other cluster. In the case of two sources, the resultant match is usually a set of binary mappings that consist of pairs of matching entities commonly known as links or match correspondence. As a basic scenario, these binary match mappings can be further post-processed to decide clusters of matching entities for example by calculating the transitive closure of the correspondence (Connected Components – CC) and other clustering approaches. This work extends this approach by enabling support for more than two sources by first generating a summary graph using binary match links among the entities and then clustering these matching entities within the summary graph. A similar use of a summary graph has been considered in [18, 19].

As shown in Figure 6.10, the data sources are first converted into graphs in stage 1, followed by populating these graphs with data within stage 2 referred to as the Unified Graph Generator. Distributed Entity Resolution is then employed to generate a summary graph in stage 3 where preprocessing of the summary graph is carried out for property values required for similarity computation are normalized. Stage 4 follows the initial clustering and decomposition of clusters based on Group-by and Similarity-based clusters. Eventually, stage 5 ensures that the summarized graph generates attributed clusters to integrate the sources as these evolve. Stage 6 finally ensures that these entities are consistent with the changes that occurred over the sources before pushing them over to the clinical data warehouse for long-term preservation

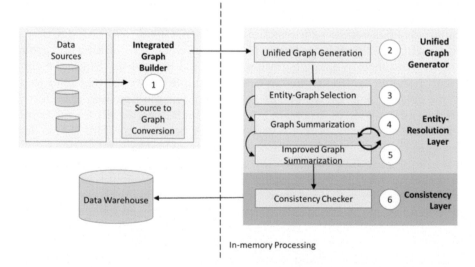

FIGURE 6.10
Data model to integrate heterogenous sources as knowledge graphs.

of data and reporting. Stages 2–6 are performed in-memory to speed up the process of integrating knowledge graphs and resolution of deduplication of records as passed on from data sources during the integration. This assists in providing the necessary performance guarantees as well as the accuracy required in the generation and integration of knowledge graphs.

6.4 Results and Discussion

The two use-cases of knowledge graphs in healthcare above help organize data in a centralized way, distribute the graphs for processing, and provide storage solutions in a data warehouse. They allow for the integration of genomic data with clinical data to get more meaningful insights. They allow quick access to data by making processing quicker by distribution. They also check for consistency, so no data is missing, allowing for a better quality of analysis and reporting.

Use-case 1 extracts data from heterogeneous data sources and uses biological concepts to define ontologies and taxonomies which help organize the data in a graph. The graph can easily be traversed and data at any node can be quickly retrieved. The data is more centralized and organized. It eliminates the need to look at different data sources to get information. It acts as a knowledge base for the diseases, linking them to genomic datasets.

Use-case 2 integrates the data from different data sources while ensuring that it is consistent and there is no data loss at any stage. It uses in-memory to speed up the process in addition to performing the tasks in a distributed environment for quicker processing. It provides a solution of consistent data integration in near to real-time for report generation and analyses.

Both the use-cases show how powerful knowledge graphs are in the field of healthcare and can be beneficial for data analysis.

References

[1] Sheth, A., Padhee, S., & Gyrard, A. (2019). Knowledge graphs and knowledge networks: The story in brief. *IEEE Internet Computing*, 23(4), 67–75.

[2] Ehrlinger, L., & Wöß, W. (2016). Towards a definition of knowledge graphs. *SEMANTiCS (Posters, Demos, SuCCESS)*, 48(1–4), 2.

[3] Raghupathi, W., & Raghupathi, V. (2014). Big data analytics in healthcare: Promise and potential. *Health Information Science and Systems*, 2(1), 1–10.

[4] Subhani, M. M., Anjum, A., Koop, A., & Antonopoulos, N. (2016, December). Clinical and genomics data integration using meta-dimensional approach. In *2016 IEEE/ACM 9th International Conference on Utility and Cloud Computing (UCC)* (pp. 416–421). IEEE.

[5] Zhang, Y., Sheng, M., Zhou, R., Wang, Y., Han, G., Zhang, H., ... & Dong, J. (2020). HKGB: An inclusive, extensible, intelligent, semi-auto-constructed knowledge graph framework for healthcare with clinicians' expertise incorporated. *Information Processing & Management*, 57(6), 102324.

[6] Rotmensch, M., Halpern, Y., Tlimat, A., Horng, S., & Sontag, D. (2017). Learning a health knowledge graph from electronic medical records. *Scientific Reports*, 7(1), 1–11.

[7] Park, J., Cho, Y., Lee, H., Choo, J., & Choi, E. (2021, October). Knowledge graph-based question answering with electronic health records. In Machine Learning for Healthcare Conference (pp. 36–53). PMLR.

[8] Bean, D. M., Wu, H., Iqbal, E., Dzahini, O., Ibrahim, Z. M., Broadbent, M., ... & Dobson, R. J. (2017). Knowledge graph prediction of unknown adverse drug reactions and validation in electronic health records. *Scientific Reports*, 7(1), 1–11.

[9] Chen, T., Yu, W., Chen, R., & Lin, L. (2019). Knowledge-embedded routing network for scene graph generation. In Proceedings of the IEEE/CVF Conference on Computer Vision and Pattern Recognition (pp. 6163–6171).

[10] Mohamed, S. K., Nováček, V., & Nounu, A. (2020). Discovering protein drug targets using knowledge graph embeddings. *Bioinformatics*, 36(2), 603–610.

[11] Ernst, P., Siu, A., & Weikum, G. (2015). Knowlife: A versatile approach for constructing a large knowledge graph for biomedical sciences. *BMC Bioinformatics*, 16(1), 1–13.

[12] Aizad, S., & Anjum, A. (2019, August). Graph Data Modelling for Genomic Variants. In 2019 IEEE SmartWorld, Ubiquitous Intelligence & Computing, Advanced & Trusted Computing, Scalable Computing & Communications, Cloud & Big Data Computing, Internet of People and Smart City Innovation (SmartWorld/SCALCOM/UIC/ATC/CBDCom/IOP/SCI) (pp. 1577–1584). IEEE.

[13] Ensembl database. https://www.ensembl.org/

[14] Mihaylov, I., Kańduła, M., Krachunov, M., & Vassilev, D. (2019). A novel framework for horizontal and vertical data integration in cancer studies with application to survival time prediction models. *Biology Direct*, 14(1), 1–17.

[15] Tripathi, D., & Joshi, N. K. (2019, February). Towards introducing and verifying heterogeneous data integration model for cloud. In Proceedings of International Conference on Sustainable Computing in Science, Technology and Management (SUSCOM), Amity University Rajasthan, Jaipur, India.

[16] Chen, Y., Argentinis, J. E., & Weber, G. (2016). IBM Watson: How cognitive computing can be applied to big data challenges in life sciences research. *Clinical Therapeutics*, 38(4), 688–701.

[17] Arshad, B., & Anjum, A. (2019, December). High performance dynamic graph model for consistent data integration. In Proceedings of the 12th IEEE/ACM International Conference on Utility and Cloud Computing (pp. 263–272).

[18] Pershina, M., Yakout, M., & Chakrabarti, K. (2015, October). Holistic entity matching across knowledge graphs. In 2015 IEEE International Conference on Big Data (Big Data) (pp. 1585–1590). IEEE.

[19] Saeedi, A., Nentwig, M., Peukert, E., & Rahm, E. (2018). Scalable matching and clustering of entities with FAMER.*Complex Systems Informatics and Modeling Quarterly*, 16, 61–83.

[20] Arshad, B. (2022, October). Graph-based data integration for system integrity and scalable analytics. PhD diss., University of Derby.

7

Explainable Machine Learning-Based Knowledge Graph for Modeling Location-Based Recreational Services from Users Profile

**Daniel Ekpenyong Asuquo[a,b], Patience Usoro Usip[b],
and Kingsley Friday Attai[c]**

[a]TETFund Center of Excellence in Computational Intelligence Research,
University of Uyo, Nigeria

[b]Department of Computer Science, Faculty of Science, University of Uyo, Nigeria

[c]Department of Mathematics and Computer Science, Ritman University, Nigeria

CONTENTS

7.1 Introduction

An interconnected structure of web contents, which provides access to a huge collection of web pages containing graphics, text, audio, and video using hyperlinks, is known as World Wide Web (WWW). Most web resources are unstructured, making information extraction an intricate task, which led the WWW consortium (W3C) to develop a technology to support "web of data," known as the semantic web. Semantic web is an effort to label and connect web content in a way that makes it significant to systems. This ensures that the delineated and connected web contents are more meaningful to machines compared to previously known "web of documents."

It has been established that data is not information, and information is not yet knowledge (Mohajan, 2016). To structure the huge array of information to a more meaningful format that machines can easily process, the concept of ontology was introduced (Ortíz-Rodriguez et al., 2022a). Ahmed and Gerhard (2010) define ontology as the assemblage of interrelated semantic-based concepts, which depend on a limited set of terms. Ontologies provide an inclusive description of a particular domain and are efficient because they present reusable knowledge representation and improve the knowledge about a domain. On the other hand, knowledge graph (KG) acquires and integrates information in ontology by using a reasoner to derive new knowledge. Thus, with KG, a better functional knowledge management system can be developed to enable semantic content classification, contextual search, and a more precise relevancy calculation.

A KG, also known as semantic network, describes a network of real-world objects and the relationship between them. Information is typically stored in a graph database and visualized as a graph structure, prompting the phrase "knowledge graph." Hahn and Vertan (2005) reviewed semantic web technologies, their impact on the multilingual web, and the mechanisms for enhancing the quality of online translation systems. The authors argued that the vast amount of information available in the WWW makes it difficult to retrieve needed information using the standard keyword or lexical search approach. Thus, a standard semantic representation with ontologies and inferences among ontology objects is required.

The idea is that semantic web facilitates the existence of a systematic conceptual description of facts or the availability of a domain with the relations between entities. With this in place, any information provider can use ontology to represent information and illustrate the content with possibilities to map user query on the ontology. Consequently, an ontology developed by domain specialists, encoded in a standard web ontology language (OWL), is highly necessary and required. The text described semantically in a resource description framework (RDF) can be annotated and linked in the ontology. A searching machine on the server can compare the RDF annotated text and the query with the OWL-ontology and retrieve appropriate information, especially in cases where lexical search proves ineffective.

Customer 360 initiatives or Know Your Customer (KYC) uses linked and holistic views of the customer, enriched with contextual information, to develop personalized communication and make informed decisions. KGs automatically generate unified views of heterogeneous data sources, providing reusable datasets for analytics platforms or training machine learning (ML)

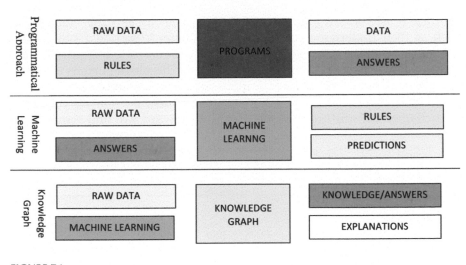

FIGURE 7.1
Toward eXplainable AI.

algorithms. On this basis, advanced applications for knowledge discovery, data, and content analytics can then be developed using a semantic layer. Figure 7.1 shows the developmental efforts toward eXplainable AI (XAI). It reveals that even though data scientists use traditional ML, knowledge scientists are the ones who deal with semantic AI and XAI efforts and are involved in the entire KG life cycle.

Recreation is a vital part of every human life, with different varieties shaped naturally by individual interests and the surrounding acceptable practice. It could be active or passive, outdoors or indoors, communal or solitary. Research indicates that access to exercise and leisure facilities may help to reduce the risk of obesity and other related health problems. Residents and tourists can improve their physical activity levels with a good exercise infrastructure. According to Ortíz-Rodriguez et al. (2022b), although government services target all citizens, most of its physical and technology-based services do not cover all people. This chapter presents a framework based on KG and ontology with ML technique to provide semantic context for knowledge sharing and context reasoning. The developed recreational facility KG supports pervasive context-aware AI applications where recommendations can be made to mobile users requesting recreational services such as gym, sports, live shows, café, parks, or health/beauty shops. The deployment of this framework can demonstrate the benefits of integrating KGs and ML to improve automatic reasoning, ontology enrichment, context-aware service delivery, data interpretability, and reusability.

The rest of this chapter is structured as follows. Section 7.2 presents related works on ontology, KG and multilingual semantic web, as well as ML-assisted KG generation and refinements with observed performance metrics. It also reviews the main XAI approaches in existing literature as well as their underlying strengths and limitations. Section 7.3 highlights components of the proposed ML-based KG framework and presents the developed recreational facility KG. Section 7.4 discusses current trends in the semantic web and KG applications, open issues and major research challenges of semantic web adoption. In contrast, Section 7.5 concludes this chapter with future research directions toward ML and semantic AI approaches with KG.

7.2 Related Works

This section reviews related literature on semantic web technologies, multilingualism in semantic web, ontology development, ML and KG, RDF and OWL. The connections and AI applications of semantic web to other disciplines including open issues and research challenges are also presented.

7.2.1 Semantic Web Languages

Tim Berners-Lee, an inventor of WWW, published an article in 2001 with James Hendler and OraLassila, promoting the semantic web concept. In 2006, Tim Berners-Lee, Nigel Shadbolt, and Wendy Hall outlined developments, methodologies, techniques, and challenges of the semantic web. Shadbolt et al. (2006) identified the need for data integration in semantic web. Berners-Lee et al. (2001) pointed out that semantic web facilitates the growth of the existing web of documents, where information is assigned precise denotation to enhance cooperation and understanding between tasks performed by computers and people. According to Ahmed and Gerhard (2010), semantic web is an intelligent improvement in WWW to gather, analyze, annotate, and present information in a machine-readable format for classification and consistent access to resources. Such structured information allows programs to interact easily with the web, enabling intelligent agents or software agents – which are autonomous computer programs that perform a task in place of humans, to automate tasks which will significantly augment the online experience.

In summary, there are numerous applications of semantic web in Healthcare (Abatal et al., 2018; Dissanayake et al., 2020), Internet of Things (Andročec et al., 2018; Antoniazzi and Viola, 2019; Corno et al., 2017; Lanza et al., 2019), Urban Traffic (Tan et al., 2021), Surveying and Remote Sensing (Hao et al., 2021), Education, Research, and Industry (Feldmann et al., 2016; Pauwels et al., 2017). The diverse areas of the application and interoperability of semantic web provide easy and timely access to accurate information that can help in critical decision-making processes.

7.2.2 Multilingual Semantic Web

A multilingual semantic web ensures that web resources are organized and delivered in a machine-readable format regardless of the language. Gracia et al. (2012) reported that though the web of data contains several kinds of information in numerous languages, it lacks specific means to spontaneously resolve such information when communicated in different languages. This raises new concerns, including the necessity to deal with information expressed in diverse natural languages because data communicated in a particular language are not always accessible to those who speak other languages. They proposed a set of explicit approaches to implement multilingual access, such as ontology mapping, localization, and cross-lingual ontology-based information access and presentation.

Multilingualism is an essential concern, and addressing it on semantic web could significantly improve access to knowledge and data (Ehrmann et al., 2014). According to Hahn and Vertan (2005), deploying multilingualism in semantic web can transform websites, improve knowledge management, and internationalized communication base for industry and commerce. Multilingual semantic web's major challenge is ontology localization (Espinoza et al., 2009; Gracia et al., 2012; León-Araúz and Faber, 2014), which requires an ontology to be translated to specific language and culture (Suárez-Figueroa and Gómez-Pérez, 2008). Adjusting ontology to suit different cultural contexts especially linking up web documents in different languages will be a significant advancement in the multilingual semantic web. By so doing, the multilingual web of data can be understood as a layer of resources with services placed above the current linked data infrastructure (Gracia et al., 2012). Consequently, it can add information for vocabularies and data in different languages, map between data with labels in these languages, provide services to gain access, and navigate linked data across them.

7.2.3 Ontology

Gruber (1995) describes ontology development as the task of specifying concepts in order to assist software agents and humans share meaningful knowledge. According to Asikri et al. (2017), people, applications, and databases can utilize ontology to enhance domain information sharing. Ontology explains the terms used to illustrate and represent a sphere of knowledge. It ensures that knowledge about a specific domain or several domains is properly represented. The two major interests of ontologies in Lamy (2016) are that they can be applied to perform logical inferences for inferring new facts and connect numerous chunks of knowledge from distinct ontologies in the semantic web.

Authorized languages for ontology representation includes, OWL, RDF Schema language (RDFS), and Open Biomedical Ontologies format (OBO).

Ontology can be categorized into domain ontology (DO), natural language ontology (NLO), and Ontology Instance (OI). NLO considers ontology as part of both natural language semantics and metaphysics (Moltmann, 2020). DO, as the name implies, is the presentation of domain-specific concepts. DO can define a semantic model of the data merged with the associated domain knowledge, and OI generates automatic object-based web pages (Ahmed and Gerhard, 2010). The fields in which ontology can be applied include medicine, e-science, organizing complex and semi-structured information, military/government, social media analysis, semantic web, and semantic grid (Mohan and Venkataraman, 2017). A class is the main component of ontology. Classes are structured with "is-a" relations. The task of defining excellent class hierarchy for a knowledge base in order to permit efficient access from numerous AI tools including information retrieval and natural language processing (NLP) is challenging. Moreover, to manually organize a class hierarchy for a distinct KG is very tedious and costly. Gupta et al. (2016) and Velardi et al. (2013) proposed the automatic extraction of class hierarchies when dealing with extensive automatically acquired knowledge bases.

7.2.4 Resource Description Framework and OWL

RDF is simply a framework that aids resource description. It is a language created to support knowledge representation on the semantic web (Gibbins and Shadbolt, 2010; Powers, 2003). RDF is the structure or data model for linked data. It provides useful facilities that aid data merging and interchange on the web, despite diverse underlying schemas (Jevsikova et al., 2017; Mitchell, 2013). Its emergence is aimed at providing a logical infrastructure for sharing, querying, and publishing organized data. However, the accomplishment of RDF and semantic web depends on the availability of applications that verify the appropriateness of concepts and programming interfaces that permit such applications development, as well as databases and inference systems that manipulate RDF to classify and retrieve significant web resources.

Ristoski (2019) formally defined an RDF graph as a labeled graph G = (V, E), where V and E denote a set of vertices and a set of directed edges, respectively. Typically, a unique identifier identifies each vertex, and every edge is labeled from a defined set of edge labels. The fundamental unit of knowledge representation in RDF is the triple <subject, predicate, object>, where the subject and object make up the nodes of a graph, and the predicate specifies how the subject and object are related. The web of data constitutes directed labeled graphs, and these semantic graphs depend on the three-way structure, targeting syntactic as well as semantic description of information, to become reusable by systems and humans (Bizer et al., 2011; Faith and Chrzanowski, 2015; Gibbins and Shadbolt, 2010; Petrova, 2019). Thus, RDF, shown in Figure 7.2a–c, arranges knowledge in statements, associating two entities in a directed labeled KG by an edge, Alternatively, an RDF

(a) RDF, as directed, labelled KG

:Mobile_Device   : User   :Content_Provider

(b) RDF as a triple <subject, predicate, object>

User(Mobile_Device, Content_Provider)

(c) RDF as binary predicates

FIGURE 7.2
Examples of RDF statement.

statement can also be expressed as consisting of a subject, a predicate, and an object or as binary predicates. Although there are different formal languages to ensure the RDF model, Extensible Markup Language (XML) is the most appropriate for the semantic web.

However, RDF modeling alone is insufficient for the semantic web as no information is given between the numerous predicates. For instance, there is a need for language that gives the main aspects by which classes, sub-classes, properties, and sub-properties can be illustrated. Consequently, OWL was designed as a stand-alone language for ontology description (Bechhofer et al., 2004). OWL has exchange syntax with RDF/XML and a number of OWL expressions with modeled inference rules create a knowledge base.

7.2.4.1 Ontology and Multilingualism in Semantic Web

According to Hahn and Vertan (2005), web data's multilingual character should be considered when building ontological meta-data. They observed that the documents on the web written in languages other than English have vividly increased in recent years with a rising interest in German, French, and Japanese, amid others. However, the difficulty in designing ontologies with multilingual instances is that words in a specific language frequently project concepts within the ontology and lack one-to-one mapping to the meaning in other languages. Vertan (2004) proposed a framework that can extract translation correspondences, keeping in mind their annotations in RDF. The semantic web is naturally believed to be language-independent, such that information is provided with explicit meaning through properly defined ontologies built on standard representation languages. Consequently, the commanding importance of the semantic web cannot be overemphasized, given the great opportunity it offers to ensure that web information are generally accessible and independent of native language and culture. The primary challenge in constructing a "multilingual semantic web" is to link the information needs of users in a specific language with the language-independent content of the web.

7.2.5 Linked Open Data

Semantic web KGs are the foundation of countless information systems requiring structured knowledge access. Such KGs contain unbiased knowledge about real-world entities and the relations between them, usable in diverse data mining applications including NLP and information retrieval. KGs are widely accessible as linked open data – a linked assemblage of datasets in machine-readable format that handle major real-world entities (Schmachtenberg et al., 2014). Bizer et al. (2011) define linked data as a collection of best practices for connecting and publishing structured RDF data (Manola et al., 2004) via a uniform resource locator (URL) on the web. Linked data guarantees that the corresponding data are in a format that can easily be interpreted by machines and accessible by people on the web. This transforms the web into a "global database" where resources from various sites and interrelated knowledge can be retrieved or extracted by the use of developed AI applications. According to Faith and Chrzanowski (2015), linked data provides an avenue for integrating many people with meaningful information. McCrae et al. (2015) presented recently developed tools that can be used to create and publish language resources as linked data for multilingual access. The authors assert that linked data enables excellent data integration which allow semantic web to characterize data categories and facilitate improved resource interoperability.

7.2.6 ML and Knowledge Graph

Although, a generally accepted definition of the term "knowledge graph" does not exist (Ehrlinger and Wöß, 2016), the characteristics expressed in Paulheim (2016) indicate that it represents domain entities with the relations between them as a graph. Google coined the term when it introduced its KG in 2012 as a structure of a new web search strategy to migrate from ordinary text processing to a symbolic knowledge representation. KG collects and put together information in ontology before applying a reasoner to derive new knowledge (Ehrlinger and Wöß, 2016; Ji et al., 2022). The graph is constructed by representing entities as nodes and connecting them via edges or relations (Duan et al., 2018). According to Chen et al. (2018), a KG acts as an integrated information repository, interconnecting varied data out of diverse disciplines. When effectively organized to represent knowledge, it can be utilized in advanced applications to provide semantics to textual information (Chen et al., 2020; Duan et al., 2018). Nevertheless, Chen et al. (2019) and Wang et al. (2021) assert that the quality of KG can be evaluated to enhance its performance in terms of accuracy, timeliness, worthiness, completeness, consistency, interpretability, robustness, availability, etc. This evaluation is necessary for building high-quality applications and could be achieved through detection of errors in entity types, attributes, and relations as well as local and global update of the KG.

Paulheim (2016) stated that KGs had been the structure of numerous information systems that necessitate access to domain-independent or

TABLE 7.1

The Size of Some Public Cross-Domain KGs

KG	# of Entities	# of Facts	# of Classes	# of Properties
OpenCyc	118,499	2,413,894	116,822	165
NELL	1,974,297	3,402,971	290	1,334
YAGO	5,130,031	1,435,808,056	30,765	11,053
Dbpedia	5,109,890	397,831,457	754	3,555
DbkWik	11,163,719	91,526,001	12,029	128,566
Wikidata	44,077,901	1,633,309,138	30,765	11,053
WebIsALOD	212,184,968	400,533,808	–	1

domain-specific structured knowledge. The author identified DBpedia (Auer et al., 2007) and Wikidata (Vrandečić and Krötzsch, 2014) as large-scale cross-domain KGs that are mostly used datasets for semantic web as well as the use of ML algorithms to improve KG tasks in recommender systems. Other well-known public KGs include YAGO (Suchanek et al., 2007); OpenCyc (Färber et al., 2015), which was shut down in 2017, Freebase, acquired by Google and shut down in 2015; NELL, DBkWik, and WebIsALOD. Nevertheless, some company-owned KGs seem to lack the capability for in-depth analysis and are considered not suitable for developing applications by the public. They include Yahoo's KG, Google's Knowledge Vault, Google KG, Microsoft's Satori, and Facebook's KG. Table 7.1 summarizes the features of the afore-mentioned KGs. The table describes the size of each KG and presents the number of entities, relations, classes, and properties. A class, in a KG, refers to a category of entities while property refers to a category of relations. For example, Organization, Country, City, Person, etc. are classes that may form hierarchies while height, birth date, etc. are properties.

KGs provide the following summarized goals: use of data for automatic reasoning; higher data quality; better interpretability of data and content; reusability of data; automated processes for networking and analyzing data; finding relevant data, personalizing and contextualizing it.

After decades of developing KGs, the discipline has also been influenced by many other knowledge domains, including mathematical logic, graph theory, information retrieval, computational linguistics, knowledge representation, reasoning, and, most recently, semantic web and ML. Some application scenarios of KGs include

- Orchestrating knowledge workflows in a collaborative setting
- Unify structured and unstructured data in a Smart Data Catalog
- Search and Analytics with KGs
- Deep Text Analytics (DTA)
- Excellent Customer Experience

Seeliger et al. (2019) reviewed current research directions on merging semantic web technologies with ML due to the latter's potential in predictive tasks and ability to proffer semantically interpretable solutions that facilitate reasoning on knowledge bases by the former. Since large-scale KGs are very difficult and challenging to create manually, ML techniques can be used to provide needed heuristics for the creation and refinement of generated KGs (Tiddi and Schlobach, 2022). They offer capabilities to fine-tune parameters and obtain optimal prediction performance using metrics like precision, accuracy, recall, area under the precision-recall curve (AUG-PR), and area under the receiver operating characteristic curve (AUC-ROC). Mainly supervised (classification) (Alirezaie et al., 2019; Che et al., 2015; Chen et al., 2018; Choi et al., 2017; Clos et al., 2017; Geng et al., 2019; Ma et al., 2018; Sarker et al., 2017; Wang et al., 2017) and unsupervised (clustering, embeddings) (Aditya et al., 2018; Ai et al., 2018; Batet et al., 2010; Bellini et al., 2018; Choi et al., 2017; Gusmão et al., 2018; Huang et al., 2018; Liao et al., 2018; Ma et al., 2019; Wang et al., 2018; Zhang et al., 2019) eXplainable ML models have been deployed with semantic expressiveness for ontology, KG, and taxonomy.

ML techniques can create, extend, or map a KG to existing ones. This could be achieved by a manually coded training set or by employing knowledge previously established in a KG for training models to enhance or authenticate existing information. While KGs are often times separately generated, it would be exciting to apply them as training data to enhance each other and allow them to cross-fertilize knowledge. However, Kotis et al. (2021) pointed out that hidden bias at different levels of graph representation in KGs is an issue that requires concern.

Recommender systems have changed how people discover and pay for services and products. The advancements in web technology and the continuous increase in online services and products have made recommender systems a valuable tool for categorization of vast amount of information. The emergence of semantic web and linked open data has also resulted in extensive application of recommender systems. KGs provide contextual information needed to extract relevant product features for enhanced recommendation results. It is possible to utilize KGs in collaborative, content-based, and hybrid techniques for diverse recommendation tasks, namely, Top-N recommendations, rating prediction, and cross-domain recommendation in content-based recommendations. Consequently, with linked open data, a much better perception and representation of user preferences, contextual signs, and item features can be created in recommender systems.

7.2.7 Context-Aware Pervasive Computing

Context plays a significant role in ubiquitous environments. According to McGrath et al. (2003), applications in pervasive environments should be context-aware to adapt themselves to the fast-changing technological landscape. Such applications utilize different context information including informational, personal, physical, environmental, application, social and system contexts, such as weather, activities and location of people, etc. Distributed infrastructure, specifically Context Toolkit (Dey, 2001), provides suitable middleware for building context-aware applications.

Pervasive computing environments comprise numerous independent entities that aid in the transformation of physical spaces into computationally active and intelligent spaces. Users, devices, services, or applications could make up these entities. Lately, improvements in middleware have permitted dissimilar entities to interact, even though the challenge to understand the "semantics" of the environment by autonomous entities still exists. This problem can be handled by semantic web technologies. Ontologies or KGs can be developed to describe different aspects of these environments to ensure those information systems are more adaptable, enabling different entities to understand numerous terms and concepts, thus, presenting seamless interaction. This will permit the discovery of entities and generation of intelligent interfaces that allow users to interact effortlessly with the entities. Typical examples include MyCampus (Sadeh et al., 2002) – an agent-based environment for context-aware mobile services – and Rcal (Payne et al., 2002) – a distributed meeting scheduling software that negotiates meeting times based on user's availability and preferences. The former uses ontologies to describe contextual attributes, user preferences, and web services but does not utilize any reasoning method to guarantee the correctness of the ontologies. The latter has a reasoning scheme that automatically integrates published schedules on semantic web into users' schedules.

7.3 ML-Based KG for Modeling Users' Profiles for Context-Aware Content Delivery

The development of adaptive and interactive systems in various domains, including recommendation tasks, has become an important driver of research in ML integration with semantic web technologies. With this combination, the prediction performance is expected to increase with higher explainability and interpretability. This work presents an ML-based KG for ontology modeling user profiles to achieve personalized recommendations or content delivery of recreational services and their geographic locations in Uyo metropolis, Akwa Ibom State (AKS), Nigeria. This work adapts the ontology in Asuquo and Usip (2018) for its KG construction. Mobile users' social role ontology was created as a sub-ontology under telecommunication service domain ontology (TSDO). It proposes the deployment of ML techniques first to train and, later, test data obtained from users' profiles and

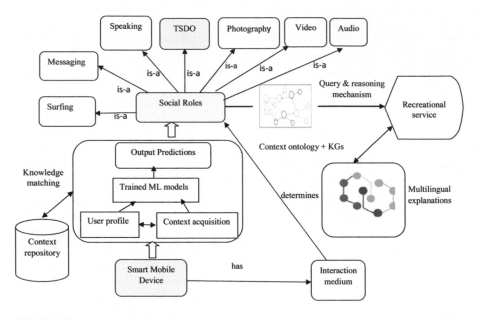

FIGURE 7.3
Proposed ML-based KG framework for constructing context-aware applications.

preferences as well as other contextual information. The output predictions from the learned models, along with the interaction medium of the smart mobile devices, are then used to determine a user's social role in some mobile service delivery. The components of the framework, shown in Figure 7.3, are explained as follows.

The Smart Mobile Device, furnished with context-aware sensors, collects a user's request and acquires the contextual information therein. During Context Acquisition, contextual information stored in the repository may be captured and managed due to their heterogeneity. Data from such requests forms inputs to the ML models for classification, clustering, and regression analysis. The Output Predictions from the ML models are used to generate Context Ontology and KGs. At the same time, the Query and Reasoning module uses inference rules to deduce new situations from semantically represented context. The Service Adaptation module permits content providers to adapt recreational services to a user's context in real time based on recommendations derived from query and reasoning mechanisms. The recommendations can be explained in diverse languages to express multilingualism.

To deduce high-level contexts from low-level ones, context ontology is utilized as input to the context processing and reasoning module. A two-tier hierarchy describes it: the general, domain-independent and the domain-dependent, application-specific levels. The first level may indicate the user's profile and preferences, activity, service requested, and device and environment-related properties. The numerous social functions a user can perform are ascertained by the competence of a particular interaction medium.

It has been debated that adequate access to exercise and recreational facilities stimulates general physical activity. Recreation is an activity of leisure. Access to these facilities may help people to engage more in exercises and recreational activities, thus, encouraging running, walking, or cycling to and from these facilities. It is also believed that the presence of a decent exercise infrastructure in the neighborhood can encourage residents to workout thus, increasing their physical activity levels. Research reveals that access to fitness facilities may help to reduce the risk of obesity, among other health challenges. While Table 7.2 presents details of 16 recreational facilities in the Uyo metropolis, Figure 7.4 shows the developed recreational facility KG, where services provided include a gym, park, sports, café, live show, bar, health/beauty shop, etc. The users of the recommendation system can also view the center name, operational hours, address, and location in terms of coordinating to access a nearby recreational center or one that provides explicit service demand. The KG also contains the center's contact information; including phone number, website, and social media handle for inquiry, advanced booking, and feedback. Our KG is generated from clarafinds.com.[1] On deployment by content providers, the proposed framework and its KG can facilitate personalized recommendations with increased prediction performance, higher explainability, interpretability, and reusability. A number of studies indicate the proficiency of KGs in discovering meaningful knowledge in a variety of domains. The emerging Graph Neural Networks (GNN) and Deep Learning (DL) can extract relations and object characteristics from KGs (Futia and Vetrò, 2020).

The KG in Figure 7.4 shows the various recreational facilities in the Uyo metropolis with services offered. Additional information, such as location with longitude and latitude and all contact details such as email, phone, address, social media links, etc., about each of the facilities can be obtained by clicking the node. Tourists will find the KG useful as filters are easily made on facilities that can provide required services. Let us consider two tourists, for example, Tourist A and Tourist B. Tourist A likes a party, hanging out, and alcohol consumption and will prefer facilities that offer park, bar, and live show services, while Tourist B is a female tourist with a medical condition who prefers facilities with gym, café, and health_and_beauty_shop as major required services as well as having a strong dislike for facilities with a live show. Filters for Tourist A and Tourist B are provided in Figures 7.5 and 7.6, respectively, with details of the facilities. The filter result shows two facilities (G-Park Global Resort and Discovery Park) for Tourist A and three facilities (Ibom Golf Resort, Ultrafit Fitness Center, and The Gym Least Pay Group) for Tourist B. With fewer results, the tourists can easily view and make their choices, making the decision-making process or task speedily and less cumbersome.

TABLE 7.2

Brief Detail of Some Recreational Facilities in Uyo Metropolis, AKS, Nigeria

Center Name	Location/ Coordinates	Operational Hours	Facilities/Services Offered						
			Gym	Sports	Live Show	Park	Health/ Beauty Shop	Cafe	Bar
Ibom Golf Resort	5.054561631878505065, 8.0377562243417846	24/7	Yes	Yes	No	Yes	Yes	Yes	Yes
Discovery Park	5.0199144197815, 7.9269767347470552	8 am–11 pm Daily	No	Yes	Yes	Yes	No	Yes	Yes
G-Park Global Resort	5.0409697431450935, 7.9096978389626066	8 am–11 pm Daily	No	No	Yes	Yes	No	Yes	Yes
Iconic Fitness Room	5.038887371889059, 7.9128577985464945	6 am–6 pm Daily	Yes	No	No	No	No	Yes	No
Metroflex Gym	5.029150007658079, 7.9329878889121968	6 am–9 pm Mon–Sat	Yes	No	No	No	No	No	No
West Itam Mini Stadium	5.048128915230136, 7.886745296634592	6am–5pm daily	No	Yes	No	Yes	No	No	No
Godswill Akpabio International Stadium	5.006492806105149, 7.884999496634551	24/7	No	Yes	No	Yes	No	No	No
Ultrafit Fitness Center	5.022212957135705, 7.9425922384139095	6:30 am–8 pm Mon–Sat	Yes	Yes	No	No	Yes	Yes	No
Truth Fitness Center	5.00918655091473, 7.928503857626108	Daily	Yes	No	No	No	No	No	No
Bubble Healthcare Pharmacy & Stores	5.000233317244198, 7.9657118676768456	Daily	No	No	No	No	Yes	No	No
The Gym Least Pay Group	5.02047964043979, 7.9227897659465755	Daily	Yes	No	No	No	Yes	Yes	Yes
Newtraford Fitness Centre	5.029909917198005, 7.949421671633873	Daily	Yes	No	No	No	Yes	Yes	Yes
Fonz Natural	5.044786774597501, 7.9235008038583175	Daily	No	No	No	No	No	No	No
Basketball and Handball Court	5.046474623542985, 7.9246682416862795	Daily	No	Yes	No	Yes	No	No	No
Green World Africa	5.028350661003441, 7.929474814856342	Daily	No	No	No	No	Yes	No	No
Lindoirs Beauty Shop	5.028099444039574, 7.9430789295971495	Daily	No	No	No	No	Yes	No	No

FIGURE 7.4
Recreational facility KG.

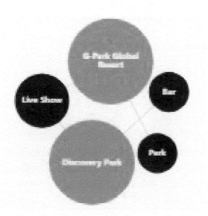

G-Park Global Resort

LOCATION/COORDINATES
5.0409697431450935, 7.909697838962606

ADDRESS
162 Ikot Ekpene Road

PHONE
+2349038438182

Discovery Park

LOCATION/COORDINATES
5.01991441978015, 7.92697673470552

ADDRESS
Obio Imoh Street by Udoumana

PHONE
+2348065188616

FIGURE 7.5
KG filter showing suitable facilities for Tourist A with details.

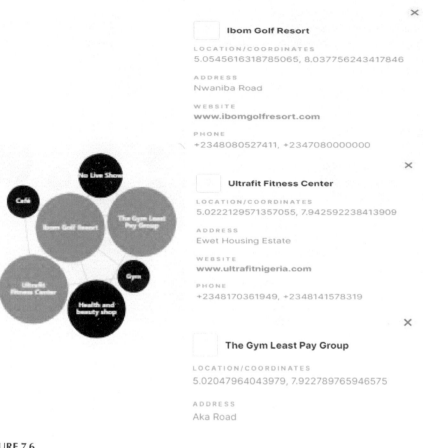

Ibom Golf Resort

LOCATION/COORDINATES
5.0545616318785065, 8.037756243417846

ADDRESS
Nwaniba Road

WEBSITE
www.ibomgolfresort.com

PHONE
+2348080527411, +2347080000000

Ultrafit Fitness Center

LOCATION/COORDINATES
5.0222129571357055, 7.942592238413909

ADDRESS
Ewet Housing Estate

WEBSITE
www.ultrafitnigeria.com

PHONE
+2348170361949, +2348141578319

The Gym Least Pay Group

LOCATION/COORDINATES
5.02047964043979, 7.922789765946575

ADDRESS
Aka Road

FIGURE 7.6
KG filter showing suitable facilities for Tourist B with details.

7.4 Challenges and Opportunities in Semantic Web

The evaluation of entity relatedness and similarity has been a difficult task especially during knowledge extraction from websites, information retrieval, and other NLP tasks. Whereas similarity solely assesses the likeness of two objects, relatedness considers an extensive array of relations. For instance, "country" as a class has two entities – "USA" and "Canada" where both possess high scores for similarity and relatedness analyses. Alternatively, "USA" and "Joe Biden" are not similar in any way but are very related. Furthermore, "Canada" and "Joe Biden" have no similarity whatsoever but have lower relatedness score. Apart from word distributions, the KG approach can effectively evaluate entities' semantic relatedness.

The literature shows six known challenges of semantic web: ontology and content availability; ontology modeling and evolving improvement; scalability of semantic web content; multilingualism; visualization; and semantic web languages standardization. It can be inferred that semantic web implementation is seriously faced by the challenges of processing and combining noisy and varied data, mismatched data models, mislaid standards, and application programming interfaces (APIs) between components. Nevertheless, large-scale KG is difficult to be created manually, making demands for the use of heuristics. Thus, ML heuristics can be applied in creating KG and refining the generated KG, but without a substitution between data volume and the resultant KG's accuracy as well as a certain level of noise.

7.5 Conclusion

Traditional content-based recommendation approaches lack sufficient information to extract users' profile and characterize every facet of their interaction with the system. Findings from our study indicate that semantic-aware content-based recommender systems that incorporate ontological knowledge can be developed to surmount the shortcomings of their traditional content-based counterparts. This implies that KGs and associated query languages can be used to discover entities, facts, and other relationships based on appropriate algorithms and node similarity metrics. To help tourists and residents in the Uyo metropolis boost their health condition and well-being, a recreational facility KG was developed to recommend centers and geographic locations (coordinates) where precise service demands like sports, gyms, cafes, live shows, and beauty shops are provided. Even though KGs are simple to understand by people, they contain complex information about specific domains that are not easy to exploit for ML tasks. As an AI paradigm driven toward creating systems that require data training, ML techniques have the potential to advance accuracy performance of many data analytic tasks.

Alternatively, KGs provide needed capability for knowledge representation about entities and the relations between them with better explanation, improved reliability, and reuse. It is believed that the integration of ML and KG can significantly improve the recommendation system's explainability, accuracy, and reuse, thereby intensifying the capabilities of ML techniques. Future work shall address the integration of heterogeneous data to build KG with a common API for multilingual visualization of context-aware recreational services in TSDO.

Acknowledgments

The authors would like to thank all the reviewers for their constructive comments and the University of Uyo for creating a conducive environment for conducting research. This research was supported by Tertiary Education Trust Fund (TETFund), through TETFUND Center of Excellence in Computational Intelligence Research, Nigeria..

Note

1 https://depot.clarafinds.com/graphs/rec-facilities/

References

Abatal A, Khallouki H, Bahaj M. "A semantic smart interconnected healthcare system using ontology and cloud computing." 2018 4th International Conference on Optimization and Applications (ICOA), Mohammedia, Morocco, 2018, pp. 1–5. https://doi.org/10.1109/ICOA.2018.8370595.

Aditya S, Yang Y, Baral C. "Explicit reasoning over end-to-end neural architectures for visual question answering." 2018 Proceedings of the AAAI Conference on Artificial Intelligence. Vol. 32, No. 1, 2018.

Ahmed Z, Gerhard D. "Role of ontology in semantic web development." *Computer Science*, 2010. https://arxiv.org/abs/1008.1723.

Ai Q, Azizi V, Chen X, Zhang Y. "Learning heterogeneous knowledge base embeddings for explainable recommendation." *Algorithms*, Vol. 11, No. 9, 2018, p. 137.

Alirezaie M, Langkvist M, Sioutis M, Lout A. "Semantic referee: a neural symbolicframework for enhancing geospatial semantic segmentation." *Semantic Web*, Vol. 10, No. 5, 2019, pp. 863–880.

Andročec D, Novak M, Oreški D. "Using semantic web for internet of things interoperability: A systematic review." *International Journal on Semantic Web and Information Systems*, Vol. 14, No. 4, 2018, https://www.doi.org/10.4018/IJSWIS.2018100108.

Antoniazzi F, Viola F. "Building the semantic web of things through a dynamic ontology." *IEEE Internet of Things Journal*, Vol. 6, No. 6, 2019, pp. 10560–10579.

Asikri ME, Krit S, Chaib H, Kabrane M, Ouadani H, Karimi K, Bendaouad K, Elbousty H. "Mining the web for learning ontologies: State of art and critical review." *International Journal of Sensors and Sensor Networks*, Vol. 5, No. 5–1, 2017, pp. 13–17. https://doi.org/10.11648/j.ijssn.s.2017050501.13.

Asuquo DE, Usip PU. "Ontology modeling of social roles of users in mobile computing environments." *Advances in Science, Technology and Engineering Systems Journal*, Vol. 3, No. 2, 2018, pp. 319–328.

Auer S, Bizer C, Kobilarov G, Lehmann J, Cyganiak R, Ives Z. "Dbpedia: anucleus for a web of open data." *The Semantic Web*, 2007, pp. 722–735, Springer, Berlin, Heidelberg.

Batet M, Valls A, Gibert K. "Performance of ontology-based semantic similarities in clustering." 2010 International Conference on Artificial Intelligence and Soft Computing, 2010, pp. 281–288, Springer, Berlin, Heidelberg.

Bechhofer S, van Harmelen F, Hendler J, Horrocks I, Mcguinness DL, Patel-Schneider PF, Stein LA. "OWL web ontology language reference." *W3C Recommendation*, Vol. 10, No. 2, 2004, pp. 1–53.

Bellini V, Schiavone A, Di Noia T, Ragone A, Di Sciascio E. "Knowledge-aware autoencoders for explainable recommender systems." Proceedings of the 3rd Workshop on Deep Learning for Recommender Systems, 2018, pp. 24–31.

Berners-Lee T, Hendler J, Lassila O. "Web semantic." *Scientific American*, Vol. 284, No. 5, 2001, pp. 28–37.

Bizer C, Heath T, Berners-Lee T. "Linked data: the story so far." In *Semantic Services, Interoperability and Web Applications: Emerging Concepts*, 2011, pp. 205–227, IGI Global, Hershey, PA.

Che Z, Kale D, Li W, Bahadori MT, Liu Y. "Deep computational phenotyping." Proceedings of the 2015 21th ACM SIGKDD International Conference on Knowledge Discovery and Data Mining, 2015, pp. 507–516.

Chen H, Cao G, Chen J, Ding J. "A practical framework for evaluating the quality of knowledge graph." *CCKS 2019, CCIS 1134*, X. Zhu et al. (eds.), 2019, pp. 111–122. https://doi.org/10.1007/978-981-15-1956-7_10.

Chen J, Lecue F, Pan JZ, Horrocks I, Chen H "Knowledge-based transfer learning explanation." 2018 16th International Conference on Principles of Knowledge Representation and Reasoning, 2018.

Chen L, Xu S, Zhu L, Guancan Y. "A deep learning based method for extracting semantic information from patent documents." *Scientometrics*, Vol. 125, No. 1, 2020, pp. 289–312. https://doi.org/10.1007/s11192-020-03634-y.

Choi E, Bahadori MT, Song L, Stewart WF, Sun J. "GRAM: Graph-based attention model for healthcare representation learning." 2017 Proceedings of the 23rd ACM SIGKDD International Conference on Knowledge Discovery and Data Mining, 2017, pp. 787–795.

Clos J, Wiratunga N, Massie S. "Towards explainable text classification by jointly learning lexicon and modifier terms." In IJCAI-17 Workshop on Explainable AI (XAI), 2017, pp.19–23.

Corno F, Russis LD, Roffarello AM. "A semantic web approach to simplifying trigger-action programming in the IoT." *Computer*, Vol. 50, No. 11, 2017. https://www.doi.org/10.1109/MC.2017.4041355.

Dey AK. "A conceptual framework and a toolkit for supporting rapid prototyping of context-aware applications." *Human-Computer Interaction*, Vol. 16, No. 2–4, 2001, pp. 97–166.

Dissanayake PI, Colicchio TK, Cimino JJ. "Using clinical reasoning ontologies to make smarter clinical decision support systems: A systematic review and data synthesis."*Journal of the American Medical Informatics Association*, Vol. 27, No. 1, 2020, pp. 159–174. https://doi.org/10.1093/jamia/ocz169.

Duan Y, Shao L, Hu G, Zhou Z, Zou Q, Lin Z "Specifying architecture of knowledge graph with data graph, information graph, knowledge graph and wisdom graph." *International Journal of Software Innovation*, Vol. 6, No. 2, 2018, pp. 10–25. https://doi.org/10.4018/IJSI.2018040102.

Ehrlinger L, Wöß W. "Towards a definition of knowledge graphs." *SEMANTiCS (Posters, Demos, SuCCESS)*, Vol. 48, Nos. 1–4, 2016, p. 2.

Ehrmann M, Cecconi F, Vannella D, McCrae J, Cimiano P, Navigli R "Representing multilingual data as linked data: The case of BabelNet 2.0." Proceedings of 2014 Language Resource Evaluation Conference, 2014, pp. 401–408. http://www.lrec-conf.org/proceedings/lrec2014/pdf/810_Paper.pdf.

Espinoza M, Montiel-Ponsoda E, Gomez-Perez A. "Ontology localization." Proceedings of 2009 5th International Conference on Knowledge Capture (KCAP 2009), Redondo Beach, CA, USA, 2009, pp. 33–40.

Faith A, Chrzanowski M. "Connecting RDA and RDF: Linked data for a wide world of connected possibilities." *Pennsylvania Libraries Research and Practice*, Vol. 3, No. 2, 2015, p. 122. https://doi.org/10.5195/palrap.2015.106.

Färber M, Ell B, Menne C, Rettinger A. "A comparative survey of DBpedia, Freebase, OpenCyc, Wikidata, and YAGO." *Semantic Web Journal*, Vol. 1, No. 1, 2015, pp. 1–5.

Feldmann S, Kernschmidt K, Vogel-Heuser B. "Applications of semantic web technologies for the engineering of automated production systems – three use cases." In *Semantic Web Technologies for Intelligent Engineering Applications*, S Biffl and M Sabou (eds.), 2016, pp. 353–382. Cham: Springer International Publishing.

Futia G, Vetrò A. "On the integration of knowledge graphs into deep learning models for a more comprehensive AI – three challenges for future research." *Information*, Vol. 11, No. 2, 2020, p. 122. https://doi.org/10.3390/info11020122.

Geng Y, Chen J, Jiménez-Ruiz E, Chen H. "Human-centric transfer learning explanation via knowledge graph." 2019; arXiv preprint arXiv:1901.08547.

Gibbins N, Shadbolt N. "Resource description framework (RDF)." *Encyclopedia of Library and Information Sciences*, 2010, pp. 4539–4547.

Gracia J, Montiel-Ponsoda E, Cimiano P, Gómez-Pérez A, Buitelaar P, McCrae J. "Challenges for the multilingual web of data." *Journal of Web Semantics*, Vol. 11, 2012, pp. 63–71.

Gruber TR. "Toward principles for the design of ontologies used for knowledge sharing." *International Journal of Human-Computer Studies*, Vol. 43, No. 5–6, 1995, pp. 907–928.

Gupta N, Podder S, Sengupta S, Annervaz KM. "Domain ontology induction using word embeddings." 2016 15th IEEE International Conference on Machine Learning and Applications (ICMLA), IEEE, 2016, pp. 115–119.

Gusmão AC, Correia AHC, De Bona G, Cozman FG. "Interpreting embedding models of knowledge bases: A pedagogical approach." 2018. arXiv preprint arXiv:1806.09504.

Hahn W, Vertan C. Textstruktur und Pragmatikoder: Wiekann man Texteplanen? oder: Dr. OetkersPragmatischesKochbuch, 2005.

Hao X, Ji Z, Li X, Yin L, Liu L, Sun M, Liu Q, Yang R. "Construction and application of a knowledge graph." *Remote Sensing*, Vol. 13, No. 2511, 2021. https://doi.org/10.3390/rs13132511.

Huang J, Zhao WX, Dou H, Wen JR, Chang EY. "Improving sequential recommendation with knowledge-enhanced memory networks." 2018 41st International ACM SIGIR Conference on Research & Development in Information Retrieval, 2018, pp. 505–514.

Jevsikova T, Berniukevičius A, Kurilovas E. "Application of resource description framework to personalize learning: Systematic review and methodology." *Informatics in Education*, Vol. 16, No. 1, 2017, pp. 61–82. https://doi.org/10.15388/infedu.2017.04.

Ji S, Pan S, Cambria E, Marttinen P, Yu PS. "A survey on knowledge graphs: representation, acquisition and applications." *IEEE Transactions on Neural Networks and Learning Systems*, Vol. 33, No. 2, 2022, pp. 494–514. https://doi.org/10.1109/TNNLS.2021.3070843.

Kotis KI, Zachila K, Paparidis E. "Machine learning meets the semantic web." *Artificial Intelligence Advances*, Vol. 3, No. 1, 2021, pp. 71–78. https://doi.org/10.30564/aia.v3i1.3178.

Lamy J-B. "Ontology-oriented programming for biomedical informatics." *Studies in Health Technology and Informatics (STC)*, Vol. 221, 2016, pp. 64–68.

Lanza J, Sánchez L, Gómez D, Santana JR, Sotres P. "A semantic-enabled platform for realizing an interoperable web of things." *Sensors*, Vol. 19, No. 4, 2019. https://doi.org/10.3390/s19040869.

León-Araúz P, Faber P. "Context and terminology in the multilingual semantic web." In *Towards the Multilingual Semantic Web*, Paul Buitelar and Philipp Cimiano (eds.), 2014, pp. 31–47, Springer, https://doi.org/10.1007/978-3-662-43585-4_3.

Liao L, He X, Zhao B, Ngo CW, Chua TS. "Interpretable multimodal retrieval for fashion products." Proceedings of 2018 26th ACM International Conference on Multimedia, 2018, pp. 1571–1579.

Ma F, You Q, Xiao H, Chitta R, Zhou J, Gao J. "KAME: Knowledge-based attention model for diagnosis prediction in healthcare." Proceedings of 2018 27th ACM International Conference on Information and Knowledge Management, 2018, pp. 743–752.

Ma W, Zhang M, Cao Y, Jin W, Wang C, Liu Y, Ma S, Ren X. "Jointly learning explainable rules for recommendation with knowledge graph." The World Wide Web Conference, 2019, pp. 1210–1221.

Manola F, Miller E, McBride B. "RDF primer." *W3C Recommendation*, Vol. 10, No. 1–107, 2004, p. 6.

McCrae JP, Moran S, Hellmann S, Brümmer M. "Multilingual linked data." *Semantic Web*, Vol. 6, No. 4, 2015, pp. 315–317.

McGrath RE, Ranganathan A, Campbell RH, Mickunas MD. "Use of ontologies in pervasive computing environments." Report number: UIUCDCS-R-2003-2332 UILU-ENG-2003-1719, 2003.

Mitchell ET. "Building blocks of linked open data in libraries." *Library Technology Reports*, Vol. 49, No. 5, 2013, pp. 11–25.

Mohajan H. "Sharing of tacit knowledge in organizations: A review." *American Journal of Computer Science and Engineering*, Vol. 3, No. 2, 2016, pp. 6–19.

Mohan AK, Venkataraman D. "The forensic future of social media analysis using web ontology." 2017 4th IEEE International Conference on Advanced Computing and Communication Systems, ICACCS 2017, Coimbatore, India, https://doi.org/10.1109/ICACCS.2017.8014682.

Moltmann F. "Natural language ontology." *Routledge Handbook of Metametaphysics*, R Bliss and J Miller (eds.), 2020, pp. 325–338.

Ortíz-Rodriguez F, Medina-Quintero JM, Tiwari S, Villanueva V. "EGODO ontology: Sharing, retrieving, and exchanging legal documentation across e-government." 2022a, https://doi.org/10.4018/978-1-6684-4225-8.ch016.

Ortíz-Rodriguez F, Tiwari S, Panchal R, Medina-Quintero JM, Barrera R "MEXIN: Multidialectal ontology supporting NLP approach to improve government electronic communication with the Mexican ethnic groups." 2022 23rd Annual International Conference on Digital Government Research, Association for Computing Machinery, New York, NY, USA, 2022b, pp. 461–463. https://doi.org/10.1145/3543434.3543590.

Paulheim H. "Knowledge graph refinement: A survey of approaches and evaluation methods." *Semantic Web*, Vol. 8, No. 3, 2016, pp. 489–508.

Pauwels P, Zhang S, Lee Y. "Semantic web technologies in AEC industry: A literature review." *Automation in Construction*, Vol. 73, 2017, https://doi.org/10.1016/j.autcon.2016.10.003.

Payne TR, Singh R, Sycara K. "Rcal: A case study on semantic web agents." Proceedings of 2002 1st International Joint Conference on Autonomous Agents and MultiagentSystems: Part 2, 2002, pp. 802–803.

Petrova EA. *"AI for BIM-based sustainable building design: integrating knowledge discovery and semantic data modelling for evidence-based design decision support."* Aalborg Universitetsforlag. Ph.d.-serien for Det Ingeniør- ogNaturvidenskabelige-Fakultet, Aalborg Universitet, 2019.

Powers S. *Practical RDF: Solving Problems with the Resource Description Framework.* O'Reilly Media, Inc., Sebastopol, CA, 2003.

Ristoski P. *Exploiting Semantic Web Knowledge Graphs in Data Mining*. Vol. 38, IOS Press, Amsterdam, 2019.

Sadeh N, Chan E, Shmazaki Y, Van L. "MyCampus: An agent-based environment for context-aware mobile services." Proceedings of the Workshop on Ubiquitous Agents on Embedded, Wearable, and Mobile Devices, 2002, pp. 34–39.

Sarker MK, Xie N, Doran D, Raymer M, Hitzler P. "Explaining trained neural networks with semantic web technologies: First steps." 2017; arXiv preprint arXiv:1710.04324.

Schmachtenberg M, Bizer C, Paulheim H. "Adoption of the linked data best practices indifferent topical domains." 2014 International Semantic Web Conference, 2014, pp. 245–260, Springer, Cham.

Seeliger A, Pfaff M, Krcmar H. "Semantic web technologies for explainable machine learning models: A literature review." *PROFILES/SEMEX@ ISWC, 2465*, 2019, pp. 1–16.

Shadbolt N, Berners-Lee T, Hall W. "The semantic web revisited." *IEEE Intelligent Systems*, Vol. 21, No. 3, 2006, pp. 96–101.

Suárez-Figueroa MC, Gómez-Pérez A. "First attempt towards a standard glossary of ontology engineering terminology." 2008 8th International Conference on Terminology and KE (TKE 2008), 2008, pp. 1–15, Copenhagen, Denmark.

Suchanek FM, Kasneci G, Weikum G. "Yago: A core of semantic knowledge." Proceedings 2007 16th International Conference on World Wide Web, 2007, pp. 697–706.

Tan J, Qiu Q, Guo W, Li T. "Research on the construction of a knowledge graph and knowledge reasoning model in the field of urban traffic." *Sustainability*, Vol. 13, No. 3191, 2021, https://doi.org/10.3390/su13063191.

Tiddi I, Schlobach S. "Knowledge graphs as tools for explainable machine learning: a survey."*Artificial Intelligence*, Vol. 302, 2022, https://doi.org/10.1016/j.artint.2021.103627.

Velardi P, Faralli S, Navigli R. "OntoLearn reloaded: A graph-based algorithm for taxonomy induction." *Computational Linguistics*, Vol. 39, No. 3, 2013, pp. 665–707.

Vertan C. "Language resources for the semantic web-perspectives for the machine translation." Proceedings of 2004 2nd International Workshop on Language Resources for Translation Work, Research and Training, Coling Conference, Geneva, Switzerland, 2004, pp. 37–42.

Vrandečić D, Krötzsch M. "Wikidata: A free collaborative knowledge base." *Communications of the ACM*, Vol. 57, No. 10, 2014, pp. 78–85.

Wang H, Zhang F, Wang J, Zhao M, Li W, Xie X, Guo M. "Ripplenet: Propagating user preferences on the knowledge graph for recommender systems." Proceedings of 2018 27th ACM International Conference on Information and Knowledge Management, 2018, pp. 417–426.

Wang P, Wu Q, Shen C, Hengel AVD, Dick A. "Explicit knowledge-based reasoning for visual question answering." 2017, arXiv preprint arXiv:1511.02570.

Wang X, Chen L, Ban T, Usman M, Guan Y, Liu S, Wu T, Chen H. "Knowledge graph quality control: A survey." *Fundamental Research*, Vol. 1, 2021, pp. 607–626. https://doi.org/10.1016/j.fmre.2021.09.003.

Zhang W, Paudel B, Zhang W, Bernstein A, Chen H. "Interaction embeddings for prediction and explanation in knowledge graphs." Proceedings of 2019 12th ACM International Conference on Web Search and Data Mining, 2019, pp. 96–104.

8

Building Knowledge Graph from Relational Database

Bilal Ben Mahria, Ilham Chaker, and Azeddine Zahi

Intelligent System and Application Laboratory (SIA),
Faculty of Science and Technology, Fez, Morocco

CONTENTS

DOI: 10.1201/9781003313267-8

8.1 Introduction

Google is the first organization that used the term knowledge graph (KG) in 2012 to prove the power of semantic technologies in web search. Therefore, the Google search engine allows users to search for things like events or organizations rather than just performing the string matching as web documents did ("Things, not strings"). Recently, the term KG has also been used as a synonym for semantic web knowledge bases such as Dbpedia (Voit & Paulheim, 2021) or YAGO (Mahdisoltani et al., 2014). Currently, KGs are increasingly used as the main technology for data integration and are acknowledged by numerous businesses as an effective solution to data governance, metadata management, and data enrichment. Furthermore, KG can improve the quality of the data that can be employed later as input for machine learning (ML) algorithms (Dessì et al., 2021).

The KG consists of a number of interconnected descriptions of entities (real-world objects as documents or abstract concepts such as a Person which is a being that has attributes like morality and consciousness, etc.) where these descriptions have formal semantics that makes it possible for both humans and machines to analyze them effectively and unambiguously. Ontologies – which can be thought of as the KG's schema – are used to create a formal meaning for these entities. In this context, the ontologies work as a formal agreement that guarantees a common understanding of the data and its meaning between the creators of the KG and its consumers (Pan et al., 2017).

Understanding the primary stages and tasks necessary during the development process is one of the major elements in creating KG. The knowledge acquisition layer, knowledge storage layer, and consumption layer are the three basic levels that pertain to the use of KGs. Firstly, the knowledge acquisition layer covers the procedure for gathering data from different sources, organizing it, and then producing valuable knowledge. Secondly, after completing the data-collecting phase, the following step is to determine how to store that data (Pan et al., 2017). Finally, to increase the effectiveness of the data and address specific requirements, the phase of using the knowledge embedded in KG should be started (Pan et al., 2017).

Generally speaking, knowledge acquisition is the layer where we need to develop the ontology that represents the core elements of the KG. Furthermore, the steps to develop an ontology are somehow similar to the engineering ones. There are two basic approaches to creating an ontology: manual construction or using techniques that are relied on ML. The manual construction of the ontology (Al-Arfaj & Al-Salman, 2015; Fernández-López et al., 1997; Grüninger & Fox, 1995; Noy & McGuinness, 2001; Sure et al., 2004; Uschold & King, 1995) is a very difficult and expensive operation that typically calls for a combination of domain experts' knowledge and ontology engineers' expertise. Due to these drawbacks, the term "ontology learning" (OL) has come into use, which captures an approach to explore ontological knowledge automatically or semi-automatically from various resources such as relational databases (RDBs), text documents, etc. In fact, OL methods can in a perfect way enhance the knowledge acquisition phase and makes the process of creating an ontology easy compared with manual methods.

In this chapter, we focused on the RDB as a source of information to build an ontology for several reasons. Firstly, RDBs are used to store almost 70% of the data on the web. Secondly, full conceptual representations are presented by RDBs. Thirdly, they offer a comprehensive and complete information source. Finally, they provide one of the best mechanisms for altering and storing data. However, the lack of semantic meaning in RDBs makes it difficult to develop interoperability among information systems.

To build an ontology from an RDB, there are three main steps: mapping schema, data migration, and data accessibility. Firstly, the mapping schema includes two main steps: extraction of metadata from database models (conceptual, logical, or physical) and generating mapping rules of each component extracted in the metadata phase, then converting them into their corresponding component according to the ontology language (Spanos et al., 2012). There are three types of mapping: automatic mapping, semi-automatic mapping, and manual mapping. Without no user interaction in the mapping process, the automatic mapping approach aims to convert an RDB to ontology in an accurate manner. The semi-automatic mapping approach took a place to improve a local ontology constructed using the automatic approach by using classes and properties from existing ontologies that are already developed and published on the web. Manual mapping approaches propose an iterative process in which a domain expert evaluates the proposed mappings.

Secondly, the mapping schema is not sufficient to create ontology from the database because the RDB includes both schema information and instances data which must be also manipulated. Therefore, the way instances data is transformed into ontological instances is called data migration and two methods that can be applied to achieve the data migration phase, either static transformation or dynamic transformation. Static transformation generates an RDF graph from an RDB instance, in the same manner as data warehousing approaches using the ETL process. ETL is composed of three steps: extract, transform, and load. The dynamic transformation relies on data synchronization, which is important if the data is frequently updated. In such cases, the data resides in the RDB, and how the data is accessed comprises rewriting the semantic query to an SQL query, which is executed, and its outcome is converted back as a response to the semantic query (Spanos et al., 2012).

Thirdly, independent of the manner in which the ontology is constructed, data accessibility defines how the data is queried and retrieved from the knowledge constructed. Therefore, the ontology content can be accessed by using ontology query language or linked data (Po et al., 2020).

In this chapter, we addressed the first two steps which are schema mapping and data migration. More specifically, the principal contributions of this chapter are:

- We will focus on introducing a state-of-art ontology construction from RDBs.

- We will provide an overview of the main two approaches to build an ontology. Also, we present classification methods for constructing ontology from the RDB. Furthermore, we present two important approaches to achieve the data migration phase and we deal with the two main methods to retrieve the data from the KG constructed.

- We will sum up the main mapping languages that can be used in the process of converting the RDB to the KG.

8.2 Ontology Construction

Knowledge management refers to the acquisition, accessing, and maintenance of knowledge. Current knowledge management technology suffers from limitations in searching, extracting, maintaining, uncovering, and viewing information (Gruber, 1993). The concept of the KG appears to provide new approaches for managing information based on the use of semantic metadata, which brings machine-readable descriptions to the data and documents that exist on the web or within an organization. In fact, using semantics metadata can enhance how information is presented and is the best solution for integrating information coming from different sources, whether within one organization or across organizations.

At the heart of the KG is the use of ontologies, which have been increasingly used to solve data integration problems by making knowledge explicit through conceptualization (Swartout et al., 1996). The motivation behind using ontologies as a solution for integrating data between different information systems is summarized in five applications (Sure et al., 2004): metadata representation, global conceptualization, support for high-level queries, declarative mediation, and mapping support.

As aforementioned, the use of ontologies is necessary to achieve semantic interoperability within a heterogeneous information system. Therefore, the main question now is how to build an ontology and what are the methodologies can be used to build it? There are two main approaches for its construction – either using manual techniques or relying on ML methods.

8.2.1 Constructing Ontology from Scratch

Constructing ontology from scratch or manually (Al-Arfaj & Al-Salman, 2015; Fernández-López et al., 1997; Grüninger & Fox, 1995; Noy & McGuinness, 2001; Sure et al., 2004; Uschold & King, 1995) is a very difficult and expensive operation that typically calls for a combination of domain experts' knowledge and ontology engineers' expertise. Due to the incredible rate of knowledge development in the real world, ontology engineers must constantly update and rewrite the resulting ontologies with new concepts, terms, and lexicons. It is non-intuitive, time-consuming, error-prone, and potentially expensive (Antoniou & Van Harmelen, 2004). Due to these limitations, the term "ontology learning" has come into use, which describes a strategy for automatically or semi-automatically learning ontological knowledge from a structured, unstructured, or semi-structured source of data.

8.2.2 Ontology Learning

Ontology learning allows the automated acquisition and extraction of ontological knowledge relying on ML techniques. Ontology learning may discover ontological knowledge at a faster rate than ontology construction from scratch, and it also reduces human interactions and errors (Maedche & Staab, 2004). More precisely, when compared to the manual method, ontology learning substantially simplifies the process of creating ontologies and can eliminate the challenges associated with knowledge acquisition. As depicted in Figure 8.1, by using ontology learning methods, ontologies can be created from several sources of information sources including structured sources, such as a RDB, semi-structured sources, such as dictionaries, or unstructured sources, such as web pages. In this chapter, we focus on RDBs as a source of information.

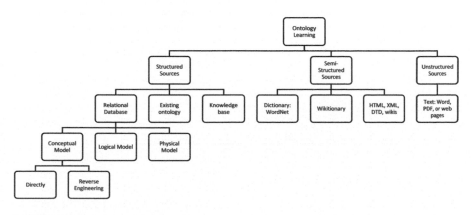

FIGURE 8.1
The classification of ontology learning source of information.

The reasons behind selecting the RDB as a source of building ontologies are the following:

- RDBs are used to store almost 70% of the data on the web.
- RDBs present full conceptual models.
- Full conceptual representations are presented by RDBs.
- RDBs provides one of the best mechanisms for altering and storing data.

The knowledge resources known as non-ontological resources (NORs) are those whose semantics have not yet been explicitly formalized using ontologies, such as RDBss.

8.3 Constructing Ontology from Relational Database

Selecting the knowledge that should be included in the KG is one of the key elements in the building process. The knowledge resources known as NORs are those whose semantics have not yet been explicitly formalized using ontologies, such as RDBs. In this context, the ontologilization of NORs has led to the design of several specific approaches. These include approaches for building the KG from RDB (Villazón-Terrazas, 2012).

In general, there are three main steps to build an ontology from RDBs: automatic mapping, semi-automatic mapping, and manual mapping.

8.3.1 Automatic Mapping

The automatic mapping approach aims to convert an RDB to a KG without user interaction to make the implicit data embedded in the RDB explicit. The direct mapping creates a KG from RDB taking as input the schema, instances, or both (Lourdusamy & Mattam, 2021). The W3C defines automatic mapping as a set of established guidelines that must be used to produce an RDF graph that accurately represents the structure and content of the RDB.

When the goal is to quickly make data sources available in a web machine-readable format, with little consideration for semantic interoperability, the automatic mapping approach is often used (Yang & Wei, 2020). In the literature, automatic mapping is often used as a synonym for direct mapping, local ontology mapping, or ad-hoc ontology mapping.

8.3.2 Semi-Automatic Mapping

Semi-automatic is also known as augmented direct mapping. In fact, an RBD does not represent a good solution to describe a domain because it does not support a full description of this domain. In order to overcome this drawback, the semi-automatic mapping approach is used to enhance the local ontology by utilizing classes and properties from ontologies that are available on the web. For example, suppose that the RDB contains a table named Person that combines all the necessary information to describe a person, such as a name, age, profession, etc. In this case, instead of using URIs that are generated from RDB, we can use a special ontology that is specific to describe an entity Person such as foaf (Friend-of-Friend) ontology (Spanos et al., 2012).

Generally speaking, when semantic interoperability is required, the automatic mapping approach is insufficient in real-world applications and we need to improve the quality of the automatic mapping. Consequently, to align the local ontology with already-existing domain ontologies, ontology alignment techniques might be applied afterward (Spanos et al., 2012).

8.3.3 Manual Mapping

Manual mapping is also known as transformative mapping or domain semantic-driven mapping. However, manual mapping does not mean building ontology from scratch with no feedback or suggestions from the application using existing tools such as Protégé editor. In contrast, after the direct mapping and the semi-automatic mapping, the domain semantic-driven mapping uses customized mapping rules generated by the user in addition to the automatically generated rules. For instance, it must be possible to manually rename the property names. Furthermore, manual mapping can also be helpful when we want to define some internal heuristics rules such as transitivity and symmetric relationships that are difficult to be identified automatically inside the RDB (Michel et al., 2014).

As we aforementioned, we will focus on developing ontology from RDB. More precisely, the RDB can be represented based on three models: conceptual, logical, and physical. Therefore, for a specific level, the ontologist can cover one of the steps or all the steps can be combined to build the ontology. The next section address all these models in more detail.

8.4 Methods for Constructing Ontology from RDB

Building the ontology from the RDB can be achieved from a conceptual model, a logical model or a physical model. As depicted in Figure 8.2, building an ontology from a conceptual model can either be done directly or via the use of reverse engineering techniques. The methods involved in each approach will be discussed in terms of their capabilities, advantages, and drawbacks.

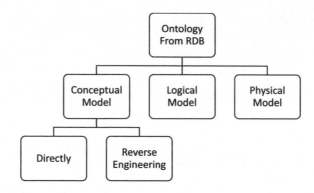

FIGURE 8.2
Methods to build ontology from RDBs.

8.4.1 Building Ontology from Conceptual Model

The conceptual model describes the semantics of a particular domain. It is more powerful than the relational model because it is simple and easily understandable, it can be understood by non-technical specialists, and it gives a higher-level description of the domain. Compared to the relational model, the conceptual model is more in line with the ontologies' semantic perspective. By using the conceptual model, we can build ontology either directly from the model or by using a reverse engineering approach.

8.4.1.1 Directly from a Conceptual Model

Peter Chen created entity relationship (ER) modeling, which was first published in 1976. In fact, the data embedded in the RDB is defined based on an abstract model that is ER. The latter is based on two concepts:

- **Entities:** They are defined as a table that contains specific data.
- **Relationships:** They are characterized as associations and interactions among entities.

ER diagrams also have several important drawbacks. Firstly, because of its graphical representation, it is difficult to parse an ER diagram to ontology (transform it into the formal language). Additionally, there is no representation of the data manipulation (ER diagram manipulates just the scheme structure), and no industry standard for notation, so it can be ambiguous. Finally, it provides limited constraints and specifications and limited expressiveness. Other problems with the entity-relationship model are the following (Thalheim, 2013):

- Hard to model IS-A relationship.
- There is no theoretical foundation for the idea of weak entities.

- Hard to represent: sets, sequences, and null-valued relationships.
- The intended semantics are not stated clearly.
- Different semantics are applied to the same concept.

All of the modeling concepts from the ER model are included in the Enhanced Entity-Relationship (EER) model. The extended ER model's main contribution is centered on data abstractions including aggregation, subclasses, superclasses, and inheritance. The EER model also uses the term "category" or "union type" to describe a group of items that are the union of objects of various entity types (Coronel & Morris, 2016).

There have several of publications in this area. All the discussed methods in Chujai et al. (2014), Fahad (2008), Lubyte and Tessaris (2007a), Myroshnichenko and Murphy (2009), Upadhyaya and Kumar (2005), Xu et al. (2004), and Zhang and Jia (2009) focused on capturing cardinality constraint and binary relationships and key constraints including a primary key and foreign key. These methods can handle different kinds of binary relationships including the one-to-one, one-to-many, and many-to-many relationships. According to Fahad (2008), the methods discussed by Lubyte and Tessaris (2007a), Upadhyaya and Kumar (2005), Xu et al. (2004), and Zhang and Jia (2009) suffer from some limitations, which include inappropriate mapping of composite attributes, where multivalued attributes are not handled. These limitations can be bypassed by defining the rules concerning all the different kinds of attributes (Chujai et al., 2014; Fahad, 2008).

We have discussed the rules that enable us to verify if these methods define all the basic components of the conceptual model and if they find the matching component in the ontology language (explained in Tables 8.1 and 8.2). Now, we will discuss the implementation details, composed of the tools and the API used to implement these methods and indicate if these methods are accompanied by accessible software. All the methods described above have accessible software except (Zhang & Jia, 2009).

Most of the methods that directly rely on the conceptual model (Chujai et al., 2014; Fahad, 2008; Lubyte & Tessaris, 2007b; Myroshnichenko & Murphy, 2009; Upadhyaya & Kumar, 2005; Xu et al., 2004; Zhang & Jia, 2009) produce ontology automatically and generate just the local ontology, which simply represents the structure of the database. In fact, the main drawback of the direct conceptual model methods is that they did not cover the data migration and the data accessibility phase.

Although previous publications (Chujai et al., 2014; Fahad, 2008; Lubyte & Tessaris, 2007a; Myroshnichenko & Murphy, 2009; Upadhyaya & Kumar, 2005; Xu et al., 2004; Zhang & Jia, 2009) do not discuss how the data is accessed after the ontology has been created, this does not imply there is no solution. In reality, the only solution is to run the SPARQL against the database where the data is stored.

Even if all these methods generate the ontology by following the automatic mapping rules, they do not capture the complicated domain semantics

TABLE 8.1

Comparison of Conceptual Model Approach Methods

| | Conceptual Model Approach | | | | | | | | | | | | | | |
| | Conceptual Model Directly Methods | | | | | | | Conceptual Model Reverse Engineering Methods | | | | | | | |
Context	Xu et al. (2004)	Upadhyaya et al. (2005)	Fahad (2008)	Lubyte et al.	Chujai et al. (2014)	Igor et al.	Zhang et al. (2012)	Astrova (2004)	Trinkunas et al.	He-ping et al. (2008)	Zhou, Meng et al.	Zhou, Ling et al.	Russo et al. (2012)	Lin et al. (2013)	Djado et al.
Concept	Y	Y	Y	Y	Y	Y	Y	Y	Y	Y	Y	Y	Y	Y	Y
Simple inheritance	N	Y	N	Y	N	N	Y	Y	N	Y	N	Y	N	Y	N
Multiple inheritance	N	Y	N	Y	N	N	N	Y	N	Y	N	N	N	Y	N
Value restriction	N	N	N	N	N	N	N	N	N	N	N	N	N	N	N
Has value restriction	N	N	N	N	N	N	N	N	N	N	N	N	Y	N	N
Transitive property	N	N	N	N	N	N	Y	N	N	N	N	N	N	N	N
Symmetric property	N	N	N	N	N	N	N	N	N	N	N	N	N	N	N
Inverse property	Y	Y	N	Y	Y	Y	N	Y	N	N	Y	Y	Y	N	N
Equivalence class	N	N	N	N	N	N	N	N	N	N	N	N	N	N	N
Equivalence property	N	N	N	N	N	N	N	N	N	N	N	N	N	N	N
Enumerated class	N	N	N	N	N	N	N	N	N	N	Y	N	N	N	N
Disjoint class	Y	Y	N	Y	Y	N	N	Y	N	N	N	N	N	N	N

(Continued)

TABLE 8.1 (Continued)

Comparison of Conceptual Model Approach Methods

| | Conceptual Model Approach | | | | | | | | | | | | | | |
| | Conceptual Model Directly Methods | | | | | | | Conceptual Model Reverse Engineering Methods | | | | | | | |
Context	Xu et al. (2004)	Upadhyaya et al. (2005)	Fahad et al. (2008)	Lubyte et al.	Chujai et al. (2014)	Igor et al.	Zhang et al. (2012)	Astrova (2004)	Trinkunas et al.	He-ping et al. (2008)	Zhou, Zhou, Meng et al.	Zhou, Ling et al.	Russo et al. (2012)	Lin et al. (2013)	Djado et al.
Individuals	Y	N	N	N	N	N	N	Y	N	Y	N	N	N	N	N
Same/different individuals	N	N	N	N	N	N	N	N	N	N	N	N	N	N	N
Sub-properties	N	N	N	N	Y	N	N	N	N	N	N	N	N	N	N
Keys	N	Y	N	Y	Y	Y	Y	Y	Y	Y	Y	Y	Y	Y	Y
Ternary and higher order relations	Y	Y	N	N	N	Y	N	Y	N	Y	Y	N	N	N	N
Functional property	N	Y	N	N	Y	Y	Y	N	N	N	N	N	Y	N	Y
Inverse functional property	N	N	N	N	Y	Y	N	N	N	N	N	N	N	N	Y
Cardinality restriction	Y	Y	Y	Y	Y	Y	Y	N	N	Y	N	N	Y	Y	Y
Some value from	N	N	N	N	N	N	N	N	N	N	N	N	N	N	N

Note: Y = Yes; N = No.

TABLE 8.2

Comparison of Logical and Physical Approach Methods

Context	Logical Model Approach Methods			Physical Model Approach Methods								
	Telnarova (2010)	H. Zhang et al. (2012)	Li et al. (2005)	Ghawi & Cullot (2007)	Astrova et al. (2007)	Nyulas et al. (2007)	Tirmizi et al. (2008)	L. Zhang & Li (2011)	Yiqing et al. (2012)	Buccella et al.	Sedighi & Javidan (2012)	Bakkas et al. (2013)
Concept	Y	Y	Y	Y	Y	Y	Y	Y	Y	Y	Y	Y
Simple inheritance	N	Y	Y	Y	Y	N	Y	Y	N	N	Y	N
Multiple inheritance	N	N	N	Y	N	N	N	N	N	N	N	N
Value restriction	N	N	Y	N	Y	N	Y	N	N	N	N	N
Has value restriction	N	N	N	N	Y	N	N	N	N	N	N	N
Transitive property	N	N	N	N	Y	N	Y	N	N	N	N	N
Symmetric property	N	N	N	N	Y	N	Y	N	N	Y	N	N
Inverse property	Y	N	Y	Y	Y	N	Y	Y	Y	Y	Y	Y
Equivalence class	N	N	N	N	N	N	N	Y	N	N	N	N
Equivalence property	N	N	N	N	N	N	N	Y	N	N	N	N
Enumerated class	N	Y	N	N	Y	N	Y	N	N	N	Y	N
Disjoint class	N	N	N	N	N	N	N	N	N	N	N	N
Individuals	N	N	Y	N	Y	Y	N	N	N	N	N	Y
Same/different individuals	N	N	N	N	N	N	N	N	N	N	N	N
Sub-properties	N	N	N	Y	Y	N	Y	Y	Y	Y	N	N
Keys	Y	Y	Y	Y	Y	Y	Y	Y	Y	Y	Y	Y
Ternary and higher order relations	N	N	Y	N	Y	N	N	N	Y	N	Y	N
Functional property	Y	N	N	Y	Y	N	Y	Y	N	Y	Y	N
Inverse functional property	N	N	N	N	Y	N	Y	Y	N	N	Y	N
Cardinality restriction	Y	N	Y	N	N	N	Y	Y	N	N	Y	N
Some value from	N	N	N	N	N	N	N	N	N	N	N	N

Note: Y = Yes; N = No.

needed by many applications and systems, and the generated ontology is local. The direct conceptual model approach cannot be a solution for the data integration problems. Therefore, this approach is valuable when the goal is to provide the data sources in machine readable format. In brief, all the methods described above (Chujai et al., 2014; Fahad, 2008; Lubyte & Tessaris, 2007a; Myroshnichenko & Murphy, 2009; Upadhyaya & Kumar, 2005; Xu et al., 2004; Zhang & Jia, 2009) are unable to express the property characteristics such as symmetry and transitivity.

8.4.1.2 Reverse Engineering

Reverse engineering is the process of converting a physical model into a conceptual one to identify every component and its relationships. As illustrated in Figure 8.3, the main objective of database reverse engineering is to examine an existing database system (Chiang et al., 1994):

- Recognize the elements of the database (in an RDB, the relations, and attributes) and how they relate to one another.
- Recover domain semantics that isn't explicitly expressed in the subject system (keys, cardinality ratios for relationships, etc.).
- Find domain semantics that a forward engineering approach would find challenging or impossible to get.
- Based on the discovered semantics, suggest potential design guidelines that might result in the current system.
- Create an entity-relationship model (or other conceptual representation) of the outcome to help with data interpretation for the application domain.

As previously discussed, the reverse engineering technique is the process of transforming the physical model into the conceptual model. Therefore, several approaches consist of building ontology by using this technique.

FIGURE 8.3
Reverse engineering steps.

The methods described in Astrova (2004), Dadjoo and Kheirkhah (2015), He-ping et al. (2008), Lin et al. (2013), Russo et al. (2012), Trinkunas and Vasilecas (2007), Zhou, Ling et al. (2010), and Zhou, Meng et al. (2010) speci-fied a set of mapping rules, including entity mapping, attribute mapping, primary key mapping, and foreign key mapping. For relationship manipula-tion, the binary relationship is handled by Astrova (2004), Lin et al., (2013), Russo et al. (2012), Trinkunas and Vasilecas (2007), and Zhou, Meng et al. (2010), whereas the ternary relationship is covered by Astrova (2004), He-ping et al. (2008), and Zhou, Ling et al. (2010). Therefore, the cardinality constraint is missed in all approaches except Dadjoo and Kheirkhah (2015), He-ping et al. (2008), Lin et al. (2013), and Russo et al. (2012); the unique constraint and the Not Null constraint are handled only by Dadjoo and Kheirkhah (2015). Table 8.1 provides further details and compares all the methods based on the extracted metadata. Only the approaches described in He-ping et al. (2008), Lin et al. (2013), Trinkunas and Vasilecas (2007), Zhou, Ling et al. (2010), and Zhou, Meng et al. (2010) are implemented.

Most of the methods that belong to the reverse engineering approach fol-low the procedure described in Figure 8.3. Automatic mapping is used to build an ontology in most cases (Dadjoo & Kheirkhah, 2015; Lin et al., 2013; Trinkunas & Vasilecas, 2007; Zhou, Ling et al., 2010; Zhou, Meng et al., 2010) except for Russo et al. (2012), which relies on the automatic and semi-automatic mapping. As we already discussed, semi-automatic mapping is needed when the aim is to achieve semantic interoperability. In fact, semi-automatic map-ping enhances the local ontology that results from automatic mapping by using existing domain ontologies or vocabularies such as WordNet.

In contrast to the previous approach, this approach takes into account the data migration process, which describes how the data is transformed from the RDB to the RDF triple store. Some approaches use static migra-tion employing the ETL process (Dadjoo & Kheirkhah, 2015; Lin et al., 2013; Trinkunas & Vasilecas, 2007; Zhou, Ling et al., 2010; Zhou, Meng et al., 2010) whereas dynamic migration is used in an alternative approach (Astrova, 2004). As already mentioned, static migration is not executed against the most recent version of data, whereas dynamic migration relies on data syn-chronization, which becomes important if the data is updated.

Unlike the direct conceptual model approach, which handles only the transformation schema, the reverse engineering approach covers the trans-formation schema and the data migration. To decide which of the two approaches is to be used, it is necessary to determine the aim of the work and the problem to be solved. For instance, if the goal is to solve a data integration problem, it is preferable to choose a reverse engineering approach. Besides the overall aim, the major benefits of the reverse engineering approach are evident in the metadata extraction step because it can take advantage of the metadata residing in the physical and the conceptual models.

In short, all the above methods that include building ontology from a conceptual model directly or using a reverse engineering approach are summarized in Table 8.1. Table 8.1 highlights the differences and similarities between these methods based on the metadata provided by ontology and the conceptual model. Our goal in identifying these differences and similarities is to show the context where the domain expert must focus when improving or building ontology.

8.4.2 Building Ontology from Logical Model

The logical model offers the abstraction structure of a domain of information and should be based on the structure identified in the conceptual model. Indeed, the conceptual model represents the meaning of information that can be stored in an RDB. In contrast, the logical model provides the foundation for designing a database, and it identifies the requirements of the data as much detail as possible, without taking into consideration how they will be physically embedded in the RDB.

Telnarova (2010) and Zhang et al. (2012) focus on the principles of automatic conversion of the RDB, especially the logical model into an ontology. The set of rules that allows the process of transformation of the logical model into ontology is included: table, columns, primary key, foreign key, binary relationship, unique constraint, and not null constraint. In fact, Telnarova (2010) provides 11 mapping rules but there is no implementation for these rules whereas Zhang et al. (2012) propose a method for extracting and visualizing ontology from a logical model with web interfaces. The prototype of this method is the EVis system, which comprises three modules. Firstly, the database to ontology module provides the corresponding rules for the table, attribute, and primary key, foreign key, binary relationship, unique constraint, and not null constraint. Secondly, the ontology editing module allows the user, after extracting ontology from the database, to correct the resulting errors, finally, loading of the resulting ontology and the transformed database for the evaluation phase. The input database must be in third form normal (3NF).

The main problem in converting the logical model into ontology comes from relationships. One-to-many (or one-to-one) relationships without attributes are easily found through a foreign key. If the foreign key is a subset of the primary keys, it is almost certain that the one-to-many relationship links a weak entity to a strong one. Indeed, the many-to-many relationships, if they include attributes, are somehow hidden, because they generate new tables that are identical to entity tables. Finally, the participation and cardinalities of the relationships are also difficult to represent (Telnarova, 2010). Table 8.2 displays the metadata that can be extracted from the logical model.

Although the previous methods use the logical model approach to construct ontology, they do not profit from the benefits presented by this model. Therefore, we notice no differences between the previous approach and this approach due to two main reasons: they do not know the main basis behind the logical model, and they do not answer an important question that justifies the choice of the approach, namely what is the aim of the work.

Similarly to the direct conceptual model approach, the logical model approach does not handle the data structure. Therefore, the data migration and the data accessibility phases are missed. The data may remain in the RDB, and to access this data it must use the SAPRQL query language against the RDB. It is the same solution as is used in the direct conceptual model approach. The two methods already discussed generate the local ontology automatically.

8.4.3 Building Ontology from Physical Model

The RDB's actual design blueprint is represented by the physical model. It is crucial to take into account the conventions and limitations of the DBMS used during designing a physical model because it describes how data should be organized and handled in particular DBMS.

Table 8.2 listed all the possible metadata we can obtain from this model. Fortunately, there are many publications in this area. The main difference between these methods is in the steps which each method follows to build ontology as well as the metadata extracted and mapping rules proposed.

All the methods described in Astrova et al. (2007), Bakkas et al. (2013), Buccella et al. (2004), Ghawi and Cullot (2007), Li et al. (2005), Nyulas et al. (2007), Sedighi and Javida (2012), Tirmizi et al. (2008), Yiqing et al. (2012), and Zhang and Li (2011) take into account the table mapping, columns mapping, primary key mapping, foreign key mapping. However, the binary relationship is missed in Nyulas et al. (2007), Yiqing et al. (2012), and Zhang and Li (2011) in addition to the ternary relationship which is not manipulated in Bakkas et al. (2013), Ghawi and Cullot (2007), Nyulas et al. (2007), Yiqing et al. (2012), and Zhang and Li (2011). Only Astrova et al. (2007) and Buccella et al. (2004) can handle the check constraint, Not Null constraint, and unique constraint, whereas Li et al. (2005), Sedighi and Javidan (2012), Tirmizi et al. (2008), and Yiqing et al. (2012) can cover the cardinality constraint. Consequently, all the previous methods are implemented except Tirmizi et al. (2008) and Zhang and Li (2011).

The advantage and drawbacks defined by the logical model are also applied to the physical model. However, the physical model is more robust because it can add expressivity that is not available in the logical model. For example, attribute domains may be more specific, and many different sorts of constraints may be specified, either through the use of a column of table constraints or more sophisticated methods such as the use of triggers.

In contrast to the two previous approaches, the physical model approach takes in account the structure and content of the database whereas the conceptual model approach relies just on the structure. The structure means all the metadata that we can extract from the physical model as displayed in Table 8.2, whereas the content means the instances or the individuals of the database.

The main benefit of the physical model approach is that it can cover all the phases shown in Figure 8.3: Mapping Scheme, data migration, ontology resulting, and data accessibility. For the first phase, which is the mapping schema, all the methods described above rely on automatic mapping. For the data migration phase Astrova et al. (2007), Bakkas et al. (2013), and Nyulas et al. (2007) follow the static migration, while Ghawi and Cullot (2007) cover the dynamic migration, but Buccella et al. (2004), Sedighi and Javidan (2012), Tirmizi et al. (2008), Yiqing et al. (2012), and Zhang and Li (2011) do not handle the data migration phase, which plays an important role in determining the type of the data accessibility that can be used to describe how the data is retrieved.

The type of ontology obtained after the mapping schema and the data migration is local ontology (Buccella et al., 2004; Sedighi & Javidan, 2012; Tirmizi et al., 2008; Yiqing et al., 2012; Zhang & Li, 2011). In fact, the quality of the ontology obtained in this approach depends on the quality and sophistication of the data modeling effort. Therefore, if greater-scale interoperability is desired, the local ontology still needs to be integrated with a global domain ontology.

The last phase is data accessibility, which describes how the data is queried from the source. All the methods described above do not explain how the data is queried after the ontology construction except (Ghawi & Cullot, 2007), which relies on the SPARQL language query. Table 8.2 displays the metadata that can be extracted from the physical model as well as exhibits the differences and similarities between these methods based on the metadata provided by the ontology and physical models.

8.5 Data Migration

The mapping schema phase covered thus far involves analyzing the database schema in detail. However, the mapping schema is not sufficient to create ontology from the database because the RDB must include both schema information and instances data which must be also addressed. Therefore, the way instances data is transformed into ontological instances is called data migration which is also referred to in the literature as Mapping Implementation or Data Exposition. Two methods can be applied to achieve the data migration phase, either static transformation or dynamic transformation.

8.5.1 Static Transformation

Static transformation generates an RDF graph from an RDB instance, in the same manner as data warehousing approaches using the ETL process. ETL is composed of three steps: extract, transform, and load. Data extraction means extracting data from the source followed by data transformation where the data is converted into the proper structure for storage purposes. Finally, data loading is performed where the data is loaded into the final target database in the triple store. Other terms used in the literature for a static transformation are data materialization, batch transformation, ETL, or massive dump.

The major benefit of ETL is evident in data integration problems where large amounts of data from multiple sources can be centralized. However, the ETL process does not guarantee that the returned data is updated because of the absence of the data synchronization criteria and does not give access to the data in its original form. Therefore, to keep a copy of the original data, users must perform extract, load, and then transform (ELT). In this case, the data is extracted and loaded into the triple store, where the user can transform the data into a new state or leave it in its original format (Services, 2015).

ETL is a part of data migration, which is the process of moving data from the RDB into the RDF store, unlike Spanos et al. (2012) and Michel et al. (2014), which consider ETL as a part of the data accessibility process that explains how the requested data is accessed.

8.5.2 The Dynamic Transformation

As mentioned before, one of the main drawbacks of the ETL is that the query is not always executed against the most recent version of the data. Consequently, the dynamic transformation relies on data synchronization, which is necessary if the data is regularly changed. In these scenarios, the data is stored in an RDB, and accessing it entails converting the SPARQL query into an SQL query, running it, and then converting the result back to the SPARQL.

The dynamic transformation suffers from some limitations concerning how to deal with the reasoning processing, including the execution of the inference rules (Michel et al., 2014; Press, 2008). An alternative term, on-demand mapping, can be used to refer to dynamic transformation.

8.6 Data Accessibility Approaches

Independent how the ontology is constructed, data accessibility also known in the literature as data retrieval, query implementation, or access paradigm, defines how the data is queried from its source. Therefore, the ontology content can be accessed by using an ontology query language and linked data. In the following section, we concisely describe these methods.

8.6.1 Query-Based Access

Based on the resulting ontology from the mapping process, several query languages have been developed (Zhang & Miller, 2005) to handle the data stored either in the RDF store, where the data entity is composed of subject-predicate-object, or in the RDB, where the RDF statement can be considered as a table with three columns: the subject column, the predicate column, and the object column. Early approaches suggested query languages rather than

SPARQL. Nevertheless, they were abandoned when SPARQL became the de-facto standard (Alaoui, 2019).

8.6.2 Linked Data

The linked data access signifies that the mapping's outcome is provided online on the web based on the principles of linked data (Wood et al., 2014): all URIs should employ the HTTP method and, when they are dereferenced, they give important information about the site they designate.

Each entity that is converted into RDF during the mapping process has an exclusive IRI that identifies it in the data graph. Using this IRI in an HTTP GET request, it ought to be feasible to dereference any such IRI following the linked data standards (Wood et al., 2014). The entity identified by the IRI should be represented in the HTTP response. Typically, the output format of the data is decided upon by the client and the web server during a routine HTTP content type negotiation process (Po et al., 2020).

8.7 Mapping Languages

The RDB-to-RDF mapping languages used to construct KGs from various sources of information, including RDBs, were compared based on a set of properties outlined in this section. These characteristics ought to serve as the foundation when choosing an RDB-to-RDF mapping language for a particular application situation (Hert et al., 2011).

8.7.1 The D2RQ Mapping Language

The "D2RQ Mapping Language" (Bizer & Cyganiak, 2006; Bizer & Seaborne, 2004) is a declarative language used to describe the relationship between an RDFS vocabulary or OWL ontology and an RDB architecture. Without needing to duplicate the content into an RDF store, D2RQ provides RDF-based access to RDB content. The mapping creates a virtual RDF graph from the database. This virtual graph is an RDF graph rather than a virtual relational table, which is comparable to the idea of views in SQL. Depending on the implementation, there are numerous ways to access the virtual RDF graph (Bizer & Seaborne, 2004).

8.7.2 Triplify (SQL Mapping Language)

Triplify (Auer et al., 2009) is a mapping language that is based on creating a configuration file that can be manually changed and improved by reusing terms from existing ontologies (Wood et al., 2014).

8.7.3 R2O

R2O is a stand-alone high-level language that may be used with any DB that adheres to the SQL standard. R2O is designed to be sufficiently expressive to handle difficult mapping (Barrasa et al., 2004).

8.7.4 Relational.OWL

Relational.OWL is introduced by de Laborda and Conrad (2005). It defines an OWL Full ontology using as input the schema and data of an RDB. The goal of this mapping is data exchange in peer-to-peer databases. It defines mapping rules for tables, columns either as primary or foreign keys, and data types (McGuinness & Van Harmelen, 2004).

8.7.5 Virtuoso RDF Views (Meta Schema Language)

The Virtuoso RDF Views feature provides capability similar to D2RQ. The Virtuoso RDF Views feature provides capability similar to D2RQ. In the former, an RDFS ontology is created following the basic approach, while in the latter, a mapping expressed in the proprietary Virtuoso Meta-Schema language is manually defined (Erling & Mikhailov, 2010).

8.7.6 eD2R

eD2R could handle normalized and non-normalized databases. It supports complex transformation on attribute values based on techniques such as keyword search, regex matching, NLP (natural language processing), etc. The mappings have relied on SQL queries that extract instances from the RDB and transformation functions that can be applied to the constructed values (Barrasa et al., 2003).

8.7.7 R2RML

R2RML is used in the development of many RDB-to-RDF tools. It is based on mapping document called R2RML mapping graph. This document is written in RDF with the Turtle syntax serialization. R2RML supports both transformative mapping and the direct mapping. Furthermore, it supports virtual mapping and data materialization (de Medeiros et al., 2015).

8.7.8 RML

The RDF Mapping Language (RML) is an improved version of R2RML (World Wide Web Consortium, 2012) that can support not only RDB but also other data formats such as CSV, TSV, XML, JSON (Dimou et al., 2014).

8.8 Mapping Languages Comparison Criteria

To create an effective comparison between the mappings languages described above, we introduced a set of criteria. These criteria represent a set of features that each mapping language supports (Table 8.3). We can enumerate 15 features (Hert et al., 2011).

8.8.1 Comparison Criteria

F1. Logical Table to Class: The RDF statements are constructed from RDB due to an SQL query. This SQL query could be a view that is already embedded in RDB or could be the base table. Therefore, the result of the SQL query is called a Logical Table (Neto et al., 2013).

F2. Many-To-Many Relationships: To describe Many-To-Many relationships between tables in RDBs, a unique construct known as join tables is required. Therefore, RDF properties should be used to map join tables that are resulted from a many-to-many relationship (Hert et al., 2011).

F3. Project Attributes: Some attributes may be irrelevant or sensitive such as a password. In this case, the mechanism of project attributes should be applied to filter data and select only the relevant portion (Neto et al., 2013).

F4. Select Conditions: Some data may be outdated and should not be transformed into RDF representation. For this reason, the mechanism of applying conditions is created to filter only relevant pieces of information (Hert et al., 2011).

F5. User-Defined Instance IRIs: Instances from RDB are transformed into RDF instances with IRIs as their identifiers. This feature allows

TABLE 8.3

Mapping Languages Comparison

	F1	F2	F3	F4	F5	F6	F7	F8	F9	F10	F11	F12	F13	F14	F15
Direct mapping	Y	N	N	N	N	N	N	N	N	N	N	N	N	N	Y
Relational.owl	Y	N	Y	N	N	N	N	N	Y	N	Y	Y	N	N	Y
Virtuoso	Y	Y	Y	Y	Y	Y	Y	Y	Y	Y	Y	Y	N	Y	N
D2RQ	Y	Y	Y	Y	Y	Y	Y	Y	Y	N	Y	Y	Y	Y	N
Triplify	Y	Y	Y	Y	Y	Y	Y	Y	Y	N	N	Y	N	Y	N
R2RML	Y	Y	Y	Y	Y	Y	Y	Y	Y	Y	Y	Y	Y	Y	Y
RML	Y	Y	Y	Y	Y	Y	Y	Y	Y	Y	Y	Y	Y	Y	Y
eD2R	Y	Y	Y	Y	Y	Y	Y	Y	Y	N	Y	Y	N	Y	N
R2O	Y	N	Y	Y	Y	Y	Y	Y	Y	N	Y	Y	N	Y	N

Source: Adopted from Hert et al. (2011).

the user to identify the form of the IRI. At the same time, the user could create these IRIs relying on the RDB schema and instances (Hert et al., 2011).

F6. Literal to IRI: The possibility of creating IRIs from literal values is ensured thanks to this feature (Hert et al., 2011).

F8. Transformation Functions: Some attributes that resided in RDB may demand specific treatments before converting them into RDF representation such as temperature that can be in Centigrade inside RDB but the RDF requirements want it as Fahrenheit value. Therefore, to ensure this functionality, a set of functions are constructed to perform the desired transformation (Hert et al., 2011).

F9. Data Types: This feature allows data typing such as int, float, double, etc. Thanks to this feature, the process of mapping the data types from RDB to RDF is achieved (Hert et al., 2011).

F10. Named Graphs: RDF data sets may have numerous named graphs. Therefore, a mapping may assign particular RDB components to a specific named graph (Hert et al., 2011).

F11. Blank Nodes: According to Antoniou and Van Harmelen (2004) blank nodes are a type of existential quantification that is used in RDF to describe instances that lack an RDF URI reference identifier (Hert et al., 2011).

F12. Integrity Constraints: This feature is helpful to identify mapping rules that are responsible to distinguish between RDB constraints (PK, FK, etc.) and RDF constraints (Hert et al., 2011).

F13. Static Metadata: This feature is helpful to track the source of data (provenance) and how the data should be used (licensing information) (Hert et al., 2011).

F14. A Table to Many Classes: In the cases where the RDB is not normalized. The table could be mapped multiple times and each time with a different set of attributes (Hert et al., 2011).

F15. Write Support: The mapping languages should support write access (Hert et al., 2011).

8.9 Conclusion

In this chapter, we have presented a detailed state-of-art of construction ontology from RDB. In fact, three main steps have been presented over the last years to enable the construction of ontology from the RDB. These steps are automatic mapping, semi-automatic mapping, and manual mapping. We then highlighted the main methods that we can face when we deal with an RDB as a source of information to build ontology. Independently of the way a transformation is implemented, the migration of the instances from the RDB to the ontology can be retrieved using two main methods: static transformation and dynamic transformation. We then described how the resulted can be exploited by sending a query to a query processing engine or using the linked data paradigm. The choice of the appropriate method largely depends on how the data should be exploited.

In order to make the transformation process solid and respect standards, a set of mapping languages are proposed in the literature. In this context, we presented the main languages that we can use to convert the RDB to KG. W3C recognized this gap and proposed R2RML language as a representation language for RDB to KG mapping. R2RML is currently under development, it is expected to be adopted by software tools in the near future. Other languages are presented and a relevant comparison is created in order to show the robustness of the R2RML language. More precisely, we enumerate 15 features that each mapping language covered.

References

Alaoui, K. (2019). A categorization of rdf triplestores. *Proceedings of the 4th International Conference on Smart City Applications*, 1–7.

Al-Arfaj, A., & Al-Salman, A. (2015). Ontology construction from text: Challenges and trends. *International Journal of Artificial Intelligence and Expert Systems (IJAE)*, 6(2), 15–26.

Antoniou, G., & Van Harmelen, F. (2004). *A Semantic Web Primer*. MIT Press.

Astrova, I. (2004). Reverse engineering of relational databases to ontologies. In *The Semantic Web: Research and Applications: First European Semantic Web Symposium, ESWS 2004 Heraklion, Crete, Greece, May 10–12, 2004. Proceedings 1* (pp. 327–341). Springer, Berlin, Heidelberg.

Astrova, I., Korda, N., & Kalja, A. (2007). Rule-based transformation of SQL relational databases to OWL ontologies. *Proceedings of the 2nd International Conference on Metadata & Semantics Research*, 415–424.

Auer, S., Dietzold, S., Lehmann, J., Hellmann, S., & Aumueller, D. (2009, April). Triplify: Light-weight linked data publication from relational databases. *Proceedings of the 18th International Conference on World Wide Web*, 621–630.

Bakkas, J., Bahaj, M., & Marzouk, A. (2013). Direct migration method of rdb to ontology while keeping semantics. *International Journal of Computer Applications*, 65(3).

Barrasa, J., Corcho, O., & Gómez-Pérez, A. (2003, October). Fund Finder: A case study of database-to-ontology mapping. *Semantic Integration Workshop (SI-2003)*, 9.

Barrasa, J., Corcho, Ó, & Gómez-Pérez, A. (2004). R2O, an extensible and semantically based database-to-ontology mapping language. Proceedings of the 2nd Workshop on Semantic Web and Databases, Toronto, Canada, 14.

Bizer, C. (2003). *D2r map-a database to rdf mapping language*.

Bizer, C., & Cyganiak, R. (2006). D2r server-publishing relational databases on the semantic web. *Poster at the 5th International Semantic Web Conference*, 175.

Bizer, C., & Seaborne, A. (2004). D2RQ-treating non-RDF databases as virtual RDF graphs. *Proceedings of the 3rd International Semantic Web Conference (ISWC2004)*, *2004*.

Buccella, A., Penabad, M. R., Rodriguez, F. J., Farina, A., & Cechich, A. (2004, September). From relational databases to OWL ontologies. *Proceedings of the 6th National Russian Research Conference* (Vol. 29).

Chiang, R. H., Barron, T. M., & Storey, V. C. (1994). Reverse engineering of relational databases: Extraction of an EER model from a relational database. *Data & Knowledge Engineering*, *12*(2), 107–142.

Chujai, P., Kerdprasop, N., & Kerdprasop, K. (2014). On transforming the ER model to ontology using protégé OWL tool. *International Journal of Computer Theory and Engineering*, *6*(6), 484.

Coronel, C., & Morris, S. (2016). *Database Systems: Design, Implementation, & Management.* Cengage Learning.

Dadjoo, M., & Kheirkhah, E. (2015). An approach for transforming of relational databases to OWL ontology. *ArXiv Preprint ArXiv:1502.05844*.

de Laborda, C. P., & Conrad, S. (2005). Relational. OWL: A data and schema representation format based on OWL. *Proceedings of the 2nd Asia-Pacific Conference on Conceptual Modelling, Volume 43*, 89–96.

de Medeiros, L. F., Priyatna, F., & Corcho, O. (2015). MIRROR: Automatic R2RML mapping generation from relational databases. In *Engineering the Web in the Big Data Era: 15th International Conference, ICWE 2015, Rotterdam, the Netherlands, June 23–26, 2015, Proceedings 15* (pp. 326–343). Springer International Publishing.

Dessì, D., Osborne, F., Recupero, D. R., Buscaldi, D., & Motta, E. (2021). Generating knowledge graphs by employing natural language processing and machine learning techniques within the scholarly domain. *Future Generation Computer Systems*, *116*, 253–264.

Dimou, A., Vander Sande, M., Colpaert, P., Verborgh, R., Mannens, E., & Van de Walle, R. (2014). RML: A generic language for integrated RDF mappings of heterogeneous data. *Ldow*, *1184*.

DuCharme, B. (2013). *Learning SPARQL: Querying and Updating with SPARQL 1.1.* O'Reilly Media, Inc.

Erling, O., & Mikhailov, I. (2010). Virtuoso: RDF support in a native RDBMS. In *Semantic Web Information Management* (pp. 501–519). Springer.

Fahad, M. (2008). Er2owl: Generating owl ontology from er diagram. *International Conference on Intelligent Information Processing*, 28–37. http://link.springer.com/chapter/10.1007/978-0-387-87685-6_6.

Fernández-López, M., Gómez-Pérez, A., & Juristo, N. (1997). *Methontology: From ontological art towards ontological engineering*.

Ghawi, R., & Cullot, N. (2007, September). Database-to-ontology mapping generation for semantic interoperability. In *Third International Workshop on Database Interoperability (InterDB 2007)* (Vol. 91).

Gruber, T. R. (1993). A translation approach to portable ontology specifications. *Knowledge Acquisition*, *5*(2), 199–220.

Grüninger, M., & Fox, M. S. (1995). The role of competency questions in enterprise engineering. In *Benchmarking—Theory and Practice* (pp. 22–31). Springer.

He-ping, C., Lu, H., & Bin, C. (2008). Research and implementation of ontology automatic construction based on relational database. *2008 International Conference on Computer Science and Software Engineering, 5,* 1078–1081.

Hert, M., Reif, G., & Gall, H. C. (2011, September). A comparison of RDB-to-RDF mapping languages. *Proceedings of the 7th International Conference on Semantic Systems,* 25–32.

I. Myroshnichenko and M. C. Murphy, "Mapping ER schemas to OWL ontologies," in Semantic Computing, *2009. ICSC'09. IEEE International Conference on,* 2009, pp. 324–329.

Jun, H.-G., & Im, D.-H. (2020). Semantics-pserving RDB2RDF data transformation using hierarchical direct mapping. *Applied Sciences, 10*(20), 7070.

L. Lubyte and S. Tessaris, "Extracting Ontologies from Relational Databases.," in Description Logics, 2007.

Li, M., Du, X.-Y., & Wang, S. (2005). Learning ontology from relational database. *2005 International Conference on Machine Learning and Cybernetics, 6,* 3410–3415.

Lin, L., Xu, Z., & Ding, Y. (2013). OWL ontology extraction from relational databases via database reverse engineering. *JSW, 8*(11), 2749–2760.

Lourdusamy, R., & Mattam, X. J. (2021). Resource description framework based semantic knowledge graph for clinical decision support systems. In *Web Semantics* (pp. 69–86). Elsevier.

Lubyte, L., & Tessaris, S. (2007a). Extracting Ontologies from Relational Databases. *Description Logics.*

Lubyte, L., & Tessaris, S. (2007b). Extracting Ontologies from Relational Databases. *Description Logics.* https://www.researchgate.net/profile/Volker_Haarslev/publication/277282932_dl07-proceedings___2007521__1539__page_ii__2/links/55b51b5708ae092e9655831a.pdf#page=397

M. Dadjoo and E. Kheirkhah, "An approach for transforming of relational databases to OWL ontology," ArXiv Prepr. ArXiv150205844, 2015.

Maedche, A., & Staab, S. (2004). Ontology learning. In *Handbook on Ontologies* (pp. 173–190). Springer.

Mahdisoltani, F., Biega, J., & Suchanek, F. (2014). Yago3: A knowledge base from multilingual wikipedias. *7th Biennial Conference on Innovative Data Systems Research.*

McGuinness, D. L., & Van Harmelen, F. (2004). OWL web ontology language overview. *W3C Recommendation, 10*(10), 2004.

Michel, F., Montagnat, J., & Zucker, C. F. (2014). *A survey of RDB to RDF translation approaches and tools* [PhD Thesis]. I3S.

Myroshnichenko, I., & Murphy, M. C. (2009). Mapping ER schemas to OWL ontologies. *2009. ICSC'09. IEEE International Conference on Semantic Computing,* 324–329. http://ieeexplore.ieee.org/xpls/abs_all.jsp?arnumber=5298643

Neto, L. E. T., Vidal, V. M. P., Casanova, M. A., & Monteiro, J. M. (2013). R2RML by assertion: A semi-automatic tool for generating customised R2RML mappings. *Extended Semantic Web Conference,* 248–252.

Noy, N. F., & McGuinness, D. L. (2001). *Ontology development 101: A guide to creating your first ontology.*

Nyulas, C., O'connor, M., & Tu, S. (2007, July). DataMaster–a plug-in for importing schemas and data from relational databases into Protege. *10th International Protégé Conference,* 15–18.

Pan, J. Z., Vetere, G., Gomez-Perez, J. M., & Wu, H. (2017). *Exploiting Linked Data and Knowledge Graphs in Large Organisations.* Springer.

Po, L., Bikakis, N., Desimoni, F., & Papastefanatos, G. (2020). Linked data visualization: Techniques, tools, and big data. *Synthesis Lectures on Semantic Web: Theory and Technology, 10*(1), 1–157.

Press, R. (2008). Ontology and database mapping: A survey of current implementations and future directions. *Journal of Web Engineering, 7*(1), 001–024.

World Wide Web Consortium. "R2RML: RDB to RDF mapping language." (2012) from https://scholar.google.com/scholar?q=R2RML%3A+RDB+to+RDF+Mapping+Language&hl=en&as_sdt=0%2C5&as_ylo=2012&as_yhi=2012.

Russo, G., Anastasio, F., Pipitone, A., Gentile, A., & Pirrone, R. (2012). VEBO: Validation of ER diagrams through ontologies and WordNet. *2012 IEEE Sixth International Conference on Semantic Computing*, 342–344. IEEE.

S. R. Upadhyaya and P. S. Kumar, "ERONTO: a tool for extracting ontologies from extended E/R diagrams," in *Proceedings of the 2005 ACM symposium on Applied computing*, 2005, pp. 666–670.

Sedighi, S. M., & Javidan, R. (2012). A novel method for improving the efficiency of automatic construction of ontology from a relational database. *International Journal of Physical Sciences, 7*(13), 2085–2092.

Services, E. E. (2015). *Data Science and Big Data Analytics: Discovering, Analyzing, Visualizing and Presenting Data*. Wiley.

Spanos, D.-E., Stavrou, P., & Mitrou, N. (2012). Bringing relational databases into the semantic web: A survey. *Semantic Web, 3*(2), 169–209.

Sure, Y., Staab, S., & Studer, R. (2004). On-to-knowledge methodology (OTKM). In *Handbook on Ontologies* (pp. 117–132). Springer.

Swartout, B., Patil, R., Knight, K., & Russ, T. (1996). Toward distributed use of large-scale ontologies. *Proceedings of the Tenth Workshop on Knowledge Acquisition for Knowledge-Based Systems, 138*(148), 25.

Telnarova, Z. (2010). Relational database as a source of ontology creation. *Proceedings of the International Multiconference on Computer Science and Information Technology*, 135–139. IEEE.

Thalheim, B. (2013). *Entity-Relationship Modeling: Foundations of Database Technology*. Springer Science & Business Media.

Tirmizi, S. H., Sequeda, J., & Miranker, D. (2008). Translating sql applications to the semantic web. In *Database and Expert Systems Applications: 19th International Conference, DEXA 2008, Turin, Italy, September 1–5, 2008. Proceedings 19* (pp. 450–464). Springer, Berlin, Heidelberg.

Trinkunas, J., & Vasilecas, O. (2007, June). Building ontologies from relational databases using reverse engineering methods. *Proceedings of the 2007 International Conference on Computer Systems and Technologies*, 1–6.

Upadhyaya, S. R., & Kumar, P. S. (2005). ERONTO: A tool for extracting ontologies from extended E/R diagrams. *Proceedings of the 2005 ACM Symposium on Applied Computing*, 666–670. http://dl.acm.org/citation.cfm?id=1066828.

Uschold, M., & King, M. (1995). *Towards a Methodology for Building Ontologies*. Citeseer.

Villazón-Terrazas, B. M. (2012). *A Method for Reusing and Re-Engineering non-Ontological Resources for Building Ontologies* (Vol. 12). IOS Press.

Voit, M. M., & Paulheim, H. (2021). Bias in Knowledge Graphs – An Empirical Study with Movie Recommendation and Different Language Editions of DBpedia. *ArXiv Preprint ArXiv:2105.00674*.

Wood, D., Zaidman, M., Ruth, L., & Hausenblas, M. (2014). *Linked Data*. Manning Publications Co.

World Wide Web Consortium. (2012). R2RML: RDB to RDF mapping language.

Xu, Z., Cao, X., Dong, Y., & Su, W. (2004). Formal approach and automated tool for translating ER schemata into OWL ontologies. *Pacific-Asia Conference on Knowledge Discovery and Data Mining*, 464–475. http://link.springer.com/10.1007%2F978-3-540-24775-3_57.

Yang, S., & Wei, R. (2020). Semantic interoperability through a novel cross-context tabular document representation approach for smart cities. *IEEE Access, 8,* 70676–70692.

Yiqing, L., Lu, L., & Chen, L. (2012). Automatic learning ontology from relational schema. *2012 IEEE Symposium on Robotics and Applications (ISRA)*, 592–595. IEEE.

Yu, L. (2011). *A developer's Guide to the Semantic Web*. Springer Science & Business Media.

Zhang, G., & Jia, S. (2009). Ontology-based knowledge extraction for relational database schema.. *ISECS'09. Second International Symposium on Electronic Commerce and Security, 2009, 1,* 585–589. http://ieeexplore.ieee.org/xpls/abs_all.jsp?arnumber=5209855

Zhang, H., Diao, X., Yuan, Z., Chun, J., & Huang, Y. (2012). EVis: A system for extracting and visualizing ontologies from databases with web interfaces. *2012 Fourth International Symposium on Information Science and Engineering*, 408–411. IEEE.

Zhang, L., & Li, J. (2011). Automatic generation of ontology based on database. *Journal of Computational Information Systems, 7*(4), 1148–1154.

Zhang, Z., & Miller, J. A. (2005). *Ontology query languages for the semantic web: A performance evaluation* [PhD Thesis]. Citeseer.

Zhou, S., Ling, H., Han, M., & Zhang, H. (2010). Ontology generator from relational database based on Jena. *Computer and Information Science, 3*(2), 263–267.

Zhou, S., Meng, G., & Ling, H. (2010). Ontologies acquisition from relational databases. *Computer and Information Science, 3*(1), 185.

Index

Note: **Bold** page numbers refer to tables and *italic* page numbers refer to figures.